A
Compassionate
Peace

A Report Prepared for the
American Friends Service Committee

ⱳ HILL AND WANG · New York

"A Compassionate Peace"

A Future for the Middle East

A division of Farrar, Straus and Giroux

Library of Congress Cataloging in Publication Data
A Compassionate peace.
Prepared by a working party appointed by the board of
directors, A.F.S.C.; Everett Mendelsohn, chairperson
and principal author.
Bibliography: p.
Includes Index.
1. Near East—Politics and government—1945–
2. Jewish–Arab relations—1973–   . I. Mendelsohn, Everett.
II. American Friends Service Committee.
DS63.1.C62 1982   956   81-23958
AACR2
ISBN: 0–8090–3575–8 (cloth); 0-8090-1399-1 (paper)

The publisher and the American Friends Service Committee
should like to thank the Christian Science Publishing Society for
the use of the following three maps:
The Middle East, by Joan Forbes, © 1982 The Christian Science
Publishing Society.
The Sinai Peninsula, by Joan Forbes, from *The Christian Science
Monitor,* June 22, 1981, © 1981 TCSPS.
Lebanon, by Joan Forbes, from *The Christian Science Monitor,*
June 5, 1981, © 1981 TCSPS

Preface

Force may subdue, but love gains. And
he that forgives first wins the laurel
. . . Let us then try what love can do.

These words, written by William Penn nearly three centuries ago, express the political philosophy that he brought with him to the new world to establish the Quaker colony of Pennsylvania.

Trying what love can do has been a Quaker mission ever since. John Woolman labored in the eighteenth century to persuade his fellow Friends to renounce slavery; in the 1820's Elizabeth Fry ministered to the wretched in Newgate Prison; in the 1850's English Friends cared for the wounded in the Crimea; and in the 1890's Joseph Sturge and Joseph Elkinton heeded Tolstoy's plea and brought 6,000 persecuted Russian Doukhobors to Canada for resettlement. Wherever suffering and injustice have been acute, Friends have wanted to help.

In our own violent century, part of the Quaker experiment to try what love can do has been carried into the world by the American Friends Service Committee, beginning with the rebuilding of French villages, and the feeding of millions of German children in the wake of World War I, and continuing with humanitarian service among the homeless and the suffering in the years since, working as far as we've been permitted, on every side. Indeed, it is a commentary—and an indictment—of our age that there have been only two years since the committee was founded in 1917 that we have not been called upon to minister to the needs of refugees driven from their homes by the ebb and flow of human warfare.

More recently, the committee has gone beyond only providing immediate aid in the wake of war to try to deal with the roots of violence, which lie in injustice and the denial of human rights and the terrible poverty that afflict so many millions at home and around the world. To change these conditions is to build the foundations of peace, which must be the concern of all men and women of goodwill.

In these difficult enterprises, we have often known disappointment. Our workers have provided food, comforted the homeless, marched for justice, and stood beside the outcast, but they have failed to reach to the hatreds and the despair that corrode the soul and alienate the human family across neighborhoods and across nations.

But we have also seen miracles, where humanity and caring were reborn and compassion returned, where hatred has given way to forgiveness and where community has been rebuilt. These miracles happened because special individuals dared to live as if change was possible, and it became possible. They were competent people; able to understand difficult problems, able to find places to take hold, and able to discover what tasks needed to be done. But competency wasn't enough, it had to be undergirded with the certain faith that human beings can rise above their baser natures and respond to stimuli other than fear and threat and naked power.

These pioneers, the known and the unknown, have shown us how to challenge the harsh evils and animosities that divide mankind. The problem does not lie in the inadequacy of the messages in the great world religions, but in the timidity and the lack of imagination of men and women in applying them. We need to be as wise as serpents and as gentle as doves, as the Scriptures advise us, but neither will avail without the courage to dare.

It is in this context that the American Friends Service Committee has undertaken this fresh exploration of the tangled web that is the Middle East, twelve years after our first such study, *Search for Peace in the Middle East,* appeared. As in that earlier effort, we have drawn on our own long experience in the area, buttressed by the judgments of scholars and diplomats and tested against the viewpoints of moderates on all sides of the conflict, to suggest approaches to peace that flow from our Quaker religious faith.

We know the dangers of entering this arena. Emotions run deep on the Middle East. The passion of centuries inflames every issue to make rational analysis difficult and to obscure the road to settlement. These problems are intractable enough in isolation, but they are more and more being compounded by the politics of oil and the rivalry of great powers, which make even more volatile an already explosive scene.

Under these melancholy circumstances, whoever offers suggestions for a way out will likely be seen by all sides as partial to its enemies, and by those obsessed with the instruments of power as naïve. We assume that risk, acknowledging that our recommendations don't represent final answers, since human wisdom is finite and human judgment fallible. What we do claim, and affirm to the world, is that the approach here undertaken represents the best hope for an end to violence in the Middle East. There will never be peace for either Israeli or Arab without the effort to understand the measure of legitimacy in the enemy's views and a willingness to seek accommodation with him. The alternative of continued belligerence and intransigence and the mindless accumulation of ever more terrible weapons on every side may be the way of today's realist, but it is also the way of madness. We see nothing but disaster lying down that road.

Therefore, we call on our own nation and all men and women everywhere to turn away from the politics of violence and dare to explore the politics of reconciliation. This study attempts to do this by approaching the problems of the Middle East in the spirit of reason and compassion.

The Board of Directors of the American Friends Service Committee, mindful that they do not speak for all Friends, endorses this report. It approves the publication of this study as a contribution to the dialogue now underway about the Middle East.

On behalf of the Board of Directors
American Friends Service Committee

Stephen G. Cary, Chairperson
December 1981

The Working Party

The Working Party that prepared this report was appointed by the Board of Directors of the American Friends Service Committee. The Working Party is composed of the following members:

Everett Mendelsohn—Chairperson, Middle East Working Party; member, Middle East Panel, AFSC; Professor of the History of Science, Harvard University

Arthur Day—Executive Vice President, United Nations Association; former Consul General, United States Consulate in Jerusalem; former Deputy Assistant Secretary of State for Near Eastern and South Asian Affairs. Mr. Day participated in a purely private capacity.

Joseph Elder—Professor of Sociology and South Asian Studies, University of Wisconsin; Consultant to AFSC for Exploratory Trip to Afghanistan in 1980; former member of the Board of Directors of the AFSC and consultant to the International Division

Marcia Sfeir-Cormie—Former AFSC Middle East Staff person in AFSC Chicago office

Gail Pressberg—Director, Middle East Programs, AFSC

Everett Mendelsohn is the principal author of the paper. All Working Party members participated in writing or editing drafts of various chapters. During the course of its deliberations, the Working Party consulted with a number of Israelis, Palestinians, and other Arabs. In addition, some members of the Working Party participated in a trip to the Middle East to gain firsthand insight.

This report and the Working Party have benefited greatly from the work of past and present staff of the AFSC.

• The field reports of James Fine, written during his term as Middle East representative, have been extremely valuable, both for their firsthand observations from numerous trips through the region and for the access they have provided to thought and research of individuals and groups in the Middle East. We have drawn particularly heavily on his work for the section on Lebanon and the section on the occupation of the West Bank and Gaza.

• The AFSC Washington representative for Middle East issues, Max Holland, has done valuable work on the Middle East Arms race and on aspects of U.S. policy in the region.

• During his term as director of the AFSC Jerusalem Legal Aid Program, Jonathan Gans developed materials helpful to understanding legal issues of Palestinian life in the West Bank.

• Ann Mosely Lesch was a member of the Working Party from the time of its formation until her work took her back to the Middle East. Her very useful reports written during her term as associate Quaker international affairs representative in the Middle East in Jerusalem have focused primarily on Israeli-Palestinian relations.

In preparing this report, the working group has received valuable advice, insight, and perspective from people too numerous to mention. We met with individuals in government, academic, political, and private life in the Middle East, Europe, and the United States. While we are grateful for the information and views they shared, they and we know that this report reflects the policies and perspectives of the AFSC and not necessarily that of any of the thoughtful individuals who aided us.

The Working Party is also grateful to Catherine Essoyan for extensive research and editorial assistance, to Charles Kimball for research assistance, and to Mary Baughman Anderson for extensive editorial advice. Ruth Bartholomew and Margaret Moncell rendered valuable help in preparing the manuscript.

Contents

MAPS

A
Compassionate
Peace

1

Introduction

This report is frankly biased and unashamedly visionary. It is biased toward people and against arms, toward peace and against strife and suffering, toward justice and against fear and insecurity. It is visionary because we believe, in spite of all the difficulties and setbacks, that peace, justice, and security can be achieved in the Middle East.

Our bias is based on realism. The many and long-term experiences of the American Friends Service Committee (AFSC) in the Middle East keep us aware of the intense, multi-layered conflicts that have flared into open warfare and may do so again. We also know that the Middle East is a region of strong traditions that is undergoing rapid change. It is a region where nationalism has been closely linked to religion and where religious beliefs continue to influence government policies.

Our concern is for all the people of the Middle East. The years of AFSC work with refugees, from the Holocaust in Europe and the wars and oppression in the Middle East, have given us firsthand knowledge of the human costs of conflict. We are, however, also aware that the people of the Middle East live within a political matrix of contending states and movements and that suffering cannot be lessened until the nations and movements of the region take seriously the process of peacemaking. While outside influences and interference have often fed the conflicts and while external aid may well be helpful in seeking resolutions, the fundamental responsibility for achieving a just peace lies with the people of the Middle East themselves.

The AFSC involvement with the peoples of the Middle East dates back to its work during and after World War II with Jewish and non-Jewish refugees. The intimate involvement in programs of feeding and relocation gave us a personal understanding of the plight of European Jewry. The AFSC received, jointly with British and Irish Friends, the Nobel Peace Prize in 1947 for the wartime work. On the basis of that experience and previous efforts at refugee aid, the AFSC was called upon by the United Nations in 1948 to work with the 200,000 Arab refugees who had fled to the Gaza Strip during the first Arab-Israeli war. In the wake of the third Arab-Israeli war (1967) the AFSC in 1969 returned to Gaza to establish and run a series of preschool/kindergarten centers in the refugee camps. This program continues today administered by the United Nations Relief and Works Agency (UNRWA) and partially funded by the AFSC.

Believing that an important element in dealing with relieving suffering is to prevent it, the AFSC assigned a Quaker International Affairs Representative to the Middle East in 1967. This Representative developed channels through which differing perceptions of the conflicts in the region could be shared despite the conflicts. Through personal visits, group conferences, and meetings, the AFSC gained many insights and helped many people in the Middle East cross long-standing barriers to communication and exchange of views.

Other projects of ongoing aid were established by AFSC, one in Jerusalem to give legal aid assistance to Arabs of East Jerusalem and the West Bank, and another in Beersheba to provide a variety of services to mentally retarded individuals and their families in the Israeli community.

The day-to-day experiences of AFSC workers among Israelis and Palestinian Arabs have led to personal friendships and relations of deep trust. We have heard fears and concerns behind political expressions and seen justice and right on all sides of the conflict. We also have seen error, prejudice, mistrust, and mistakes on all sides. The knowledge we have gained and the responsibility we feel to help relieve and prevent suffering have led us to this book.

The same spirit of seeking to bring an end to conflict prompted the AFSC to publish *Search for Peace in the Middle East* in 1970. That book dealt with the problems generated by the 1967 Arab-Israeli war, and it outlined steps that could lead to stability, justice, and peace in the Middle East. It recognized the depths of division and the seriousness of the situation. "Time," the authors wrote, "is working against everyone." Indeed, within three years of publication the fourth Arab-Israeli war, of 1973, broke out. We expressed the deep commitment of the AFSC and of humane people everywhere to the safety and security of Israel and its people and the book endorsed U.N. Security Council Resolution 242 as the most practical and acceptable basis for achieving peace. But *Search for Peace in the Middle East* also recognized and identified an important new factor in the Arab-Israeli equation, that is, the explicit and self-conscious role of the Palestinians who sought to have their voices heard in the search for a solution. Indeed, the 1970 book played a significant role in focusing attention on the pivotal position of the Palestinians in the Middle East. The importance of this realization has been borne out. It is now even more apparent that solving the Palestinian problem is critical to solving the Arab-Israeli conflict.[1]

Our new book renews the AFSC commitment to seek ways to end the tragic Arab-Israeli dispute. In numerous ways the Palestinian problem seems to be more deadlocked in 1982 than it was a decade before. But there also have been significant positive changes. Palestinians and other Arabs have moved toward recognition of the reality of Israel and there is in Israel a growing recognition of Palestinian nationalism and more open and realistic discussion of the rights of the Palestinian people. As we examine those trends, we are led to a cautious optimism. In 1970 the necessity of war dominated the Israeli-Arab conflict, today we find a habit of war. We shall suggest ways to break this habit and to create a will to peace.

Events in the Middle East since 1970 have demonstrated how issues and problems of the region are often interrelated; several such critical issues have become focal points for international attention and U.S. policy. The conflict in Lebanon is closely linked to the Israeli-Palestinian-Arab conflict. The tragic manner in which Lebanese soil has become the surrogate battlefield for that conflict is finally recognized. That a solution to the problems in Lebanon remains hostage to resolution of the Palestine problem is all too apparent, but the extent to which Lebanon's political problems are exacerbated by external pressures can be reduced. The United Nations has a valuable role that was assigned to it at the end of the Civil War in 1976, and the U.S. should support its efforts to reduce the external interference of Israel and Syria and to strengthen Lebanese government authority and integrity.

The Iranian revolutionary movement that overthrew the government of the Shah in January 1979 and replaced it with an Islamic fundamentalist government has sent shock waves throughout the Islamic Middle East. While circumstances are different in each country, the implications of an Islamic revolution with its anti-Western outlook must be examined in each of the Muslim states in the region. For the U.S., Iran under the Shah represented a staunch friend and military ally, and the collapse of that supposedly strong government has had profound effects on U.S. Middle East policy. Another staunch friend of the U.S., President Anwar Sadat of Egypt, became the focus of Islamic fundamentalist opposition which led to his assassination.

There have also been changes in Afghanistan. The rapid deterioration of authority in the new Marxist-led government in Afghanistan brought a Soviet invasion in late December 1979. Our report explores the meaning of this use of Soviet military power outside the socialist block and its implications for the Middle East.

The U.S. responded to the Soviet invasion with the Carter Doctrine and the dispatch of a sizeable U.S. naval contingent to the Indian Ocean and Arabian Sea. U.S. moves to introduce substantial military power into the Middle East with the focus on the Persian Gulf and Arabian Peninsula, which began prior to the Soviet move, were escalated in its wake. These moves were based on the U.S. perception of the strategic location of the region and the importance of the enormous oil deposits that lie under the desert.

The emerging issues around oil and the buildup of vast armaments in the Middle East must also be dealt with in the context of the Middle East. The U.S. tendency to subordinate these issues to the U.S.-Soviet dispute distorts their real nature and dangerously skews U.S. policy. Nonetheless, it is important to examine carefully Soviet policy and actions in the region. The Soviet Union, with its substantial Muslim population and lengthy border to the north of the region, has obvious interests in the ebb and flow of Middle East life. For us, a key question is how to reintegrate the Soviet Union into the processes of peacemaking and peace maintenance in this volatile area.

There is one important shift in emphasis that emerges in our new report. In 1970 it seemed obvious that the contending parties—Israel, the Arab nations, and the Palestinians—could not reach a meaningful settlement on their own and therefore vigorous and sustained outside initiatives were needed. After a decade of efforts at peacemaking and a decade of changes in the Middle East itself, it now seems clear that no one from the outside can make peace for the Middle East. No one from outside can save the nations of the Middle East from themselves. While important initiatives must come from the nations and peoples of the Middle East, the U.S. should play a catalytic role in bringing the conflicting parties together to confront and resolve the most intractable issues.

External parties, especially the U.S. and U.S.S.R., must not thwart the peace process by further arming the nations of the region and thus making conflict more likely. Instead, they should work vigorously with Israel, the Arab states, and the Palestinians to take the hard steps now necessary to assure a realistic and just peace for all the parties.

The imposition of the U.S.-Soviet conflict on the already troubled Middle East is fundamentally wrong. It limits the extent to which either the U.S. or the Soviet Union can act as an effective party to peacemaking. The temptation, which too often has taken over the past, has been to search for Middle East surrogates for a U.S.-Soviet confrontation. Increasingly, nations in the Middle East, and the Third World in general, have resisted efforts to make them extensions of superpower interests and have asserted their control over their futures. The current U.S. emphasis on forging an anti-Soviet "strategic consensus" involving Saudi Arabia, Egypt, Israel, and others and the Soviet movement to alliances with Syria, Lybia, and South Yemen run directly counter to these attitudes.

Therefore, we envision a different role for the U.S. Being aware of world trends toward greater independence from power blocks, the U.S. is no longer in a position to dictate events around the world. We support a more appropriate image of the U.S. role as being one among many nations, acting cooperatively on issues and problems. We believe that a policy of superpower intervention to defend in far corners of the globe what each superpower defines as its national interest is fundamentally flawed. Indeed, we will recommend for the Middle East an explicit policy of superpower nonintervention and call instead for the powerful nations to cooperate with the states in the region in local efforts to achieve local security. From our point of view we would reverse the current thrust toward bipolar division and encourage instead the development of regionally oriented nonalignment and would keep superpower conflicts out of the Middle East.

We are led, therefore, in our conclusions to be more demanding of the Middle Eastern parties to assume greater initiative in designing and pursuing steps to peace. We are led to demand of our own government that it not use the Middle East as a surrogate battlefield, that it not assert claims to special interests in the Middle East, and that it stop serving as the arsenal for Middle East wars.

Our interest in the life of the people in the Middle East leads us to restate the urgent necessity of rejecting violence and terror. Certainly we are aware that even the most ardent peacemaking efforts will not easily erase decades of distrust and conflict. Political agreements, as important to peace as they are, will not fully resolve all conflicts and differences. But a just peace can dramatically reduce and finally eliminate the killing and destruction that has disrupted Middle Eastern life for too long.

We are aware that even as we write, the situation in the Middle East is rapidly changing. No report can be fully current or predict events with certainty; witness the revolution in Iran and the assassination of President Sadat. But even rapid change has left fundamental issues unresolved. It is to these that we turn.

2

Israel

An Israeli author was overheard in 1978, at the time of a West Bank protest, to comment that Israel had to decide whether it wanted to live in the West Bank or the Middle East. Conflict over the first, he said, would preclude peace in the second.

The stunning Israeli military victory in the Six Day War of June 1967 left Israel in control of all the land from the Jordan River and Golan Heights in the east to the Mediterranean Sea in the west, from the Lebanese border in the north to Sharm el Sheik at the southern tip of the Sinai peninsula. Israeli control extended across the Sinai desert to the eastern shore of the Suez Canal and the Red Sea. There was more than territory involved. Over a million human beings lived in the occupied areas largely clustered in the West Bank, the Gaza Strip, and the Mediterranean northern shore of the Sinai peninsula.

Some Israelis saw in the conquered territory a chance to achieve militarily important strategic depth. For others concerned with the implications of including more than a million Arabs in Israel's population or presiding over a hostile, occupied population, the victory raised new problems. The ensuing years have been marked with conflict—a war of attrition with Egypt, another full-scale Arab-Israeli war in 1973, and continued hostilities with the Palestinians. Today Israel faces the fundamental issue of how to deal with the people in the occupied territories. The Egyptian-Israeli peace treaty of 1979 has served to underscore the problem of how to deal with the West Bank and Gaza Strip, how to come to terms with a more articulate Palestinian nationalism and with the Palestinian people.

In 1970 the American Friends Service Committee wrote in *Search for Peace in the Middle East:*

> It is the judgment of the authors of this paper that the long-held Israeli policy of maintaining indefinitely the military occupation of Arab territories and of disclaiming responsibility for the plight of the Arab refugees . . . must be abandoned if an Arab-Israeli settlement is to be made. It is our further judgment that by using flexibility Israel can bring an end to the conflict and the change needed to build a firm national security upon the basis of slowly emerging trust between the Arabs and the Israelis.[1]

The book declared that the United Nations Security Council Resolution 242 is "the most practical and acceptable basis for achieving a peaceful settlement . . ." and called on Israel to undertake a firm commitment to withdraw from Arab lands contingent upon Arab commitments to accept the existence of Israel. It asked that the Arabs accept an Israeli state within mutually agreed and recognized borders as part of a total peace settlement. These aims, spelled out with hope tempered with realism, remain critically important more than a decade later.

The report of 1970 and this report strongly affirm the AFSC's belief in Israel's right to live in peace, with secure borders, among her Arab neighbors. Modern Israel has several roots, each with its own history. Each has a different influence on the state today and each projects a different image in the community of nations. One tradition connects modern Israel with the ancient Jewish kingdom of Biblical times; it has continued meaning not only for those who live in Israel but for others around the world for whom the Scriptures are a religious and moral guide. While a remnant of the ancient Jewish community remained in the Holy Land through the centuries, active Jewish settlement began in the late nineteenth century guided by a new social movement. This movement, Zionism, was in part a response to the pogroms carried out against the Jews of Europe. This attempt to gather Jews from centuries of living in the diaspora was very much a political event, reaffirming the land of Palestine as the Jewish homeland. Migration was slow until war and the Holocaust made the homeland into a haven vital for Jewish survival. What did not enter deeply enough into the consciousness of the early twentieth-century settlers was the extent to which their national aspirations conflicted with legitimate Arab claims to the same land. The need to resettle the hundreds of thousands of Jewish refugees from Europe pushed such awareness even further into the background. Few thought to ask the other residents in the land, the Arabs, how to resolve the desperate need of the refugees. To ask today whether the refugees could have been settled differently is to engage in nonproductive discussion. To ask now how to reconcile the needs of two peoples within the same area can lead to innovative solutions.

The experience, anguish, and commitment of many Israelis can be understood through reading their autobiographical writings. Arie "Lova" Eliav, former Knesset member and former General Secretary of the Labor Party, wrote of himself:

A Jew born in Russia to refugees from violence in the midst of a bloody civil war; a man whose Zionist parents brought him to the Land of Israel as an infant and planted him in the golden sands of Tel Aviv; . . . a Jew, who, after fighting as a youth in the battlefields of the Western Desert and Europe in World War II, was among those who opened up the Nazi death camps and helped to save the survivors; a man who went on to fight in the War of Independence and the wars of Israel that followed, until he was sent back to the rear; a father whose son continued to fight in the Yom Kippur War, while he himself was called to serve in the most terrible unit he had ever known, whose task it was to tell the parents about the deaths of their sons . . .[2]

If the experiences of history have produced one sort of anguish and commitment, recent developments have strengthened it. Israelis remain aware of the depth of Arab hostility and the recurrent wars and continued conflicts have led to a profound preoccupation with security in all segments of the population. The actuality, the fear, the propaganda about terrorist actions—a bomb in a bus or marketplace, a settlement attacked—have assumed large proportions in the lives and perspectives of Israelis. It has fueled their distrust of the very idea of a negotiated settlement with those who directly or indirectly have caused terrorism. It has deeply marked Israeli attitudes toward their Arab neighbors.

Within Israel the past decade has witnessed economic and social growth coupled with significant political change. Two major groups of immigrants have made their special mark on Israeli society and consciousness. The first came from communities across North Africa, the Arab countries and Iran in the wake of the wars of 1948 and 1956. They fled from countries in which hostility toward Israel was frequently vented upon the indigenous Jewish populations. Restrictions of varying severity on human and civil liberties, expropriation of property, and various forms of religious persecution became more and more common. Jews from these countries accordingly either elected or were forced to leave their homeland.

At least 550,000 Jews have left Arab lands to come to Israel since the establishment of the state of Israel; others have migrated elsewhere. Flourishing Jewish communities have been decimated. Yemen today has 1,000 to 1,500 Jews living in scattered groups; there are 300 Jews in Egypt; 5,000 in Syria; 350 in Iraq.[3] A substantial Jewish population remains in Morocco though there has been a significant emigration to France and Israel. Today Jews who remain in Arab countries, with the exception of Egypt, live in uncertainty. Recent intense pressures on the Jewish community in Iran threaten its existence. In a meeting with a Syrian Jewish leader of Damascus in 1979, an AFSC delegation was told when it asked to visit a synagogue that it would not be possible. "It would not be a good idea for you to be asking around for Jewish institutions." As the delegation left, he told an AFSC representative, "Please do not forget us if trouble should develop."[4]

Jews from Arab countries, Iran, and Turkey brought their traditions with them—traditions at variance with the outlook of European refugees from the Holocaust or earlier Zionist immigrants from Europe. The Sephardic and Oriental Jews tend to be orthodox in their religious practices and more traditional in their social behavior. Their families are often larger and their growth rate is more rapid than their Ashkenazi, or European, fellow citizens. Their communities often remain separate and their integration into the mainstream of Israeli life is slower. By the mid-1970's Oriental and Sephardic Jews were a majority of the Israeli population, but in jobs, education, income, and social status they were clustered at the lower end of Israeli society. By 1977 their social disaffection from the Labor Party leadership of Israel resulted in a striking shift of political power as they provided the margin of victory for the Likud conservative coalition to come to power.

The other noticeable group of immigrants were those fleeing direct religious persecution within the Soviet Union. Many who had not been practicing Jews in their early life discovered their heritage while still in the Soviet Union, through awareness of the experiences of the Jews of Israel. More highly educated and trained than their Sephardic co-immigrants, they made their way into Israeli society. They brought with them a greater awareness of anti-Semitism in the outer world and often through their experiences in the Soviet Union communicated an anticommunist and antisocialist outlook.

The decade of the 1970's witnessed sharp economic problems within Israel as the burdens of military defense and the costs of occupying the West Bank and Gaza Strip created inflation of over 100 percent per year. The rate for 1980 was 130 percent. Because wages and social services are indexed to the rate of inflation, individuals do not suffer as sharply as expected from these rates. The national economy, however, falls deeper into debt, and the balance of payments suffers. Without substantial external aid, the Israeli economy would have difficulty surviving.[5] Despite social and economic problems that would tear most societies apart, Israel maintains a high degree of cohesion due in part, it is claimed, to the continuing sense of external threat that Israelis share.

However, in the 1970's, Israel experienced the loss of a significant number of its population through emigration. For some years during the decade this trend outward was probably greater than immigration. Howard Sachar, in his major popular history of Israel, blames the trend on economic pressures and a decline in spirit and values in the society:

> At the least, an insight into what was happening should have been provided by the hemorrhage of emigration. Few spoke of the phenomenon openly. The statistics of departure rarely were published by the newspapers, and least of all by the government . . . Yet in the very midst of the post-1967 prosperity, with the nation's tastes whetted for a less arduous existence, with its tolerance fading for drudgery and danger of endless military reserve service, Israelis were leaving the country by the thousands . . .[6]

Sachar estimates that by 1975 at least 300,000 Israelis had settled in the United States alone.

The Yom Kippur War of October 1973 shocked Israel. Carefully planned by Egyptian President Anwar Sadat, Egyptian troops defeated the Israelis at the Suez Canal and crossed into the Sinai peninsula. Although the war was fought to a stalemate and much territory was recaptured by the Israelis, the Egyptians and Syrians who fought acquitted themselves extremely well in the eyes of the Arab world. The image of defeat that the Arab nations found humiliating in 1967 was reversed. One school of analysis links Sadat's victory in 1973 to his surprising and important trip to Jerusalem in 1977. As early as 1975, when Egypt entered a second disengagement agreement with Israel in the Sinai under U.S. auspices, there were signs that Sadat was charting an independent course from the other Arab countries and had already begun to rupture the close Egyptian ties to the Soviet Union. For Israel this represented a lessening of military tensions and threats to the south and west and ultimately led to the first break in Israel's isolation from her Arab neighbors since 1948.

A second event of 1973 indirectly affected Israel quite deeply. This was the decision of the Arab oil-producing states to sharply increase oil prices and to impose a partial embargo on oil shipments to the United States and Europe in reprisal for the aid they gave Israel before and during the war. The resulting shift in wealth and political power to the Arab states led many European states to reassess their Middle East policies and to enter a series of new relationships with the Arab states, often at the expense of their relationships to Israel.

The wars of 1967 and 1973 demonstrated that Israel remained the preeminent military power in the region. With its technically superior weapons and better trained army, Israel offset the numerical imbalance in population and troops that favored the Arab states.[7] But the 1973 war in which Israel was caught off guard began raising for some Israeli analysts questions about long-term security and the extent to which military might alone can guarantee security. This issue became particularly acute after 1973 as the Arab states accelerated their weapons-acquisitions programs, particularly highly sophisticated weapons in which Israel had previously enjoyed the advantage. To Israel's chagrin western-oriented Arab states found the United States to be a willing supplier of the newest high-technology armaments.[8] Even the Israeli peace with Egypt resulted in substantial arms shipments from the United States to Egypt. Indeed, securing modern arms and economic aid from the U.S. was a high priority for Sadat. The European states, anxious to sell their own advanced weapons systems, also have arranged weapons contracts with many Arab states.

Security has particular meaning for the Israelis. For people who have been hated, persecuted, and killed, whose Jewish identity often made them targets—whether incidental or disastrous—in other lands where they have lived, the security of their land is essential. We deeply appreciate this and support it. However, for Israel, the certainty of maintaining continued military superiority over the Arabs is thoroughly in question and a new look at the security issue is necessary. On what, Israelis now must ask, is true security based?

One Israeli who asked this question and proposed a visionary answer was the well-known historian Jacob Talmon. In an open letter to Prime Minister Begin published in the Hebrew daily *Ha'aretz* shortly before he died, Talmon made the case for Israel's giving up the occupied territories as part of a solution involving security considerations. His argument is political, responsible, and moral. He wrote:

> There are those who say, "But our vital security interests make it imperative that we hold on to our sovereignty over *all* of the present territories of the Land of Israel and settlements in the territories are crucially needed for our defense" . . . Such claims . . . are mere rationalizations for the pursuit of other goals. On the contrary, these settlements are at present destructive to our vital interests and our Zionist goals—and especially of peace with our neighbors, which is the precondition for achieving all other goals.[9]

Referring to the settlers moving into West Bank areas, Talmon compares them unfavorably with the original pioneers who established the Jewish homeland. These new settlements, he claims, are a "political act" having as their primary purpose to determine who will rule ". . . or as the settlers put it, 'to show the Arabs who is boss here . . . to put the Arabs in their place.' " He is fearful of this meaning and attitude: "[S]uch settling, it seems to me, is tantamount to conducting a kind of war."

For Talmon the basic moral issue was his greatest concern:

> For all the shame and pain we feel over the harm done to us by our neighbors because of anachronistic perverse policies, our fear should be greater over what these acts will do to us, to the Jewish people and to our dream of social and moral justice and renaissance. For this dream was one of the vital and beautiful aspects of Zionism . . .

Like a number of other thoughtful Israelis, Talmon was concerned that Israel's leaders had become blinded to any changes occurring in the mind of the potential enemies and had become so convinced of the implacable resolve of the Arabs to annihilate Israel that the Israelis were forced to act accordingly; despairing of any possibility of peace, of international guarantees of borders, or of demilitarization or other solutions. "I am afraid, Mr. Prime Minister, that this attitude is likely to become a self-fulfilling prophecy," he wrote. When he turned to the question of peace talks or negotiations, Professor Talmon was unafraid. "We should talk with anyone who is prepared to talk with us . . . and by talking with Israel engages in recognizing its existence and right to continue."[10]

THE BEGIN GOVERNMENT AND THE PEACE PROCESS

Since November 1977 when Egyptian President Anwar Sadat broke the tradition of decades of Arab-Israeli hostility and visited Jerusalem to launch a new peace effort, Israeli politics have been dominated by the peace process. But several shifts in Israeli political life have influenced deeply Israel's policy and role in the peace efforts.

The government in office at the time of Sadat's visit was the six-month-old Likud-led coalition of Menachem Begin. It had come into office after thirty years of unbroken leadership by the Labor Party. The election of the politically more right-wing Likud government was seen as a repudiation of the lackluster performance of Labor on domestic issues, of its vacillation in foreign affairs, and of its inconclusive policy on the Palestinian problem. It also represented the emergence to political influence of the Sephardic Jewish communities, comprised of immigrants from North African and Arab countries. By 1977, although representing a majority of the Israeli population, the Sephardim felt pushed aside by the dominant European-descended Ashkenazi Jews who had led the country since its founding in 1948 and who had dominated the activities of the successive Labor governments. The Sephardim felt separated, by class and ethnic background, from the Israeli mainstream. As outsiders, largely unconnected to the kibbutz ethic and the implicit socialism of the Israeli center, they were drawn to the political and social conservatism of Menachem Begin, the charismatic leader of Israeli right-wing politics.[11] The Sephardic vote gave Begin his new strength. Also, fifteen Labor seats were lost in the election to a new middle-of-the-road coalition led by the well-known archaeologist and former general Yigal Yadin. Yadin's Democratic Movement for Change (DASH) was comprised of a split from the Labor Party by those of its traditional constituency who resented what they viewed as drift in government and laxness on issues of corruption. DASH, together with the National Religious Party (which had brought its members into coalition in every government since 1948) and Agudat Yisrael (a small ultraorthodox party) gave Begin his political majority in the ninth Knesset.

There is irony in the fact that it was Menachem Begin, from the hawkish end of the Israeli political spectrum, who was the prime minister when President Sadat chose to make his dramatic visit. Begin's politics have marked the Israeli participation in the peace process that developed and, in large measure, complicated a solution of the Palestinian problem. The events that led from Sadat's visit to Jerusalem to the faltering exchanges between the Egyptian and Israeli leadership that finally brought direct U.S. participation and the intense meetings involving President Jimmy Carter, Begin, and Sadat at the presidential hideaway at Camp David, Maryland, have been well chronicled in the press.

The peace accords between Egypt and Israel that emerged from Camp David involved two distinct sections—one focused on Egyptian-Israeli issues and the other on the Palestinian problem. The first involved a phased withdrawal of Israeli military forces and civilian settlements from the Sinai peninsula, which Israel had occupied since 1967. A small sector along the eastern shore of the Suez Canal had been returned to Egypt as part of the Sinai II agreement negotiated by Henry Kissinger in 1975 in the aftermath of the 1973 Arab-Israeli war. What is notable about the Camp David accords is that Israel agreed to a total withdrawal from all Egyptian territory in return for a formal peace treaty (signed in March, 1979), demilitarized zones in the Sinai, and the normalization of relations between Egypt and Israel. Ambassadors have been exchanged, limited tourism and trade have been arranged, and the final sector of the Sinai is scheduled to be returned to Egypt in April 1982.

Some members of Begin's own party and coalition, including Yitzhak Shamir, the present foreign minister, opposed the treaty. Guela Cohen, a long-time Begin ally in the Knesset, was so strongly opposed that she withdrew from the coalition, formed another political faction, and ran for reelection in June 1981 as part of a separate party. Opposition centered on the treaty's requirement that Israel give up the productive oil field in the Sinai peninsula, and agree to close down its settlements in the northern Sinai and move several major air bases it had earlier constructed in the eastern Sinai. Nevertheless, Israel stood to gain much from the treaty. Peace with the most populous Arab country, security along its Western borders, and realization that another full-scale Arab-Israeli war could not be fought since Egypt was no longer in military opposition were major achievements. Egypt, of course, regained significant territory and, like Israel, became a recipient of large-scale U.S. military assistance.

But there have been important failures in the Camp David process. Egypt and Israel remain alone as Middle East participants in the Camp David peace process, and the hoped-for inclusion of other key Middle East nations—Jordan and Saudi Arabia—has not materialized. Nor have the Palestinians joined the process. The second part of the Camp David accords, dealing with the Palestinian problem, has had no success and at this time (winter 1981) even minor gains are unlikely although the autonomy talks resumed in the fall of 1981, after Sadat's assassination. The accords established a framework for achieving "full autonomy" and a "five-year transition period" for the inhabitants of the West Bank and Gaza, but the meaning of autonomy, the powers to be granted to the administrative council set up to administer it, and the goal after the transition were all left so vague in the initial agreements that widely divergent interpretations have emerged. The Begin government has adopted a restrictive interpretation of autonomy and, from the beginning, rejected giving up Israeli sovereignty over the occupied territories.[12] Indeed, on assuming office in June 1977 Begin gave indication of his position when he changed the designation of the West Bank to the Biblical names Judea and Samaria. When he went before the Knesset for approval of the Camp David accords, he promised its members that the West Bank and Gaza would never fall under foreign sovereignty, that Jerusalem

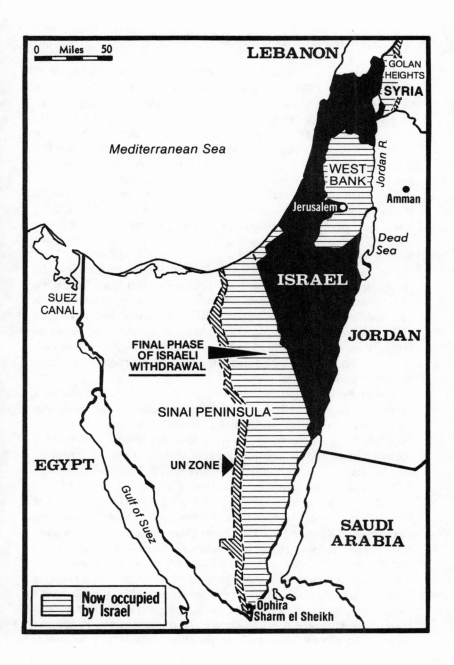

would never again be divided and would remain the eternal capital of Israel, and that a Palestinian state would never be established. The "legitimate rights of the Palestinian people" which he recognized at Camp David became the rights of the "Arabs of Judea and Samaria and the Gaza district" to cultural and religious freedoms within a very restrictive administrative autonomy. Jordan and the Palestinians felt there was nothing in Begin's formulation to encourage their involvement in the Camp David process or subsequent treaty.[13]

Though Begin's government has given the sharpest expression to the idea of an expanded Israel, including the West Bank and the Gaza Strip, elements of this position can be found in earlier Labor governments. There has been a recent growth in the Labor Party of those who envision a greater Israel. This represents a serious departure from the policy of Prime Minister Levi Eshkol, who in the early days of the occupation expressed willingness to return almost all the West Bank to Jordanian rule. By 1969, when Golda Meir became prime minister, her coalition partner, the National Religious Party, had developed strong interests in retaining the territories. Israel, then, began to retreat from the widely held interpretation of U.N. Resolution 242, which included Israeli withdrawal from occupied territories in return for peace and secure borders.

By October 1973 and the outbreak of a new Arab-Israeli war, tens of thousands of Israelis had settled in previously Arab territories largely in the greatly expanded city of Jerusalem already governed by Israeli law. Israel claims this was in response to rising Palestinian nationalism and Arab states designation of the PLO as the legitimate representative of the Palestinians; neither the PLO nor the Arab states fully accept 242 as a basis for negotiations. (Although laws had been passed in the wake of the 1967 war bringing all of Jerusalem under Israeli "law, jurisdiction and administration," it was formally annexed by the Knesset after the Camp David agreements.)[14] In addition, Jewish settlements had been established before 1973 in the Jordan Valley, in Hebron, and in the Gaza Strip. While some of these settlements represented an emerging government policy of securing borders through placing settlements in strategic areas, others were independent efforts of ultranationalist Israeli groups. The Labor Party made clear what it believed was national sentiment, that a Palestinian state would never be acceptable on the West Bank largely because of security considerations, but it also claimed in these years that the settlements were negotiable and that those considered nonstrategic would be withdrawn in return for peace agreements.

The settlement policy of the Labor government left broad ambiguity and, in the final analysis, permitted the establishment of a large number of settlements, many in places that had nothing to do with security. Strong annexationist commitments became part of the Israeli political pattern. Movements like Gush Emunim (Bloc of the Faithful) and others committed to an expanded Israel gained a government commitment to make no decision on return of the West Bank and Gaza without going to the country in a referendum or elections. In addition they created the "facts"—numerous settlements in the West Bank.

By the time that Begin won election in May 1977, Labor, during its decade of occupation, had permitted construction of 24 settlements housing 3,200 settlers in the West Bank. When Begin won his second election in June 1981, there were approximately 75 settlements with over 18,000 settlers in the West Bank. These settlements occupy over 75,000 acres of West Bank area that Israel has taken or purchased.[15] Some 70,000 Israelis now live in apartment blocks constructed in the former Arab lands to the north, east, and south of Jerusalem. The Begin government has pursued an accelerated program of appropriating occupied lands and settling them. While much of the land was identified as public land belonging previously to the Jordanian government, or absentee-owned land, some has been taken directly from Palestinian residents. Only in the latter case has compensation been offered.

This land acquisition and settlement policy has transformed the issue of eventual disposition of the settlement areas from an issue of government policy and diplomatic strategy to a question of deep national significance and stimulated expansion of the Israeli peace movement. Settlers are armed and organized into paramilitary units, and, together with their ultranationalist political supporters within Israel, they promise to resist vigorously any return of the land.

The policy is one of de facto annexation. The Begin-led coalition, defining the occupied regions as part of the Biblically promised land of Israel, envisages no acceptable plan which would allow withdrawal. The coalition has instead set about building the infrastructure for permanent control and has invested significant amounts of government money in a network of roads, settlements, and other structures.

This policy of unyielding commitment to the maintenance of Israeli sovereignty over the West Bank has brought the Begin government into conflict with Egypt, which envisages a Palestinian future for the occupied territories, and with the U.S., which has been concerned about the deadlock in the Palestinian issue. This uncompromising policy was also responsible for the resignation from the first Begin cabinet of its two senior ministers, Foreign Minister Moshe Dayan and Defense Minister Ezer Weizman. Begin's new cabinet, appointed in August 1981, elevated ultranationalists to key ministries. Former General Ariel (Arik) Sharon, who in his former position as agriculture minister coordinated the government's settlement policy, became the new defense minister, directly responsible for the military government of the occupied territories. Yitzhak Shamir assumed the position of foreign minister after Dayan's resignation. Shamir was among the handful of members of Begin's own party who refused to support the Camp David accords when Begin presented them to the Knesset, although now as a cabinet member he says he will abide by them. Yosef Burg, head of the National Religious Party and minister of the interior, is chief negotiator on autonomy. The appointment of Burg, an advocate of permanent Israeli sovereignty in the territories, to replace the then foreign minister, Moshe Dayan, as autonomy negotiator prompted Dayan's resignation. This switch from foreign to interior minister underlined the Begin position that issues concerning the West Bank and Gaza are internal matters more than foreign-policy issues. Begin apparently believed that if he negotiated the return of the Sinai to Egypt he would receive at least tacit acceptance from his negotiating partners of his plan for continued Israeli sovereignty in the West Bank and Gaza.

The annexationist policy runs head on into even the most moderate Arab's views and, of course, clashes directly with even limited Palestinian nationalist aspirations. The Israeli position on the territories has markedly hardened during the same period when there has been a perceptible moderating of some Palestinian views. But even as Begin has made his views on continued Israeli rule in the occupied territories increasingly clear, the Palestinian and Arab government positions have remained equivocal and sometimes contradictory.

The June 1981 Israeli elections made clear that Begin's policies were not rejected by the Israeli public, but the closeness of the election (48 seats for the Likud and 47 for Labor in a 120-member Knesset) by no means gave Begin an unequivocal mandate. In order to form a government, Begin had to enter into coalition with three religious or ethnically oriented parties (National Religious Party, 6 seats; Agudat Yisrael, 4 seats; Tami, 3 seats). The coalition gave him a slim one-vote majority; it therefore may force Begin to even more rigid positions on the territories and the peace process. New levels of theocratic influence have been introduced into the governing process. During the campaign, the Labor Party muted its criticisms of Begin's foreign policies, and several of the small progressive and peace parties were either severely reduced in number or eliminated from the Knesset by the election. Politically, Israel slipped further to the right, a shift that may not be transitory since it reflects deep structural changes in the society. In assessing the internal implications of the elections, and thus the political forces to which an Israeli government will have to respond, one thoughtful analyst, Bernard Avishai, lamented: "The mean-spirited campaign that preceded the June 30 election has, in fact, revealed a country passionately divided by ideology, class, age, attitudes toward Orthodox faith and law—and crucially, ethnic origin."[16]

The implications of the June 1981 election for the policy of the new Begin government toward the Palestinian problem and peace process are not encouraging. The Begin cabinet is filled with ultranationalists in key positions. The chairman of the Knesset Committee on Security and Foreign Relations, Moshe Arens, opposed the Camp David accords, and the Begin government, to remain in office, depends upon the Knesset votes of the rightist, ultranationalist, and religiously orthodox parties. A likely outcome of this political constellation will be a further hardening of the line on the Palestinian issue and an acceleration of movements in the West Bank and Gaza to support the new cabinet's claim to assure full Israeli sovereignty.

Israel's relations with Syria, which had never been good, further deteriorated during the Begin years. With the breakdown of the efforts to achieve a comprehensive peace and the focus on negotiating a bilateral treaty between Egypt and Israel, Syria's own attitudes hardened as it saw its bargaining position for the occupied Golan Heights weakened. In addition, the Syrian role in Lebanon, which involved approximately 30,000 troops, first in ending the Lebanese civil war (1976) and then in remaining as a strong military presence, increased Israeli fears of Syria's intentions. This problem came to a head in the spring and summer of 1981. Israel increased its military activities inside Lebanon, attacking suspected Palestinian targets and giving direct military support to the Lebanese Phalangist militia when it was under attack by Syrian forces in the strategic mid-Lebanese city of Zahle. Syria countered the latter Israeli action by moving sophisticated surface-to-air missiles into Lebanon near Zahle, thus denying Israel supremacy in the air. This confrontation remained unresolved in spite of the efforts of special U.S. negotiator Philip Habib, although a cease-fire was achieved and was in effect through the late fall.

As this report went to press in December 1981, Israel made the surprise move of formally annexing the Golan Heights, which had come under Israeli occupation in 1967. The move, explained by Israel in terms of the strategic nature of the Heights and the continuous threat that Syrian forces had posed in the pre-1967 years, has the broader effect of directly abrogating the terms of U.N. Security Council Resolution 242. Except for the annexation of Jerusalem and some surrounding West Bank land, this is the most serious move Israel has taken to make explicit its intention to maintain sovereignty over territories occupied in the 1967 war. It further strains the already frail peace process, and again brings Israel into sharp contest with international opinion, including that of the U.S. government. It will cause even deeper isolation of Israel and further strengthen the hand of rejectionists among the Arabs. This move deeply embarrassed the new government of Egypt and presented it with a dilemma. If it responded sharply, it would put at risk the fulfillment of the Egyptian–Israeli Treaty and the return to Egypt of the final portion of the Sanai. If Egypt did not respond, it would be more thouroughly isolated from the Arab world.

3

The Occupation

During the years of Jordanian rule of the West Bank (1948–1967), although there was some significant integration of Palestinian leadership in the governing process, Palestinian nationalism was nonetheless active and often clashed with Jordanian authority.

The Israeli occupation of the West Bank and the Gaza Strip* has extended the range of countries affected by the Palestinian problem. Over 200,000 Palestinians left the occupied territories between 1967 and 1980, with most currently living in other parts of the Arab world.[1] For Israel, the occupation affects the lives of the occupiers, the men and women of the military government. Some Israelis have asked the difficult question: Where in the dreams of the Zionist founders of Israel was there a vision of Israel as an army of occupation?

Israel, in response to complaints about the occupation, has often argued that its treatment of the Palestinian population and overall handling of occupation affairs is not severe by comparison with military occupations in other places. While this claim is probably accurate, it is a distinction made by the occupiers and not the occupied. The occupation has had a dramatic impact on the day-to-day lives of Palestinian residents. In addition, the acts of the occupation and the policy it represents have seriously complicated any search for a just, negotiated solution. General Ariel (Arik) Sharon, minister of defense

---

*The West Bank and the Gaza Strip were referred to by the Israelis as administered territories. Subsequently the Begin government referred to the West Bank as Judea and Samaria.

in the second Begin government and minister of agriculture and chairman of the Cabinet Committee on settlements in the last Begin government, has articulated one goal held by many Israelis:

> It is impossible any more to talk about Jordanian option or territorial compromise. We are going to leave an entirely different map of the country that it will be impossible to ignore. I don't see any way any government will be able to dismantle the settlements of Judea and Samaria.[2]

The first four years of the occupation under the Likud government have witnessed an accelerated and what some people believe to be an irreversible transformation of the geographic and social structures of the territories linking them ever more clearly with Israel.

THE RULE OF LAW

As the result of several wars and continuing acts of enemy terrorism, Israel views virtually all the activities in the daily life of citizens of the occupied territory through the lens of security. In the name of security virtually all actions of the occupation forces are undertaken. In establishing legal rules and procedures for the West Bank, Israel argues that the provisions of the 1949 (Fourth) Geneva Convention covering the protection of civilian persons in time of war do not apply to the West Bank and Gaza. Israel claims that these areas are not enemy territory because in its view Jordan's prior control of the territories was illegal. International legal opinion has supported the view that the Geneva Convention rules should apply to the residents of the West Bank and the Gaza Strip because the peoples of these territories are, in fact, "in the hands of an occupying power of which they are not nationals" (from the Convention Commentary). Israel has announced that in spite of the Geneva Convention's inapplicability, it will abide by the humanitarian provisions of the Convention.[3]

The Convention charges the occupying power with protecting persons under occupation. Forbidden under all circumstances are, among other things: forcible transfers or deportations (art. 49); any measures of brutality, whether applied by civilian or military agents (art. 32); collective punishments, reprisals against protected persons or their property, and all measures of intimidation (art. 33); unlawful confinement or deprivation of rights of fair and regular trial (art. 147).[4]

In place of full adherence to the Geneva Convention, Israel has chosen to rely on the Defense Emergency Regulations originally promulgated by the British in 1937 and codified in 1945. They consist of 120 sweeping orders meant to cope with the tense situation that existed in the closing years of the mandate when British authority was being challenged by advocates of the nascent state of Israel. Far-reaching powers are given to security authorities to act without due process of law. These regulations, which were vigorously opposed in 1946 by the Federation of Hebrew Lawyers in Palestine, were adopted by the new state in 1948 and applied to the Arab population of Israel until 1966. Beginning in 1967, they were applied to the Arab population in the occupied territories.

Israel announced in June 1967 that all laws in force in the occupied territories would be continued if they did not contradict the military governor's proclamations and did not conflict with changes brought by the occupation. Nonetheless, many basic laws and the system of administering justice have been broadly altered since 1967. By declaring in February 1968 that the occupied territories were no longer enemy territory, Israel relieved itself of many constraints widely accepted in international law. The area was from that time referred to as administered territory by Israel.

Since 1967 the Israeli Military government has issued 880 military orders claiming to amend existing Jordanian law on the West Bank that, in fact, replace it in many categories. Since there is no existing legislative authority in the territories, the military government has assumed that role. Powers under law previously given to Jordanian authorities and officials have been taken over by Israelis, and powers and privileges previously held by civilian authority have been shifted to military administration. Thus, for example, the Israeli officer in charge of the judiciary holds and exercises a very wide range of what were previously civil positions and powers, including minister of justice, minister of commerce, and registrar of lands, companies, trademarks, tradenames, and patents. He also holds the powers formerly held by the bar association to allow lawyers to train and law schools to be recognized.[5]

One of the most important changes effected by Israel in the West Bank legal system was an alteration of the judiciary, including abolition of the highest court, the Court of Cassation. This court had had responsibility for overseeing proper functioning of the judicial system and for being the arbiter in novel issues of law. It also operated as a special board to hear requests from government departments for interpretation of the law and its ramifications. Of these functions only that of the High Court of Justice has been retained; its functions have been passed on to the West Bank Court of Appeals.

The most controversial element of the legal system is the Military Court. Judges are appointed by the military area commander and all must be military officers or civilian lawyers doing reserve duty. Court sessions are held where and when the judge determines, and the judge generally makes the only record of what occurs. Convictions are by either a three-member court or single-judge court. The decisions may be accepted, varied, or annulled by the area commander, who, in the case of a single-judge court, may accept written representations for sentence variance but not normal appeal. No regular system of judicial appeal is possible from the decision of either of these courts. The lack of a regular appeal mechanism is viewed as one of the most serious breaches of an orderly rule of law since judicial errors cannot be corrected and proper procedures and standards of evidence cannot be guaranteed. Confessions obtained from individuals detained by the military pending trial, therefore, may not be appealed nor may objections be raised during the period while a confession is being obtained. In principle, a procedural violation could be brought to the Israel High Court of Justice, but, in practice, that court has taken an extremely restricted view of its ability to challenge military-government decisions taken on security grounds. In a limited number of cases, the Israeli Supreme Court sitting as a High Court of Justice has been willing to consider appeal petitions from the occupied territories. These largely have related to personal and property matters, but have generally excluded security-related cases.[6]

Between 1967 and 1980, over 200,000 individuals in the occupied territories have been arrested and brought to Israeli prisons, detention centers, and police stations. These arrests have occurred under the Security Provisions Orders and the Defense Emergency Regulations.

The pace of arrests doubled during 1979 and 1980. Of those arrested, 70 percent are between sixteen and twenty-three years old, and there is agreement by both the International Commission of the Red Cross and the military authorities that 90 percent of these arrests are for the sole purpose of eliciting information about political or potential security concerns. While most of those arrested have been released after several days, some, with judicial approval but not having faced trial, have been detained for extended periods.[7]

Any Israeli soldier has the authority to make an arrest without warrant of any person who commits or is suspected of committing an offense under the security provisions. No detaining order is needed; there is no law of habeas corpus allowing application to a judge for explanation, and although an arrest warrant must be obtained within four days (ninety-six hours), the warrant need not specify any charges. The detention may be extended to eighteen days before the individual must be brought before a judicial authority, who may extend confinement up to six months.

Most Israelis are not familiar with the workings of the Military Courts or, for that matter, with the administration of the law in the occupied territories. Their own experience within Israel leads them to trust the military and the justice it provides. In addition, there is a widespread sentiment that security offenders really don't deserve trials and the niceties of legal protection, since they threaten the existence of the State of Israel. For the residents of the occupied territories, however, the opposite perception prevails. Some of the feelings of bitterness, outrage, and injustice are natural, given the underlying feeling that the occupation itself is unjust. But independent observers, including Amnesty International, have factually corroborated difficulties and injustices within the military justice system.[8] International law has been distorted and violated; rules of evidence, argument, and due process have been lax or altered in ways detrimental to defendants; and the role of the defense counsel has been deeply compromised.

In the context of the broad changes in the legal systems of the occupied territories, one important progressive legal reform should be noted—the abolition of the death penalty. Though the amendments and reforms of Jordanian law made by the military government have

Israel's security as their justification, in the eyes of local residents they seem capricious and unfounded. A recent report, prepared by a West Bank barrister, assisted by a Palestinian-born, U.S.-trained lawyer, and issued by the International Commission of Jurists, puts forward this perplexity in its conclusion. They point to an "order prohibiting picking of wild thyme growing on the hills." They go on to say:

> One can but wonder, when finding such an order, whether the point of issuing it was to protect nature, to safeguard the economic interests of Israeli planters, or perhaps to deprive the Palestinian population of access to a herb which, through the many allusions to it in Palestinian literature, has come to symbolize the attachment of Palestinians to their land and their love of the herbs that are peculiar to it . . . it is much more difficult to explain the prohibition made by another [order] which prohibits the planting of azaleas.[9]

ECONOMIC LIFE

The occupation through conscious policy and by default has created a situation in which residents of the West Bank and the Gaza Strip have become heavily dependent on Israel for trade and employment. The territories currently receive 90 percent of their imports from Israel, and every day 75,000 laborers, or approximately one-third of the total Arab work force, commute to Israel. In some forms of unskilled labor, such as found in building trades and the service sector, Palestinians make up as much as 30 percent of the work force.[10] Palestinians' wages are not covered by Israeli trade-union agreements. They are ineligible for the basic social welfare benefits given Israeli workers. The Israeli National Insurance system does not include West Bank-Gaza residents. Some Israeli critics point out that the Arab labor fills jobs that are difficult to mechanize and equally difficult to convince Israeli workers to perform. It is true, on the other hand, that the wage scale of Palestinians employed in Israel is advantageous, and the earnings of Arab workers have been of great importance to the occupied territories. Employment in Israel accounts for 30 percent of the total income of West Bank and Gaza Strip Palestinians. But the importance of the territories as the largest outlet for Israeli goods has also increased. In 1979 Israel sold $300 million in goods in the occupied territories, an amount greater than in France, the next largest buyer. The large number of workers who go into Israel to work also affects the local Palestinian economy. Because most of these workers come from the agricultural sector, the area under cultivation in the West Bank and Gaza Strip has been reduced by 35 percent.[11]

Israeli taking of West Bank and Gaza land has been significant, and it is now estimated that one-third of the total area of the occupied territories has been expropriated, "closed," or otherwise seized for Israeli civilian and military purposes. In the six months prior to the June 1981 election, land seizure and settlement were accelerated. During this period, the government ordered the seizure of an additional 10 to 15 square miles of West Bank land for settlement use, approved 6 new settlements, and authorized 400 new homes for existing settlements.

In recent years, with a greatly increasing number of Israeli settlements, a system of government has been established consistent with the Likud concept of autonomy (see section on autonomy). In the West Bank, the Jewish settlements are organized into ten regional and ten local councils which operate under Israeli law, with the power to purchase land, levy municipal taxes, and negotiate with Israeli ministries for grants and aid. The settlements have also organized armed paramilitary units, linked to the Israeli Defense Forces. There has been a striking shift in land control on the West Bank. At present the municipal areas included in the Israeli West Bank settlements and subject to Israeli law are greater in size than the municipal areas of the Palestinian towns. The current approved master plan for Jewish settlement in the West Bank encompasses an area greater than the approved master plan for Arab towns and villages.[12] The current comparative population figures are approximately 20,000 Israeli settlers and 800,000 Arab residents.

In the arid conditions of much of the Middle East, few issues are more sensitive than control of water, its sources and its use. The drilling of wells is a matter of some concern, since wells in adjacent areas often compete for the same limited supplies. Israel, in assuming occupation powers, has taken control of well-drilling permits. Conflict increases as established Palestinians have difficulty obtaining permits while the new settlements drill for and use West Bank water. By 1979

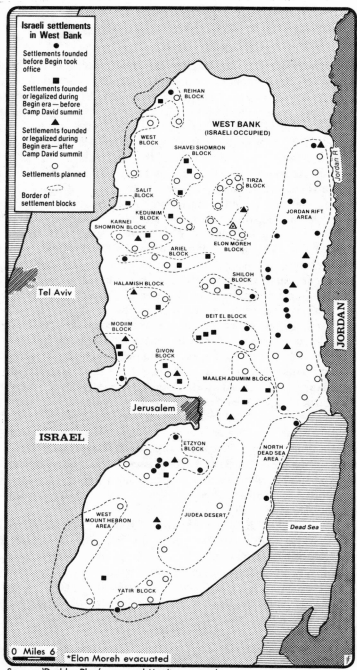

Israeli settlements
in West Bank

● Settlements founded
before Begin took
office

■ Settlements founded
or legalized during
Begin era — before
Camp David summit

▲ Settlements founded
or legalized during
Begin era — after
Camp David summit

○ Settlements planned

Border of
settlement blocks

Tel Aviv

ISRAEL

Jerusalem

REIHAN BLOCK

WEST BANK
(ISRAELI OCCUPIED)

WEST BLOCK

SHAVEI SHOMRON BLOCK

TIRZA BLOCK

SALIT BLOCK

KEDUMIM BLOCK

KARNEI SHOMRON BLOCK

ARIEL BLOCK

ELON MOREH BLOCK

JORDAN RIFT AREA

Jordan R

SHILOH BLOCK

HALAMISH BLOCK

BEIT EL BLOCK

MODIIM BLOCK

GIVON BLOCK

MAALEH ADUMIM BLOCK

JORDAN

ETZYON BLOCK

NORTH DEAD SEA AREA

WEST MOUNT HEBRON AREA

JUDEA DESERT

Dead Sea

YATIR BLOCK

0 Miles 6   *Elon Moreh evacuated

Source: 'Drobles Plan' map and Monitor research

Israeli settlers had drilled twenty-four artesian wells, seventeen for use by Jordan Valley settlements. Meters have been placed on Arab wells, limits set for amounts allowed, and penalties imposed for violations. Israel proper has diverted some water from the West Bank for use within the pre-1967 borders. A lesser amount is piped from Israel to the West Bank. The 1979 water-use deficit in Israel was 265 million cubic meters, and it is expected that this figure will rise to 500 million cubic meters by 1985.[13]

Israel has for some years been linking the electricity system of the occupied territories into the Israel grid. A recent attempt by the Israel Power Corporation to merge the old Jordanian Jerusalem Electric Company into Israel's grid was opposed by the Arab directors. The Israeli High Court supported the Arab opposition.[14] Israel's desire to merge West Bank electric systems is based on an overall plan to control West Bank economic activity and its infrastructure and to make electricity available to Israeli settlements.

ISRAELI SETTLERS

Yehuda Litani, the well-known correspondent for the Hebrew daily *Ha'aretz,* opened his news story of May 11, 1979, about settlements in the West Bank with the following observation:

> If one adds up all the recent events in which West Bank settlers have taken the law into their own hands, the description given them by the American media—"vigilantes," with all the negative connotations of the term— would appear to fit pretty well.[15]

He reported on the settlers' aim to foil any efforts by the Israeli government to implement even a very restricted autonomy plan in the area. Their efforts, he concluded, were coordinated among settlements and would be carried out even at severe disadvantage to the Arab residents. From past experience with the military government, the police, and other Israeli agencies, the settlers knew that the government would, according to Litani, "not dare mete out the full severity of the law against the Jewish settlers, while their treatment of the Arab residents is often quite severe." Litani illustrated his claim with a story about the settlers from Kiryat Arba near Hebron who, feeling that the military government was not being tough enough, took the law into their own hands in March 1976 and decided to "impose order." The settlers smashed windows in Arab homes, terrorized the people, and destroyed their vineyards. Even though the incident became widely known, up to the date that Litani wrote, no police action had been taken, although the names of the suspected perpetrators were well known and named by Litani. Litani's accounts, and those of others, have been a regular feature in the Israeli press, yet the incidents continue. The reason, pointed out by Litani, is the failure of the government, with some few exceptions, to enforce the law when illegal settlements were established, thereby letting the settlers know that they will be forgiven and that for them the law will be flexible, ignored, or changed.

DEPORTATION

The nationalist political consciousness that has developed among many West Bank and Gaza civic and political leaders has prompted a variety of official and nonofficial Israeli actions that have had the cumulative effect of breaking up any unified or organized Palestinian political organization. Numerous Palestinian leaders have been deported, others have been severely injured in bombing attacks, while still others face harassment by the military government and by organized groups of ultranationalist Jewish settlers. A detailed study of deportations, conducted by Ann Lesch and listing each name, showed that in the first decade of occupation 1,156 individuals had been deported from the West Bank and Gaza. In December 1977 the *Financial Times* of London received confirmation from the Israeli government that 1,180 deportations had occurred. Lesch identified many moderate political figures among the deported. Israel claimed only terrorists and their supporters had been forced to leave.[16]

Among those deported was Hanna Nasir, president of Bir Zeit University and the mayors Fahd Qawasmi of Hebron and Mohammed Milhem of Halhul. The mayors, deported in May 1980, were widely regarded as political moderates and had regularly met with Israeli doves. They limited their aspirations to support of a Palestinian state side by side with Israel.[17] Milhem and Qawasmi were charged (but never brought to trial) with inciting Palestinians who were involved in a terrorist attack on Jewish settlers in Hebron. The men who committed the crime and were subsequently caught, convicted, and punished were shown to have had no connections at all with the mayors. The latter have repeatedly tried to return to their homes, but in spite of an Israeli High Court recommendation that they be permitted to do so, the military government has refused permission. In 1973 the mayors at Ramallah and el Bireh were deported, and last year, the new mayors of the same cities plus the mayor of Nablus were the object of bombing attacks presumably by Israeli terrorists. Two of the three were severely injured. An Israeli soldier sent to defuse a bomb intended to harm the third man was blinded when it exploded.

DEMONSTRATIONS AND PUNISHMENT

The press in the U.S. has carried many stories of political demonstrations by Palestinians against Israel and Israelis. Rocks have been thrown, tires burned, traffic blocked, and Israelis assaulted. Israeli reprisals have varied in form and severity, and the punishment has not necessarily matched the incident. An example illustrates the variety of response to provocation.

Beit Jala is an Arab town of 8,200 people about 5 miles south of Jerusalem, just across the valley from Bethlehem. At Beit Jala, one of the more widely reported West Bank incidents occurred in late March 1978, not many days after the large-scale Israeli Army invasion of southern Lebanon. The West Bank population was restive and Israeli soldiers tense and expectant. But in Beit Jala itself there was no significant demonstration that brought approximately fifty Israeli soldiers to the local high school. The soldiers surrounded the school, rebuffed the protests of the headmaster, ordered the pupils into their classrooms, and closed the windows. The soldiers then hurled beer-can-sized cannisters of U.S.-made CS-riot control gas into the classrooms. Frightened students jumped from the second-floor windows 18 feet above the ground. Ten were hospitalized with serious fractures.

The military government, at first, denied that anything had happened at Beit Jala. *Time* magazine's Jerusalem bureau chief, David

Neff, heard about Beit Jala two days later and went to investigate. The classrooms, he wrote, still smelled of the riot control gases. Following *Time*'s report of April 3, 1978, Israeli reporters began to investigate the story. Initial reports by local military authorities attempted to cover up the incident, but persistent probing brought an inquiry by the minister of defense, Ezer Weizman. Ultimately, he found that his own officers had not provided him with accurate accounts, and he finally acted to remove the West Bank military commander from his post and to discipline several subordinates.[18]

In the annals of the occupation, the Beit Jala incident is not unique. However, in this instance Israeli authorities took corrective measures against the military governor in charge. But the legacy of mutual distrust created by such events is great and will not soon be forgotten; permanent scars will be left.

EDUCATION

The educational system in the West Bank was structured by the Jordanians during the two decades (1948–1967) of their rule. The Israeli occupation government has enacted a series of orders bringing the different sections of the educational system under the direct control of the military governor. Order No. 91 deals with the public schools and Order No. 854 focuses on institutions of higher learning. A controversy has arisen over the nature of these controls and the fairness of their administration. A recent report by West Bank Palestinian jurists claims that there has been a steady decline in quality in the public schools and a lack of new facilities in the face of considerable population increases. There have been reductions in staff, decline in the value of salaries (now paid in Israeli currency and not indexed to inflation as they are in Israel), and deterioration of morale. Strict control is exercised over all school activities, meetings, clubs, cultural events, extracurricular activities, and even sports events.

Two 1981 reports, one in the U.S. weekly *Science* and the other in the professional journal *Chronicle of Higher Education,* cite some of the difficulties in higher education. For example, the military government has refused to allow the Bir Zeit University library to acquire some 2,000 books and magazines written in Arabic and published in

Arab countries. The military government also claims the right to ban anti-Israeli and anti-Zionist publications that it feels might incite violence. Ironically, many of the banned periodicals are on the shelves of the Hebrew University in Jerusalem. The banned books range widely from Palestinian folklore to Islamic thought and include such titles as *The Islamic Dictionary* and *Arab Society and the Palestine Question.* [19] A committee of Israeli professors at the Hebrew University has, on a number of occasions, protested such book banning.

In early November 1980, Israeli authorities closed Bir Zeit University on the ground that the "Palestine Week" it was planning would provoke violence. Planned were nationalistic plays, poetry readings, and songs. Several Israeli professors, connected with Arabic studies, had expected to participate. On November 18, several days after the closing, Israeli troops broke up a student protest and shot eleven Arab students in the legs. The university after reopening for the new term was closed once again in November 1981.

Bir Zeit, with 1,000 students, is the largest of the five Palestinian colleges in the West Bank. In addition to its proximate educational responsibilities, it sees its mission among Palestinians in much the same way as early Jewish settlers saw that of the Hebrew University —to create a national identity.

The relative autonomy of the Palestinian colleges went undisturbed until 1977, when in the wake of Menachem Begin's election a new wave of Israeli settlement construction brought heightened protest, much of it from Palestinian students. In the summer of 1980, the Israeli military government issued Order No. 854, which denied the autonomy of all five colleges and placed them under direct military control. The schools were required to obtain annual licenses, revocable at will by the Israelis, and they had to live with new rules giving the army the power to pass on the hiring and firing of instructors, the admission and expulsion of students, and the nature of the academic curriculum, including the subjects taught and the textbooks used. Bir Zeit had recently been allowed to reopen for the new academic year, and the closing in November brought protests from around the world. Israeli intellectuals joined the protests, urging that "the Palestinian Arabs receive the same rights as we demand for ourselves, including the right to a higher education."[20] Nevertheless, the military government has withheld from Bir Zeit University, and other West Bank institutions, exemption from customs duties on equipment imported from abroad, a privilege accorded to Israeli universities. Israeli customs duties are very high, and the cost to West Bank institutions has been punitive. Bir Zeit claims to have paid about $250,000 in import duties.

The Bir Zeit administration claims that the military government withheld permission or refused to reply to requests for residence permits for teachers coming from other countries to work at the university. This has caused inconvenience and scheduling difficulties, since teachers, if they come anyway on shorter-term visas issued at the border, must apply for extensions, and if these extensions are not granted, the teachers are forced to leave the country. The problem has been greatest for, but is not limited to, those coming from countries which have no diplomatic relations with Israel.

Universities on the West Bank need permits to develop any new programs. For example, approval has been refused for establishing agricultural and engineering schools at an-Najah University in Nablus. Bethlehem University, a Vatican-sponsored school, was denied permission to open a program to train tour guides in its school of hotel management.[21]

While often not harsh in the sense of being violent (though a number of university students have been shot and several killed), the Israeli control of West Bank education has been arbitrary and at times punitive. It has interfered with the building of institutions to serve the long-run educational and intellectual needs of the Palestinian residents. Sahar Khalifah, a Bir Zeit instructor and talented novelist, expressed the problem this way in a seminar sponsored by the International Writers Program at the University of Iowa in 1978:

> Tension inside, tension outside . . . You feel you are in a whirlpool, a whirlwind, a pressure cooker . . . Occupation, demonstrations, news, trials, prisons, demolished houses, demolished souls. Taxes . . . a new devaluation, a new settlement there; tomorrow they'll build a new one here. Where shall I go then? To whom shall I protest?[22]

4

The Palestinians

The "Palestine problem," as it has come to be called, remains at the core of the Arab-Israeli conflict. The 1970 AFSC study, *Search for Peace in the Middle East,* offered an important though modest assessment of how to deal with it:

> Recognition in practical form of a way to build community and to establish the political rights of the Palestine people is a necessary early step toward solution of the area's problems. This must be achieved straightforwardly and honestly, with full cooperation of the international community, of Israel, and of the Arab states.[1]

More than a decade has passed and the recommendation is largely unfulfilled. While some things remain unchanged, the majority of Palestinians still live under occupation or in diaspora, there have been important developments in the Palestinian nationalist movement and an emerging vision of pragmatic nationalist goals mixed with a passionate concern for justice.

But first the people. Who are and where are the Palestinians today? What elements of their lives shape the politics of their movements and the statements of their leaders? There are two recent distinct Palestinian experiences that are critical in every Palestinian's consciousness: occupation and dispersion. Although no full census has been taken of the Palestinians, estimates suggest the population is just over 3.5 million people. Of these, slightly fewer than .5 million live in Israel and have become Israeli citizens since the 1949 truce. Another 1.25 million reside in the occupied West Bank and Gaza. The largest group

(1.1 million) living outside of their former home region of Palestine is in Jordan. There are approximately 300,000 in Lebanon; 180,000 in Syria, 170,000 in Kuwait; 40,000 in Egypt; 45,000 living in Saudi Arabia and other Persian Gulf states; 16,000 in Iraq; 7,000 in Libya; and some 50,000 spread through Western Europe, the U.S., and South America. These figures tell only part of the story. Some 643,000 of the Palestinian population, or over 20 percent of those not in Israel, are still residents of the two categories of refugee camps, established and emergency. These camps are located in Lebanon, Jordan, Syria, the West Bank, and Gaza Strip. From those who entered the camps in the wake of the 1948 war, a whole generation has been born and raised and has had children of its own within the confines of the camps.[2]

PALESTINIANS IN ARAB LANDS

No single description would fit the experiences of Palestinian communities in different parts of the Arab world. They form different proportions of the populations in their host lands, ranging from 60 percent in Jordan to below 1 percent in Iraq, so that the importance of their political and social roles varies. Although the Palestinians share Arabic as a common language and Islam as a common religion (except in Lebanon, where there is a large Christian minority), in the various societies in which they reside they have established very different forms of social and political organization and have set up different means of receiving or integrating the Palestinian inhabitants. In Jordan many have been able to achieve full citizenship and participate in the affairs of the state (including even cabinet membership), a result of the inclusion of the West Bank in the Kingdom of Jordan after the 1949 armistice agreement. In other countries, however, they remain refugees or, even in the second generation, outsiders. Many live in camps or in city districts or neighborhoods which are effectively separate, and they are often discriminated against. Like other foreign nationals they may engage in business in the Gulf or Arabian states, but a national must be either the senior partner or the business registrant. Palestinians, aware of European history, often compare their present status to that of the Jews in the ghettos of Europe. They have come to fill the role of expatriate professionals, teachers, technicians, and skilled artisans in many societies.

Because of their nationalism and the revolutionary elements of some parts of their movement, Palestinians have been politically suspect in many Arab lands and sometimes have been imprisoned for political reasons. Thus, while the Palestinian political movement has been supported for its external activities, it has been closely circumscribed in Arab host countries.

In addition, some Arab states have used or controlled Palestinian nationalist groups for their own ends. There are Syrian-, Iraqi-, and Libyan-backed Palestinian organizations; within Lebanon, the political and military operation of the PLO is mediated and constrained in large measure by Syrian military involvement. Indeed, the first Syrian involvement in the Lebanon Civil War in 1976 was in battle with the PLO and Lebanese-Muslim-Leftist alliance.

One Palestinian scholar who lives in the U.S., Edward Said, has expressed concern with ". . . the form of Palestinian survival." Divided, dispersed, without territorial sovereignty, distrusted, demeaned, faced by hostility everywhere, Palestinians face a problem of maintaining identity. He comments, "A child born since 1948, therefore, asserts the original connection to lost Palestine as a bit of symbolic evidence that the Palestinians have gone on regardless: He or she *would* have been born there but for 1948."[3] The dispersion, and the refugee camps, keep alive an image of the whole of the old Palestine.

The widely held, easy assumption of the 1950's in the U.S. and elsewhere that somehow the Palestinian problem would literally be absorbed by the Arab states has given way to the realization that the Palestinians are stateless exiles. The dynamics of the Middle East nationalist development have worked to increase rather than diminish Palestinian nationalism. It is even possible that the Palestinians might be accepted more easily as long-term residents in Arab lands if they had a passport and nationality of their own. Most Palestinians insist on their heritage and nationhood and claim that they do not seek permanent residence in the Arab countries.

THE OCCUPATION

The other commanding Palestinian experience since 1967 has been life under occupation. The largest single group of Palestinians now lives in day-to-day interaction with the Israeli military government. Although there are extensive refugee camps in the West Bank and Gaza, it is in the life of the Palestinian cities, towns, and villages that there is the greatest sense of urgency to remove the occupiers. Widely accepted U.N. Resolutions 242 (1967) and 338 (1973), calling for withdrawal by Israel from recently occupied territories and for peace and secure borders, have been seen by some Palestinians as adding a special political legitimacy to their claims for self-determination in the West Bank and Gaza Strip.[4]

The very nature of the occupation has created an international politics, an Israeli politics, and a Palestinian politics that influence the course of the development of Palestinian nationalism.

For the Palestinians who had sought the return of their entire homeland, the occupation of the West Bank and Gaza Strip has raised a pressing question. Can they afford to wait out some grand solution to the problem of *all* of Palestine or will the continued occupation of the territories mean such irreversible changes as to make them virtually part of Israel itself? Palestinians today find themselves at a critical point of decision—to enter negotiations with Israel or to disdain them.

THE PLO AND THE PALESTINIANS

Israeli leaders have often tended to belittle ideas of Palestinian national identity or to deny the existence of the Palestinians. "Who are the Palestinians?" Golda Meir asked. Begin called them the "Arabs of the Land of Israel." But in the Camp David accords, Begin initialed a document referring to the "legitimate rights of the Palestinians."[5] Now, with tacit acknowledgment of the Palestinian people, the focus for discussion has become the Palestine Liberation Organization (PLO) and its role in the political life of the Palestinians. For Israel and for the U.S., the PLO was declared an organization with which neither power would deal. For most Palestinians it is *the* representative of their nationalist activities, especially in the international arena. The Arab states, across the political spectrum, have declared that the PLO is the "sole legitimate representative of the Palestinian people."[6] The Soviet Union and many nations of the Third World accord formal diplomatic status to the PLO, and most West European nations now maintain some form of unofficial relations with the PLO. At this time it is an illusion to believe that some other group exists that can speak on behalf of the Palestinians or engage in any serious negotiations for Palestinians without PLO involvement or endorsement. We recognize that there is not always unanimity within the PLO, but it remains the strongest group by far among the Palestinians.

The history of the Palestinian nationalist organization is complex and interesting for those concerned with the manner in which religious, nationalist, political, social, regional, and personal factors interact in creating Third World liberation movements. It is important to take into consideration the broad outlines of the history of Palestinian political organizations and to understand the constraints and opportunities they face.

The PLO had its origins in January 1964 at the Cairo Summit of Kings and Presidents of the Arab states. The meeting had several purposes. Inter-Arab rivalries and the use which different states made of separate Palestinian groups for their own ends were troubling. The Arab states recognized the new organizational role that Palestinians would play in the resistance to Israel. The PLO was then formed as an organizational umbrella for Palestinian liberation. There is little doubt, however, that Egyptian President Nasser maintained the commanding influence.

After the Arab defeat in the 1967 war and the concomitant destruction of the legitimacy of almost all the existing Arab leadership, the Palestinians realized the limits to their reliance on support by the Arab states. The 1967 defeat also reshaped Arab and Palestinian thinking to focus on resolution of the Palestinian problem. The broader revolutionary purposes which had previously been a focus of Arab nationalist movements from Egypt to Iraq were overshadowed.

One recent study lists more than twenty Palestinian resistance groups. Among these, Fatah (Palestine National Liberation Movement) is the oldest, largest, and most influential. While it is only one of many units of the PLO, it now accounts for 70 percent of the umbrella group and its leadership has assumed effective control. Fatah's membership runs the spectrum of belief and social orientation in the Palestinian community. It is more conservative than other guerrilla groups and reflects a generally Arab orientation, broadly construed Islamic religious beliefs, and a politically neutralist stance.

It contains segments that are Christian and also a strong secular, socialist wing.[7]

Eight guerilla groups now make up the PLO along with Fatah, and Yasir Arafat, the Fatah leader, is Chairman of the PLO executive committee. In the wake of the 1967 war, the PLO filled a vacuum. From the point of view of outsiders, the PLO took on the qualities of a "government in exile," although in fact it has rejected that political choice. Although known in the media primarily for guerrilla military activities, and terrorism, the PLO has assumed responsibility for many aspects of Palestinian life, especially in refugee communities. It has established a social service system and formed a Palestinian branch of the Red Crescent (headed by a physician, younger brother of Yasir Arafat); it conducts schools and operates an industrial cooperative (SAMED) in Lebanon. The PLO offered a political defense for their resort to terrorism, arguing it "gives our cause resounding coverage—positive or negative it mattered little."[8]

In the aftermath of the 1973 Arab-Israeli war, an Arab summit at Rabat, Morocco, in 1974, strengthened the PLO role and designated it as "the sole legitimate representative" of the Palestinian people. This further institutionalization and legitimization of the Palestinian movement reflected several sets of interests. It strengthened the hand of the PLO at the international level, sanctioning the PLO to speak for the Palestinians and to assert greater control over all segments of the movement. It was this latter which was of particular interest to the Arab oil states that are large financial supporters of the PLO and that wanted to assure a responsible Palestinian movement. The Arab states, having achieved a new self-confidence based on wealth from oil and what they conceived to be a positive military performance in the 1973 war, asserted what one observer described as a "metaphysical right" to the West Bank and Gaza.[9] This Arab support for the PLO has been interpreted as sanctioning a conservative and largely non-revolutionary nationalism for the PLO.

Other elements served to shape the attitude of growing pragmatism toward the Arab-Israeli conflict in the Palestinian movement and the PLO, as well as in the Arab world as a whole. Walid Khalidi, a leading Palestinian political scientist, points to a growing awareness of the extent of commitment the U.S. was willing to make to the security and well-being of Israel and conversely the limited and quite cautious Soviet support to the Arabs against Israel.[10] This realization was one influence in President Sadat's decision to break ties with the Soviets. Khalidi also points to "the growing Palestinian awareness of what the revolutionary armed struggle can and cannot achieve" as important in this regard.

The PLO has been further legitimated by the extent to which it received support from Palestinian communities in the West Bank and Gaza Strip. As the occupation continued after 1967, the local Palestinian leadership that had been tied to Jordan during the two decades, 1948–1967, began to grow weaker. Jordanian influence suffered further erosion following the September 1970 clash between Jordan and the PLO, during which the latter was forced to leave Jordan and move to Lebanon. The influence of Jordan as spokesman for Palestinian interests decreased. The Israeli occupation helped create a distinct Palestinian consciousness among those living in the occupied territories and gave focus to a struggle against the occupier. When Palestinian moderates achieved no political concessions from Israel, they were replaced by more explicitly nationalist leaders. As one Israeli analyst assessed the situation: "Israeli policy with regard to the question of Palestinian leadership proved to be counter-productive."[11] Limiting local leaders to purely municipal affairs, deporting over 1,000 leading Palestinians, banning public political meetings, and expecting broader Palestinian issues to be handled by the Jordanians thoroughly undermined the credibility of the traditional West Bank leadership. The Israeli acceleration of land expropriation and Jewish settlements in the territories only strengthened these trends. The late 1960's and the 1970's was also a period of continued rise of the PLO to broad recognition and legitimacy in the Arab world. It was through the political interests of the Arab states and the Palestinian people that the PLO came to be accepted as the obvious and sole coordinator of Palestinian unity.

In 1976 the Israelis set municipal elections for the West Bank with the clear hope that a moderate leadership not linked to the PLO would emerge and provide an alternative Palestinian voice in the occupied territories.[12] Initially, the Palestinians rejected participation in the electoral process as part of their boycott of Israeli rule, but at the last moment they relented. They elected to municipal office an almost complete slate of Palestinian nationalist leaders, many fresh political faces, and primarily PLO supporters. Seventy-two percent of the eligible electorate went to the polls and overwhelmingly supported the new nationalist leadership, a victory that stunned the Israeli government.[13] Bassam Shak'a, the new mayor of Nablus, made the point: "The elections proved clearly that the Palestinians believe their sole legal representative to be the PLO."[14] Israel had underestimated the growing nationalism of the Palestinians and ignored the changes taking place in the second Palestinian generation. Educated and independent, this generation was ready to break with the traditions of an earlier compliant generation and to vote for new leadership. The Israeli unwillingness to understand that Palestinian nationalism and support for the PLO were potent forces was continued by the Likud government when it came to power in May 1977. Begin's government, with its ideological commitment to maintain sovereignty over the occupied territories that they referred to by their Biblical names, Judea and Samaria, rejected any idea of territorial compromise. It further sought to prevent Palestinian self-expression. The pro-PLO leadership on the West Bank gained in popular support, strengthened by Israeli repressive acts, and became an increasingly important political voice in both the international Palestinian nationalist movement and the PLO.

Public support for the PLO leadership also came in the form of statements and resolutions from West Bank voluntary societies, student groups, and professional organizations. In September and October 1978, in response to the search for some alternate Palestinian leadership to join in the Camp David process, the Arab Graduates Union, the Union of Professional Societies, students at the Teacher Training Institute in Ramallah, Bir Zeit University, and an Najah University adopted a resolution reaffirming the unity of Palestinian people and the fact that the PLO is their sole legitimate representative. They also rejected Begin's "self-rule" proposal and called instead for self-determination and national independence after Israeli withdrawal from the occupied territories and East Jerusalem.[15]

It is important to note that these Palestinian statements generally restricted their call to Israeli withdrawal from the West Bank and

Gaza, with Palestinian self-determination to be exercised in these limited areas. Hebron mayor, Fahd Qawasmi, even after his deportation, explicitly indicated that his vision was of Palestine living alongside Israel: "When I say I support the idea of two states this means mutual recognition and normalization."[16] But he cautioned that he was expressing a personal view and that he could not speak for the PLO. Nonetheless, his politics and his constituency represent an important influence in PLO decisionmaking.

What does the PLO believe? Yasir Arafat, the PLO leader, suggested the pattern of policy change through which his organization has gone. In an interview with *The New York Times,* May 8, 1980, he is quoted: "We are the only victims who have offered two solutions; in 1967 we suggested a democratic secular state, but people said we wanted to demolish Israel so we offered another solution. We said that we have the right to establish our independent state in any land from which the Israelis withdraw or we have liberated."[17] This has become the familiar formula that Arafat and much of the rest of the PLO has used in recent years. In his discussions primarily with Western political leaders and the Western press, Arafat has repeated this formulation. He has consistently refused to give details on its final borders, but he generally has limited his view of a Palestinian state to the currently occupied West Bank and Gaza Strip, 20 percent of the former land of Palestine. In addition, he has accepted the concept of security provisions, including joint superpower guarantees, demilitarized zones, and United Nations peacekeeping forces within the Palestinian state.[18] These issues, including careful consideration of security concerns, have been discussed in greater detail by Palestinians regarded as close to the PLO.[19]

Arafat in recent years has defended PLO discussions with progressive elements, including Zionists in Israel, and has expressed increasing confidence in political means to achieve a just settlement while not ruling out continued guerrilla warfare. On the key question of recognition of Israel he has remained equivocal, claiming that it represents his political "trump card" (see *The New York Times,* August 17, 1981), which he will not yet give up. Critics of the PLO can and do point to the Palestine National Covenant, written in 1964 and amended in 1968, which declared the original U.N. partition of 1947 illegal (Art. 19) and called for the liberation of Palestine and the elimination of the Zionist presence in Palestine (Art. 15).[20]

An accumulation of evidence suggests a shift in the PLO and Palestinian position from the extreme claims of 1968, when the revised Palestinian covenant was adopted, to the more pragmatic formulation of 1981. Careful consideration of the changing political base and their altered sense of current realities strongly suggests that the newer conceptualizations—a limited Palestinian state in the West Bank and the Gaza Strip—are not merely tactical formulations. Basic shifts in the PLO stance have developed through time.[21] Also, the very act itself of supporting a Palestinian state in the West Bank and Gaza Strip on repeated occasions increases commitment to it.

These changes did not come quickly, though they were obviously entertained for several years after the 1967 war. In 1972 King Hussein of Jordan proposed retrieving the West Bank and federating it with Jordan. During this period, the quasi-parliamentary Palestine National Council (PNC) rejected the concept of a ministate for Palestine.[22] In part their resolutions rejecting this were criticisms of King Hussein. But it was probably his suggestion that triggered the new Palestinian attitudes. The Palestinian leadership was fearful that if the West Bank was returned to Jordan, the Palestine problem would be perceived to be resolved and the PLO would have forfeited its role in deciding the fate of its own people.

A significant change in the PLO position can be dated from the period immediately following the 1973 Arab-Israeli war. As early as November 1973, Eric Rouleau, veteran Middle East correspondent for *Le Monde*, described new attitudes among the PLO leadership. Fatah leaders told him that they needed time "to prepare the grassroots psychologically for recognizing a state whose destruction they have pledged for over a quarter of a century."[23]

The twelfth meeting of the PNC in June 1974 saw the first signs of an official reformulation. A resolution, still couched in the language of self-determination for the whole land, spoke also of establishing an "independent combatant national authority over every part of Palestinian territory that is liberated."[24] A variety of statements and resolutions by Palestinian leaders continued for several years to present a mosaic of ambiguous views. The concept of a democratic secular state in all of Palestine was dropped, however, and instead "an independent Palestinian state" became the stated goal. Said Hammami, the PLO representative in London, noted in 1975 that "the Palestinian Arabs must recognize the fact that there is an Israeli people and this people has a right to live in peace in what they consider to be their own country."[25] (Said Hammami was later assassinated by an Iraqi-sponsored squad.) About this same time, Dr. Issam Sartawi, an independent among the PLO leadership, began discussions with Israeli moderate Zionists initially under the aegis of former French premier Pierre Mendès-France and later with the aid of Austrian prime minister Bruno Kreisky. These contacts continue today despite criticism from some Palestinian "rejectionists"—those who reject any dealings with Israel, including the Popular Front for the Liberation of Palestine and the Syrian-backed guerrilla groups. (A PNC resolution of July 1981 sought to restrict contacts to progressive Jews and anti-Zionists.) Another official, if still ambiguous, change came at the March 1977, thirteenth PNC meeting. Resolution 11 expressed the council's determination to pursue the struggle to establish their independent national state.[26] They still rejected explicit recognition of Israel, however, as a price for a settlement of the conflict. Unofficial attempts to bring the United States and the PLO into dialogue began in this period. The U.S. formula for permitting itself to overcome its commitment to Israel not to negotiate with the PLO was to secure PLO acceptance of U.N. Resolution 242, with the allowance for adding to the resolution claims for recognition of Palestinian national rights. Out of the PNC meeting also came intensive diplomatic efforts by the PLO to gain international political support. The results, after four years, from the Palestinian point of view have been highly successful, and some 105 nations now recognize the PLO and give it a status equivalent to that of a government in exile.

Among the international diplomatic efforts in 1977 was an October joint statement of the U.S. and the U.S.S.R. drafted by Secretary of State Cyrus Vance and Foreign Minister Andrei Gromyko. While it is not a Palestinian document, it has frequently been referred to by Palestinian sources as an acceptable basis for a solution. Israeli withdrawal to the approximate pre-1967 borders was envisioned as part of a comprehensive settlement that assumed both Israeli security and the legitimate right of the Palestinian people. The statement proposed several measures, including demilitarized zones, U.N. troop involvement, and joint superpower guarantees to protect the borders of all nations in the region. The Palestinians were to be represented at a Geneva Conference.[27] Israel objected vigorously to the formulation, and within a month Egyptian President Sadat made his surprising visit to Jerusalem. The Camp David meetings and subsequent accords left moot the statement and marked a significant shift in the U.S. approach, and effectively cut the U.S.S.R. out of the peace process.

The Palestinian movements gathered at Tripoli in December 1977 in response to the Sadat mission and issued a statement, belligerent in tone, and seeming to pull back from diplomatic efforts. The representatives, including those from Palestinian rejectionist groups, agreed to ". . . strive for the realization of the Palestinian people's right to return and to self-determination within the context of an independent Palestinian state on any part of Palestinian land without reconciliation, recognition or negotiations as an interim aim of the Palestinian Revolution."[28]

The PLO was clearly fearful of being closed out of a settlement process and thus hardened its position and rejected the legitimacy of that particular process. In part at least, these fears were confirmed by the restrictive autonomy proposal announced by the Begin government after Sadat's visit. It is also important to note, however, that the PLO explicitly included in this strident statement the concept of an independent state on part of the land of Palestine. Influences shaping this statement included international agreements for external support and the political interests of both the West Bank constituency and those within the PLO who firmly accepted the concept of a limited Palestinian state. Also the rejectionist groups in the PLO had their views expressed in the formal resolutions of January 1979. The texts of Palestinian nationalism have been as multifaceted as the Palestinian constituencies. In the resolutions of the parliamentlike PNC, the language has something in it for all participant interests. However, in the commentaries and public statement of the PLO leadership and their close supporters more subtlety is introduced, and to understand the PLO and Palestinian policy, it is necessary to read these with care.

In 1979–1980, senior PLO leaders, including Yasir Arafat and

Khalid al-Hassan, became involved in a series of initiatives in Europe, ranging from meetings with Chancellor Bruno Kreisky of Austria and former German Chancellor Willy Brandt to contacts with then French President Valéry Giscard d'Estaing and British Foreign Minister Lord Carrington. The PLO brought to these meetings a plan for Israeli withdrawal from the occupied territories and U.N.- and PLO-coordinated self-determination by the Palestinian people, including the right to establish a state. Of particular interest in this plan, prepared initially by al-Hassan, is the involvement of the U.N., the U.S., the U.S.S.R., and member nations of the European Economic Community. In addition, the plan proposed as the legal foundations for the solution of the problem the U.N. Charter and Declaration of Human Rights and "all U.N. resolutions regarding the Palestinian issue and the Zionist-Palestinian conflict." It also referred to several anti-Zionist General Assembly resolutions. The acceptance of U.N. Resolution 242 is implied. The critics noted, however, the plan's inclusion of "the principle of the right to pursue through democratic means the reunification of Palestine in a single Palestinian state."[29] This statement combined a pragmatic realism, accepting a limited state in the short run while holding out the right to renegotiate a reunification of Palestine at a future time. By stipulating that "democratic means" were those to be used to achieve what Arafat in his U.N. speech of 1974 called his "dream" of a unified Palestine, the PLO was responding to Israeli fears of violence and to international concern for peaceful resolution of the conflict. The PLO in this statement is implying that any further claims must be negotiated and not pursued by force.

The European Community meeting in Venice on June 12, 1980, responded to the Palestinian contacts with a statement on how to resolve the Arab-Israeli conflict. After strong entreaties from the United States not to undermine the Camp David process, the "European Initiative" that emerged was quite mild. It endorsed a role for the United Nations and supported the concept of Palestinian self-determination. While viewed as generally sympathetic to the Palestinian cause, the European statement did not explicitly support a Palestinian state; and while not recognizing the PLO, did say the PLO should be associated with the solution.[30]

A review of the evolution of PLO policies leaves us with the feeling that each full step forward has been followed by a half step backward. However, there is a consistently developed theme—support for an independent state. What about its borders, or its relations with Israel? In the middle of one of the debates at the PNC in March 1977 when Dr. Issam Sartawi was sharply criticized for the meetings he was holding with Zionist members of the Israel Council for Israeli-Palestinian Peace, Arafat, addressing a Palestinian audience, supported Sartawi for his work with an Israeli group. He said, "Are you willing to live together with the Jews? If not you are using false slogans since the day the Palestinian state will be created, we shall have to live with the Jews side by side and in peace."[31]

Much of the PLO and its leadership have moved from the maximalist positions of 1968 steadily if uncertainly in the direction of accommodation. They have dropped the insistence on the armed liberation of the whole of Palestine and have increasingly talked of and utilized political action as well as armed struggle to achieve their ends. Their explicit willingness to meet with progressive Jewish and Israeli groups from inside and outside Israel has not only widened contacts but given the process of peacemaking human dimensions. The AFSC has had direct involvement with several of these informal meetings and has been, on each occasion, deeply impressed to watch former combatants from both sides struggle together to identify acceptable paths to peace.

In August 1981, Crown Prince Fahd of Saudi Arabia released an eight-point peace proposal drawn largely from previously adopted United Nations resolutions (notably U.N. Resolutions 242 [Security Council] and 3236 [General Assembly]). In summary, its points included:

- Israeli withdrawal from all territory occupied in the 1967 war
- Removal of Israeli settlements from the West Bank and other occupied areas
- Guarantees of freedom of worship for all religious sects in the Holy Land
- Recognition of the right of 2 million Palestinian refugees to repatriation and compensation for those who do not wish to return

- A U.N. trusteeship in the Palestinian-populated West Bank of the Jordan River and the Gaza Strip during a transition period of a few months
- Establishment of an independent Palestinian state, with the Arab sector of Jerusalem as its capital
- Affirmation of the right of all countries in the region to "live in peace"
- Guarantees of the implementation of these principles by the United Nations or some of its members (presumably the U.S. and U.S.S.R.)[32]

The inclusion of the intent of U.N. Security Council Resolution 242 guaranteeing the right of all states "to live in peace" was an inclusion of the diplomatic language for recognition of Israel. The explicit reference to Israel's withdrawal from the territory occupied in 1967 and the mention of no other territory also imply recognition of Israel within the pre-1967 borders. While no element in the Saudi proposal is new, Crown Prince Fahd's bringing them all together represents an attempt to put forward an Arab negotiating position. Saudi Arabia, while an important state in the region and a key supporter of the PLO, must be joined by other Arab countries if its proposals are to become a realistic basis for solving the Palestinian problem. The failure of the plan to win acceptance at the Arab summit at Fez, Morocco, in November 1981 was less a judgment of the merits of the proposal than an indication of political divisions among the Arab states and the different perceptions of the national interest of each state. In this instance, Syria withheld its agreement.

Several days after the Saudi proposal was presented, Yasir Arafat termed it "A good beginning for lasting peace in the Middle East." Several months later, on October 30, 1981, in a full-page interview in the leading Beirut daily *An Nahar,* Arafat expanded his support for the proposals because they call for "coexistence" between Israel and the Arabs. He also linked the Saudi proposal to points included in the Palestine national charter.[33] The Palestinian leadership, however, still has not made explicit its terms for a settlement, its position on cessation of military actions, or the terms for its recognition of Israel. Nor has the PLO put forward its opening position for negotiations. In his comments on Fahd's proposal, Arafat again refused explicit recognition of Israel's right to exist. Nonetheless, also in the summer of 1981, the PLO engaged in indirect negotiations with Israel for a cease-fire in Southern Lebanon. Thus, the PLO has demonstrated its willingness under some circumstances to engage seriously in the diplomatic and political process.

Menachem Begin's government quickly rejected the Saudi proposal. Several Labor Party leaders, while rejecting the Saudi proposal for a Palestinian state, did, however, positively note Saudi Arabia's implicit acceptance of Israel in the region. The difference in PLO and Israeli government reaction is important. For if the trajectory of Palestinian policy has led it steadily toward limiting its claims and the acceptance of an independent state alongside Israel, the Israeli government policy, especially since 1977, has hardened appreciably, now claiming permanent sovereignty in the West Bank and Gaza Strip. The Saudi proposals also were greeted with suspicion or denounced by the rejectionists in the Palestinian movement.[34]

RESOLVING THE PALESTINIAN PROBLEM

Can the impasse be broken? Can the Palestine problem be resolved? Perhaps, if the key parties with an interest in the outcome take steps to seek a solution rather than to block one.

The United States may have lived with the illusions that Camp David is enough and that someone other than the Palestinians can speak for them, but the United States can play a vital role in bringing the Palestinians into the political discourse out of which peace may emerge. The United States need not agree with the PLO or believe that its current political expressions are adequate in order to recognize that the PLO is the legitimate representative of the Palestinian people. To begin to move toward a peaceful solution to the Palestinian problem, the United States should enter into a dialogue with the PLO. It was unwise for the U.S. to agree in 1975 to undertake no negotiations with the PLO. The changes that have occurred since 1975 plus U.S. interests—and the interests of Middle East peace—call even more strongly for a revised U.S. position.

The United States should place itself in a position to deal honestly and justly with both Israel and the PLO. This realistic view has been gaining support from many political quarters in the United States, including those who previously opposed a U.S.-PLO dialogue. In summer 1981, after he had left office, Zbigniew Brzezinski, President Carter's national security advisor, advocated opening up direct discussions with the PLO, pointing to changes that have occurred in the Middle East. "We have to take account of changing attitudes in the Arab world . . . the view that Israel must be accepted," he said.[35] Brzezinski drew an analogy to France's refusal to talk to the National Liberation Front of Algeria in the 1950's during the Algerian war for independence. Today the government of Algeria, one of the most responsible in North Africa, Brzezinski said, is led by former leaders of the Front. Hermann Eilts, the former U.S. ambassador to Egypt, has also urged direct dialogue: "Only through open U.S. contacts with the PLO leadership will it be possible to gauge whether the PLO would be willing and able to participate responsibly in broader peace negotiations."[36] This point of view gained additional support from former Presidents Ford and Carter, who, on returning from the funeral of President Sadat in October 1981, jointly expressed the conviction that the U.S. should enter into direct contact with the PLO as an element in resolving the Israeli-Arab impasse.[37] U.S. talks with the PLO cannot be expected to bring immediate solutions to Middle East problems. However, to fail to engage in probing dialogue and to thereby risk losing possible peacemaking opportunities is politically rigid and unwise.

Israeli settlements policies may fast be foreclosing options for peaceful resolution with the Palestinians. The United States, by allowing its military and economic aid to be used indirectly for Israeli settlements in the occupied territories, becomes a silent partner in thwarting the intent of U.N. Resolution 242, which calls for Israel's withdrawal from these lands.

The United States government must not only express its opposition to land expropriation, settlements, seizure of water resources, deportations of civic leaders, and those other moves aimed to insure long-term Israeli control of the West Bank and Gaza Strip, it must also take direct steps to assure that U.S. aid is not used as part of this policy. Funds given to Israel should be under regular scrutiny so that they are not diverted to building settlements in the occupied territories.

The U.S. could reduce U.S. aid in proportion to Israeli expenditures for West Bank settlements as a strong symbolic representation of U.S. disapproval of Israel's claim to full sovereignty in the West Bank and Gaza.

U.S. policies in relation to Israel and to the Palestinians should reflect a true intent to achieve peace based on a secure Israel and self-determination for the Palestinians. The Arab states have the opportunity to play a crucial role. By advancing and supporting a peace plan including Israeli withdrawal from the occupied territories, Palestinian self-determination, and recognition of Israel's right to peaceful and secure borders, these states could play an important part in bringing Israel and the Palestinians to the negotiating table. The Saudi Arabian proposal or a similar plan could serve as an important beginning since it reflects the consensus that has grown in the Arab world as well as the safeguards that have been part of the United Nations Security Council resolutions. The Arabs must understand that Israel will mistrust any such proposal and so must be ready to reiterate their intentions and pursue negotiations forcefully. They will have to be explicit in communicating to the Israeli people their respect for Israel's right to a secure existence.

The European initiatives and the important rapport they have established in the Arab world give the European states a particular opportunity and responsibility for bolstering a new peace process. As Walid Khalidi has noted, the Europeans could constructively focus attention on the two principles of "reciprocity" and "co-existence," i.e., on mutual recognition and mutual security.[38] The Europeans are particularly well placed to serve as intermediaries to draw out from the Palestinians the full implications of their statements and resolutions and from the Israelis their responses. As intermediaries, the Europeans could elucidate Palestinian moves and Israeli counter-moves in a series of steps toward peace.

Israel's current policy of sovereignty over the occupied lands seems to foreclose any solution to the Palestinian problem. If Israel wishes a solution, it should halt any further West Bank-Gaza settlements and the creation of an elaborate Israeli infrastructure. Israel could indicate the terms on which it would meet with the PLO in a process leading ultimately to negotiations. Is the call for reciprocal recognition one that could begin the process? Israel could take up the negotiating proposals of the Arab states, with their implied recognition of Israel, and use them to fashion an agenda for further exchange.

The PLO should also act to unblock the impasse. By joining an Arab peace initiative, finally making explicit what it has left implied in its statements, the PLO should set out the basis on which it would recognize Israel and be willing to engage in the too-long-delayed negotiations. A sound PLO-Arab proposal should offer peace, recognition, and security to Israel in return for Israeli withdrawal from the occupied territories and an independent state for the Palestinians. Any Israeli political leadership would find it difficult to dismiss such an offer, for the people of Israel would for the first time be able to envision a future of peaceful coexistence with their neighbors. There would be a buildup of significant political pressure. Such a move also would have important reverberations for U.S. policy and action in the Middle East.

5

Security and Terrorism

It is impossible to write about the Middle East and the central problems between Israel and the Palestinians without addressing directly the issues of security and terrorism. These issues arouse deep emotion everywhere. The AFSC feels strongly about them, and we are sure that no long-term resolutions of problems will be possible until they are dealt with satisfactorily. We, therefore, discuss security and terrorism in this chapter as prologue to our discussion about options and possible solutions to the Israeli-Palestinian impasse.

SECURITY

A central concern of every Israeli citizen is security. The country is small, and the proximity of its vital areas to the borders of potential enemies is close. Four wars in just over three decades with hostile neighbors lend credence to Israel's claim that security is a compelling issue. Israel traditionally has relied on its military prowess and its advanced weapons to counter any enemy. It has depended upon a deeply committed citizenry, willing to fight when called to war and willing to spend a significant portion of its civilian life in war readiness. When the state was formed in 1948, the defense perimeters were established by placing settlements at key points along its borders. Israelis now face the question of how to achieve security in an era of aircraft that travel faster than sound, long-distance missiles, and high fire-power weapons.

The Israelis have developed a military concept of "strategic depth."

By this is meant "the space between the furthermost line at which a country may maintain military forces for its defense without impinging upon the sovereignty of another country and its own vital area."[1] To defend its "vital areas" (areas which if occupied end the sovereignty of the state) in an era of modern weapons against potential enemies that possess a manpower advantage, Israel has depended upon rapid large-scale mobilization, high-technology weapons and intelligence systems, preemptive actions, and the element of surprise. Israel's strategy has been to fight in territories other than its own as a means of compensating for the lack of strategic depth and the proximity of its major population centers to its borders.

The 1967 war was a classic example of this strategy. It was also, in military terms, supremely successful. While it left Israel with just the sort of additional territory envisaged in the doctrine of strategic depth, it also left Israel with political, diplomatic, and human problems of great magnitude. Was security to be gained by the greatly expanded borders resulting from the 1967 war when the new territory can be protected only by fielding a permanent army of occupation? This question is vigorously debated in Israel, even among those most directly involved in and knowledgeable about military matters. Challenging the predominant views, retired general Mattityahu Peled argues that the expanded defense perimeters are actually wasteful and that Israel's security is undermined rather than served by them. He points to the much greater expense and greater troop commitment necessary to maintain the extended borders. General Peled, the commander of logistics for the Israeli army during the 1967 war, claims that the pre-1967 borders gave Israel greater security because they allowed a more effective disposition of Israeli forces in relation to Arab forces.[2]

On Israel's western borders with Egypt, the territorial security issue has been resolved. General Aharon Yariv, director of Israel's Center for Strategic Studies at Tel Aviv University, notes that in its withdrawal from the Sinai, Israel has found ways, relying on special arrangements, to ensure its margin of security. Among the arrangements which are part of the treaty with Egypt are "demilitarized areas, where only limited forces may be stationed, buffer zones, and the presence of an international force or that of a third country, as well as a variety of guarantees."[3] Aware of potential weaknesses in arrangements of this sort, Yariv names some additional elements to strengthen them. First, he believes it is necessary to be clear about what would constitute a violation of the security arrangements and bring a return to wartime status. In addition, Yariv suggests that it is possible to compensate for lack of strategic depth (space) by early warning depth (time). He discusses the real gains to Israel possible through a reduction of Arab hostility that would result from Israeli withdrawal from the occupied areas. Egypt, he believes, provides a case in point.

The most controversial element of the Israeli security discussion concerns the occupied West Bank and Gaza Strip, and particularly the West Bank. The question can be simply put. Can Israel give up its claims to sovereignty over the occupied territories and still maintain security? On this question there are sharp divisions within Israel. The Begin government and some key segments of the Labor Party respond negatively and act upon that response. A broad assortment of others, including both doves and military strategists, believes the answer is "yes, if . . ." The Begin government response is complicated by an element that has nothing to do with security, the belief in the Biblical vision of greater Israel.

Security is considered most vulnerable on Israel's eastern borders since the distance from the pre-1967 borders to the Israeli heartland is the shortest. On the other hand, analysts point to the security risks involved in occupation and policing a hostile population. Former Defense Minister Ezer Weizman, while supporting the principle of using settlements for security, is realistic about the problems: "I object to the confiscation of Arab lands because the most important component of our security is the feasibility of peaceful relations with the Palestinians and with the rest of the region. Our future depends on it."[4] Shai Feldman, from Israel's Center for Strategic Studies, discusses also an internal weakness generated by the occupation. In writing on the debates currently going on, he says "Israelis raised fundamental questions about the purposes of their state and the nature of the road it was taking. Basic political and moral objections to Israel's foreign and defense policies were raised . . ." Doubts about government purpose undermine Israel's security because security depends on citizen soldiers whose motivation must be high. "Once its national consensus is lost, Israel's very survival is in question," Feldman notes. He believes that a return to the approximate pre-1967 borders would strengthen Israel and leave no doubt about its soldiers' motivation. "This by itself is a major factor to be considered in weighing the security risks associated with giving up control over the West Bank."[5]

Withdrawal from the West Bank would be accomplished, in Feldman's plan, within the framework of a full national security plan. This would include links to the Western alliance, internal West Bank security arrangements, an international effort to make sure the West Bank economy is made viable and linked both to Israel and the pro-Western Arab states, and an Israeli nuclear deterrence strategy. Each of these involves its own questions, but the nuclear strategy is the most likely to raise serious new questions. In another paper, prepared after the Israeli raid on the Iraqi nuclear reactor, Feldman stresses the importance of rapidly resolving the Arab-Israeli conflict in order to avoid a Middle East nuclear arms race. General Yariv adds that alongside a peace agreement there should be an areawide agreement to control nuclear proliferation.[6]

Another Israeli analyst, Dr. Avi Plascov, produced a lengthy and detailed study of the alternatives facing Israel in relation to a Palestinian state. In his research, conducted at the London International Institute for Strategic Studies, he concludes that a militarily restricted, independent state of Palestine is acceptable if the Palestinians and the Arab states drop their broader territorial claims. Only through politics will Israel ultimately gain security, he believes. "New military technology," he writes, "tends to diminish the value of buffer zones and the virtues of strategic depth and it is only predictable behavior and good will—not the security arrangements as such—which can provide the parties with security. Yet, because the political arrangements will be fragile, security arrangements are of paramount importance."[7]

A variety of security arrangements have been examined and suggested by Israelis. Shai Feldman proposes several low-manpower, primarily technological arrangements aimed at giving Israel warning time and protection against attacks from east of the Jordan River. He also argues for not permitting other Arab military forces to enter Jordan to keep them distant from Israel. In addition, heavy armament, either Jordanian or Palestinian, should be prohibited on the West Bank.

A comprehensive view of the militarily related issues of importance to any agreement for West Bank withdrawal was proposed by Meir Pail, former Shelli Knesset member and reserve officer. Pail calls for Israeli evacuation in stages, with Arab authorities in the territories establishing local police and security forces equipped with the number and types of arms arrived at through negotiation. Neither Israeli nor Arab offensive weapons and forces would be allowed in the area; fortifications and minefields would also be prohibited. Aside from the existing Kalandia airfield, no other large fields could be built. Mixed Israeli-Palestinian observation units would be posted in strategic locations in the Jordan Valley, the Gaza-Egypt border, etc., and a mixed Israeli-Palestinian-Jordanian border patrol would supervise the borders to prevent terrorist infiltration. Such a plan, Pail believes, would not endanger Israeli security; it has the potential of increasing it by encouraging genuine peace initiatives.[8]

General Peled adds to these arguments that the establishment of a Palestinian state on the West Bank might give Israel a better strategic position than it enjoyed in the pre-1967 period. This is because any negotiated Palestinian state would perforce be militarily weaker than Jordan was when it held the West Bank. He notes that Jordan had tacitly accepted restriction on armor and antiaircraft systems in the earlier period, accounting in part for its inability to match Israeli force during the 1967 war and for its consequent loss of territory. Similar military restrictions would be instituted by the terms of a peace treaty. Any political misuse of the military forces of a new Palestinian state would result in war, threatening loss of all the gains the new state would have achieved.[9]

In a far-reaching article published in *Foreign Affairs* in July 1978, Walid Khalidi, outlined his conception of a Palestinian state living side by side with Israel. His appraisal of such a state's foreign and military policy was based on a realistic appraisal of options and provides a Palestinian counterpoint to the Israeli views outlined above. The Palestinian state he described would be nonaligned in relation to the superpowers and other states, particularly militarily. He uses Austria in central Europe to illustrate his point. The state, while obviously without sophisticated weapons, would have to have security forces able to handle its needs and to deal with cross-border adventurism. United Nations forces would supplement the local forces at borders and airports. Khalidi goes so far as to suggest the numbers of weapons a new state might have as compared to Israel and Jordan.

Walid Khalidi provides serious points for examination and discussion. For Palestinians who seek to establish an independent and viable state in the West Bank and Gaza Strip, he calls for full realization of legitimate Israeli interest in security. He also insists that the new state would have security problems to contend with as well. He points out that if Tel Aviv is 15 miles from the West Bank, the reverse is also true. The West Bank and Gaza Strip are easily accessible from Israel and too easily observed for much to be hidden. Palestinian territory is vulnerable from Israel; the West Bank and Gaza are largely surrounded by Israel. Their skies are visible from Israel. Khalidi puts it graphically: "The terrain on both sides of the Jordan River is an ideal burial ground for armor." He closes his analysis with the observation that ". . . any PLO leadership would take the helm in a Palestinian state with few illusions about the efficacy of revolutionary armed struggle in any direct confrontation with Israel. They would be acutely aware of its costs. They would have little incentive on national or corporate grounds to incur it."[10]

The fear of terrorism deserves to be dealt with explicitly. It has often been the focus of Israeli justifications for military strikes and for Israeli rejection of an independent Palestinian state. Shai Feldman notes that while terrorism represents great personal tragedy, it is not "a major strategic threat."[11] A strategy which is otherwise sound should not be rejected, he argues, because it fails to solve the problem of terrorism. Feldman's conclusion, similar in spirit to the one offered by Khalidi, is that Israeli withdrawal from the West Bank, by allowing a resolution of the Palestine problem, would actually lead to a decrease of terrorism.

The arguments of Israelis and Palestinians outlined above suggest that Israel's security would be as well or better served by political measures as by reliance on military strength. General Moshe Dayan maintained on many occasions that if he had to choose between the strategic site of Sharm el Sheik, at the tip of the captured Sinai Peninsula, and peace with Egypt, he would choose Sharm el Sheik. To his credit, however, Dayan later was deeply involved in negotiating the peace treaty with Egypt, under which Israel gave up Sharm el Sheik. When peace with Egypt became a real option, the loss of Sharm el Sheik represented no loss of security. While the slogan "peace through security" is frequently heard, it is important to note that true security is only realized through peace.

TERRORISM

The question of terrorism and violence must be addressed directly. Both have been so intimately a part of the Arab-Israeli conflict that only by making a clear judgment on them can those involved in seeking settlement of the strife between Israelis and Palestinians deal fully with the problem. During the final stages of the preparation of this report (summer 1981), Israeli and Palestinian violence reached another high point. Large-scale exchange of artillery fire and rockets across the Lebanese-Israeli border culminated in the Israeli air raid on the Palestinian sector of Beirut, leaving more than 300 civilians dead and 800 wounded. Once again terror and death superseded political debates.

The decade of the 1970's, the years since the first AFSC report was published, witnessed a sharp upswing in Palestinian nationalism. It was also a decade of increased use of terrorism by Palestinian groups. This was the period of the guerrilla attacks on the northern Israeli settlements, including the large-scale killing of civilians at Ma'alot and Qiryat Shemona. Terror and violence in the Middle East spilled over to the international scene with the hijacking of airplanes, with attacks on embassies, banks, oil refineries, and with the massacre of the Israeli Olympic Team at Munich, all carried out by Palestinian groups. The list is long; a recent study lists 127 international acts of terrorism by Palestinian groups between 1968 and 1979.[12]

While Israel is the prime target of Palestinian terrorism, not all of the terror was turned against Israelis; a considerable number of attacks were on European Jews, on U.S. facilities and on oil pipelines, and other Arab targets.

Not all Palestinian groups have used terrorism to the same degree. Most of the more militant acts are credited to the rejectionist wings of the Palestinian movement. All of the organizations, however, accept the concept of what they refer to as "armed struggle" or "armed resistance" in "military actions."

For the American Friends Service Committee, terrorism and violence, whether conducted by small guerrilla groups or by the military arms of a state, are inexcusable and morally unacceptable. Coming from the long-standing Quaker tradition opposed to violence, the AFSC still "utterly rejects all wars and fighting with outward weapons . . . for any cause . . ." In the specific case of the Middle East, the AFSC has been equally clear and its representatives have remonstrated with Palestinian, Israeli, and Arab leaders to urge that all parties turn away from the use of murder to gain political ends. We have been unwilling to accept the rationale that legitimates some violence and condemns other violence. We find repugnant the idea that humane rules of war can be established that allow some weapons to be used in killing putative enemies but outlaw other weapons. For in every instance we are talking about the inflicting of death by some human beings on other human beings.

In turning, therefore, to talk about terrorism, we in no way imply that the violence of armies is acceptable. But rather that acts of terror involve a special degree of inhumanity, particularly as these acts inflict harm and take the lives of the unarmed and the noncombatant.[13] We are well aware that terrorism has had political effect in the Arab-Israeli conflict and has brought perceived injustices to international attention. Indeed, there may well be justice in some of the causes for which terrorism is used, but the acceptance of terror as the weapon—the choice of a technique that kills the innocent—perverts the very justice of the cause. Alternative techniques do exist and can be found which both oppose injustice and strengthen the basis for a new justice. We believe that in the long run the legacy of bitterness and distrust engendered by terrorism outweighs any apparent gains; that the dehumanizing effects of inflicting terrorism and suffering from terrorism are not acceptable costs. Of course, the Middle East has not been alone in using terror; it is all too common a part of the arsenals of small groups and governments alike. But the legacy of terror in the Arab-Israeli conflict, dating back through the decades and practiced at times by both sides, has stood as one block to peace-making. As we have examined the record of this terror, even recognizing the instances where each side resorted to violence to set right an obvious injustice or wrong, we find it intolerable that any movement or government should revenge itself upon the unarmed, upon children.

We believe that in the long run peace must be built upon the ability to transcend the past and forgive the former enemy. This is hard enough to achieve among the soldiers who fought in the organized armies of opposing nations. It is much more difficult to wipe out the memories of cruelty or wanton murder. Jews in Israel and around the world know the Holocaust in a special way and remember the murder of the innocents—a memory that cannot be removed. For Palestinians and Israelis today it will be difficult to forget the killing of the innocents on both sides, the terror of the Palestinian attack and the Israeli reprisal, the shooting in a kibbutz or school, and the roar of jets bombing a refugee camp. David McReynolds wrote to the AFSC: "The legacy being built is one that, murder by murder, makes a peaceful settlement more difficult."

David McReynolds spoke for us when he wrote in an earlier AFSC study in 1974:

> I deeply believe that in most Israelis and Palestinians there is a knowledge that terrorism is shameful. World opinion must be clear on this point, reinforcing those who are tempted to obey their conscience rather than their commanders. The tide may not turn until a Palestinian throws down his gun rather than shoot a child, or an Israeli pilot refuses to board his jet rather than bomb a refugee camp. Terrorism has many defenders but ultimately it has no defense. Any cause—Israeli or Palestinian or any other —that is built on the bodies of children and their parents is a cause without merit, better lost than won.

CONCLUSION

The authors of this report urge soldiers and terrorists alike to let the guns fall silent, to free innocent civilians from their role as hostages to violence and to seek instead political solutions to the deeply vexing problems that face the Israeli and Palestinian people. In addition, we urge those who condemn the violence to recognize the wisdom advanced by one Israeli, Simcha Flapan, a long-time advocate of just and peaceful relations among Palestinians and Israelis:

> In the long run, the eradication of terrorism is possible only by eliminating the condition that breeds it. Palestinian terrorism is a result of statelessness and a refugee existence. Only a political solution that offers the prospects of statehood, of a normal economy and a productive life for the Palestinians might put an end to terrorism."[14]

And, it may be added, in the long run Israel's reprisals and preemptive strikes may only be ended by eliminating the conditions that breed them. Recognition of Israel's right to exist and assurance of its security are essential elements of any political solution with the Palestinians.

6

Options and Proposals

Any resolution of the Arab-Palestinian-Israeli conflict must include a solution to the Palestinian problem acceptable both to the Palestinians and to the Israelis. The situation has existed for many years, and rather than improving it gets more serious and takes on more importance with each passing year. Within Israel, various options have emerged for ways to deal with the Palestinian problem. These options and their advantages and disadvantages, as seen by their proponents and critics, will be the focus of this chapter.

THE STATUS QUO/ANNEXATION

Since 1967, Israel has maintained a status quo policy in the West Bank and Gaza largely by default. That is, Israel has not sought to change its position as occupier of these captured territories. This policy has been seen as territorially advantageous. Borders viewed by some as militarily more defensible (see the section of this report on security) have been achieved along the whole eastern front, and Israel's major population centers are farther from potential military attackers. Originally by default, and more recently by design, the occupied territories have become integrated to a great extent into the political economy of Israel. For the short term, at least, Israel has considered the status quo to be less risky militarily and more advantageous in other ways than other changes in the status of the territories would be. Through extensive Jewish settlements, primarily on the West Bank, it has permitted partial realization of the Biblical imperative to reinhabit all the land of *Eretz Israel* that is claimed by some Israelis. The continuance of the status quo has allowed Israel to avoid confronting the problem of direct negotiation with the Palestinians.

To date, Israel has refrained from making any explicit call for annexation of the West Bank and Gaza, though many see the settlements policy as tacit annexation. During Begin's first term, however, the Knesset formalized de facto annexation of an enlarged East Jerusalem.

In the long run the status quo option and de facto annexation are untenable and suffer from all the disadvantages of outright annexation. The maintenance of a long-term occupation runs counter to the preservation of democratic principles within Israel and increases the hostility of the Palestinians. De facto annexation through prolonged occupation would, through demographic changes, threaten the Jewish character of Israel itself. A recent Hebrew University study indicates that by the year 2010 (less than thirty years away) Jews would account for only 45 percent of the population of the enlarged state.[1] If West Bank and Gaza residents were given the vote, as democratic tradition would require, the character of Israel as a Jewish state would change. If Palestinians were denied the vote and other rights of citizenship, Israel would have created an equal challenge to its democracy. This demographic issue is of great concern to Israel's Labor Party. The Likud coalition response has been to believe that the Arab populations will ultimately emigrate if Israel holds the West Bank and Gaza and further integrates them into a Greater Israel.[2] Ariel Sharon, the present defense minister, has publicly advocated programs and policies to encourage Palestinians to move from the territories.

At Camp David, Prime Minister Begin made a commitment to pursue autonomy for the West Bank and Gaza. Failure to carry out this autonomy program has been criticized by Egypt and the U.S. Any move toward annexation would incur even stronger pressure from the U.S. and other countries and international bodies. The status quo option has negative demographic implications for Israel, presents moral and ideological difficulties, and projects an image of Israel as a recalcitrant rather than peace-seeking state, unwilling to move toward solutions of the Palestinian problem.

AUTONOMY/SELF-RULE

The proposal for a form of Palestinian self-rule was Prime Minister Begin's response to President Sadat's dramatic Jerusalem initiative. Autonomy negotiations became the second part of the Camp David framework and the focus for drawn-out negotiations between Egypt, Israel, and the U.S. All three parties remain formally committed to continuing these discussions.

Autonomy is the one option for movement on the Palestinian problem that has fairly broad support in Israel. Israel interprets autonomy in a much narrower manner than either Egypt or the U.S. The autonomy that Begin envisions is an autonomy *for people,* not *for land.* He proposes the establishment of an administrative council for the Palestinians of the occupied territories that would have responsibility for education, culture, religion, industry, trade, commerce, agriculture, transportation, housing, and health.[3] It would manage the day-to-day affairs of the Arab inhabitants. However, the Israeli conception includes restrictions on the council's powers. The education department of the territories would remain subject to Israeli censorship, the finance department would not issue currency, the agriculture department would not control the area's land or water, while the tourism department would not have jurisdiction over the historic and holy sites of East Jerusalem.[4] Jerusalem would remain united as the capital of Israel with no provision for Palestinian control over East Jerusalem. The territories under autonomy would have an anthem, a flag, and a local police force.

Defense and foreign affairs would be under Israeli control. The Israeli military government which currently administers the territories would be withdrawn, but not dissolved. It would be ready to intervene if the administrative council, in the eyes of the Israeli government, proved incapable of controlling the area. Israeli defense forces would be redeployed and become less visible, staying instead in "specific security locations." The borders of the territories, which would be considered Israel's borders during the five-year transition period called for in the Camp David agreement, would be controlled by Israel (and Jordan if it chose to join). Jewish settlements in the area would remain in place and be under the jurisdiction of the Israeli government, not the local administrative council. There would be no restriction on the formation of new settlements. Rather than calling upon the U.N. or other international agencies, ultimate authority for the territories during the transition period would be held by Israel and Israeli sovereignty would be maintained. Moshe Nissim, the chairman of the Likud Bloc in the eighth Knesset, commented, "We are speaking of self-rule, not of statehood."[5] Autonomy is, in this interpretation, an alternative to self-determination and an independent state.

To the Begin government, the autonomy plan is a means of offering the Arab residents of the territories the maximum degree of self-rule believed to be consonant with Israeli security and long-term plans for the maintenance of Israeli interests. By retaining control over foreign affairs and defense, controlling land and water rights, keeping limits on the administrative council, and reserving the right to intervene if it is deemed necessary, Israel is in a position to block any moves in the territories toward independence.

Through this approach, Israel would be freed from administering the affairs of a population which resents its presence. With a shift of authority in a number of fields from the military government to the elected Arab residents, clashes between the inhabitants and the authorities might be reduced. Israel would, however, continue to enjoy the defense advantages afforded by de facto boundaries along the Jordan River and on the Golan Heights.

In the Camp David framework, autonomy was considered to be a transitional arrangement. Progress toward autonomy under the Camp David process has been understood by Israel to be a quid pro quo for peace with Egypt, which both parties are reluctant to jeopardize. Israel and Egypt, however, have strikingly different visions of the final goals of autonomy. The Begin government has given signs in the past, made more explicit after the 1981 election, that it would like to see restricted autonomy continue permanently rather than as a transitional arrangement.[6] Egypt, on the other hand, conceives of autonomy as being a step toward Palestinian self-determination and the ultimate creation of a Palestinian state linked to Jordan. In its election platform the Israeli Labor Party supported autonomy as one of several possibilities for a transition period leading to a territorial compromise with Jordan involving the partition of the West Bank.[7] This sharp divergence in views on the ultimate disposition of the territories after the five years of autonomy, and on their administration during the transition, has been a basic cause of the delay in the Israeli-Egyptian negotiations.

The U.S. has viewed the scope of autonomy and the powers of the administrative council more broadly than Israel and in a manner quite similar to Egypt. During the Carter administration, the U.S. interpreted the Israeli settlements policy in the occupied territories as illegal under international law and counterproductive for the peace process. Early statements of the Reagan administration seem to alter this judgment and leave U.S. policy unclear. The Reagan administration has not, however, broken with the commitment to Camp David.

The restrictive definition of autonomy currently held has meant that no one other than the three original signatories to the Camp David framework has accepted it. Palestinian leadership in the PLO, West Bank and Gaza Palestinians, the Arab states, and the West Europeans have rejected the proposal for limited autonomy, contending that it offers little or no promise for a solution to the Palestinian problem. It is unlikely that West Bank and Gaza residents would agree to participate in the elections for an administrative council even if Egypt and Israel finally agree upon its powers and upon appropriate mechanisms for an election.

The three participants in Camp David shared a strong hope and modest expectation that Jordan and Saudi Arabia would accept the autonomy plan and participate in the Camp David peace process. The failure of either government to join and their criticism of the whole process undermines chances for success of the plan. Without Jordan's taking up the role envisaged for it and without the cooperation of West Bank and Gaza residents, the autonomy plan, if pushed ahead, will become an "imposed" solution bearing all the difficulties this implies.

There is no real hope of success for the autonomy plan without some significant changes in its projected goals and the inclusion of the Palestinians in the planning process. For Israel the restricted autonomy plan meets its desire to maintain control over the West Bank and Gaza while ceding some authority to the residents. The very restrictions and lack of a goal of Palestinian independence and self-determi-

nation, after a period of transition, reduce the chances that the autonomy plan will get under way or be successful.

AUTONOMY PLAN VARIANTS

Several variations of the autonomy plan have been proposed and
discussed within Israel. The first was suggested by President Sadat as
a means of temporarily bypassing Israeli sensitivity to plans involving
the West Bank. Try the plan in Gaza first, he suggested, since Gaza
is politically less volatile, and Egypt, already a part of the Camp
David process, could take on the sort of responsibility that Jordan has
not done. Gaza does not have the same religio-political significance
as the West Bank, and Gaza, it was noted, does not have the emotion-
filled issue of Jerusalem as one of the problems to be solved. There are
fewer Jewish settlers and settlements in the Gaza area—only 500 to
700 settlers living primarily in the south—so that it would be politically easier for Israel to invoke a moratorium on further settlement.
Gaza, it was argued, could provide a testing ground for the autonomy
concept.[8]

Although the Gaza proposal gained some acceptance from the
Labor Party and its leader, Shimon Peres, there are significant draw-
backs. Questions were raised within Israel about the reinvolvement of
Egypt in the territory. Gazans, in general, oppose this plan in keeping
with the Palestinian political leadership's rejection of the entire autonomy plan. Gaza Mayor Rashed al-Shawa said in addition, "We will
not agree to establish autonomy in the Gaza Strip first, because the
West Bank and the Strip are a single part of Palestine; they have a
common history and a common past."[9]

Significant objections came as well from Israel, where concern was
expressed for the possible success of the Gaza experiment. If successful, the plan could serve as a blueprint for later action on the West
Bank and create expectations and momentum which Israel might find
difficult to control. By finding a solution to the less sensitive and
complex Gaza situation, Israel might establish a model that it would
be pressed to repeat on the West Bank. Concessions easily made in
Gaza would be harder to grant on the West Bank, and Israel might
find less sympathy with its argument that security considerations

require a more restrictive application of autonomy on the West Bank. The proposal has largely dropped from sight, President Sadat distanced himself from it, and there is little support and considerable opposition within Israel.

Another variant of the autonomy plan was proposed by the late Moshe Dayan, former foreign minister, defense minister, and military chief. Dayan proposed that Israel announce autonomy and unilaterally carry out its parts of the plan. Israel could withdraw the military government, redeploy its forces, unilaterally decide in which areas to station its troops for security purposes, and unilaterally determine which administrative and governance functions to hold on to as a means of maintaining Israeli control in the territories. By simply implementing its version of autonomy, it would require the Arab residents to assume the functions that Israel dropped or to have them abandoned. Dayan's rationale for unilateral autonomy was based on his belief that Israel has to take a positive initiative as the means of dealing with the key question of relations with the Palestinians.[10]

The nature of the Dayan autonomy plan itself, as opposed to the means of initiating it, does not differ significantly from the Begin model. It is equally restrictive, retains land, water and commercial rights in Israel's control, and avoids any indication of relinquishing any of the occupied territories. It is a plan for retaining Israeli territorial control while permitting the inhabitants a degree of self-rule.

While the Dayan initiative would cut through the stalled negotiations and probably would be viewed sympathetically by many Israelis who are frustrated by the inability of their government to resolve the Palestinian problem, it is equally fraught with risks for Israel. If the West Bank and Gaza residents did not respond and take up the administrative duties, many basic services would come to a halt. A power vacuum might ensue, and the absence of any orderly means of assuming responsibility could create significant destabilization and civil disturbances. The local Arab leadership and the PLO might move to exploit the opening created, assume political leadership, and direct it toward the formation of an independent Palestinian state. An Israeli intervention to prevent political independence might be necessary, and any resort to coercive measures to restore control would undermine the very reasons for taking the initial unilateral steps.

Relations between Israel and the Palestinian residents would worsen rather than improve.

While an initiative like Dayan's might break the negotiating deadlock and allow Israel to decide independently which factors are crucial for its security, its sudden application might boomerang and cause a significant breakdown in order.

The moves announced by Defense Minister Ariel Sharon, in early fall 1981, to loosen restrictions, to replace a number of military government officers by civilian administrators, and to search for Palestinians willing to join the autonomy process, embody some of the Dayan proposals. But replacing military control with civilian administration while maintaining full sovereignty has many characteristics associated in the past with the establishment of colonial regimes. At least military occupation gives the appearance of being temporary.

THE JORDANIAN OPTION

The earliest of the Israeli plans for the West Bank and Gaza developed slowly during the years of occupation and recently was reformulated as part of the Labor Party position in the June 1981 elections. It is based on two key elements that have become part of Labor's viewpoint on the occupied territories. The first is that Israel should not permanently rule over the 1.3 million Palestinian inhabitants of the West Bank and Gaza. Second, Labor seeks to negotiate a territorial compromise with Jordan involving the partition of the West Bank that would turn significant segments of the West Bank and Gaza over to Jordan, while Israel would retain areas designated as necessary for security. Initially prepared by Yigal Allon, the Israeli foreign minister from 1974 to 1977, the plan called for a 10 to 15 kilometer-deep security strip along the Jordan River.[11] On the basis of this early plan, successive Labor governments encouraged the establishment of settlements in the Jordan Valley. In addition, border adjustments to the pre-1967 boundaries would include within the new borders the Etzion bloc settlements, the Latrun salient, and the southern portion of the Gaza Strip.[12] Jerusalem would remain unified and under full Israeli sovereignty. In the north, the border with Syria would run along the ridge of the Golan Heights to avoid any repetition of the pre-1967 shelling of Galilee settlements. The major populated areas of the West Bank and Gaza would be transferred to Jordan, and a land corridor would be opened connecting the two territories.

The primary argument advanced to support this plan is based on security. The readjusted borders and the advanced line on the Jordan River, it is argued, would enhance Israeli security. Jordan, under this plan, would assume responsibility for administration and security in the ceded territories, and it is noted that King Hussein, a Western-oriented, "moderate" Arab leader, would keep the area free from Soviet or radical destabilizing influences. Further, the combined Jordan-West Bank-Gaza state would be in a better position to reabsorb Palestinian refugees who return than a smaller West Bank-Gaza independent state. By transferring the populous Arab areas out of Israeli territory, the demographic threat to a Jewish Israel would be avoided. From the political point of view, the Jordanian option removes the necessity of dealing directly with the PLO, giving that problem to King Hussein's government. It attempts to resolve the Palestinian problem permanently, unlike the temporary solutions sought in the variants of the autonomy proposal.

But there are serious problems which make the Jordanian option less viable now than it might have been in the years immediately following Israel's occupation of the territories. The increasing level of politicization of West Bank Palestinians, their open sympathy with the PLO, and their reluctance to become absorbed by Jordan provide strong internal resistance to any Jordanian solution which has not received prior assent from the Palestinian leadership. To add a significant hostile Palestinian population to the large Palestinian population already in the kingdom might undermine Jordanian domestic stability. There would be little gain for King Hussein and some political liability if he took on the thorny Palestinian problem without support from potential political rivals in Iraq and Syria and his supporters in Saudi Arabia. In accepting a partitioned West Bank, he would have to give up his symbolically important quest to return East Jerusalem to Arab rule.

Another complicating factor is that the Rabat Arab summit conference of 1974 and the Baghdad resolutions of 1978 both designated the PLO as the sole legitimate representative of the Palestinian people, clearly preempting King Hussein's ability to negotiate. This joint Arab recognition of the PLO reflected, in part, the realization that relations between Jordan and the PLO were strained since the Jordanian expulsion of the Palestinian guerrilla group in 1970.

King Hussein has explicitly rejected the Jordanian option; nonetheless, his representatives have had contact with the Israelis, and the Israeli Labor party continues to espouse the plan. Jordan's most frequent response has been to call for Israeli return to the pre-1967 boundaries as required in U.N. Resolutions 242 and 338.

Earlier, Jordan had offered a "Jordanian option." In 1972, King Hussein proposed a federation (which the Labor Party rejected) between Jordan, the West Bank, and any other Palestinian territories which chose to participate. The significant difference between Hussein's plan and Israel's is that the former envisages pre-1967 Israeli boundaries and Arab Jerusalem as the capital of the Palestinian portion of the new federated kingdom. Jordan also expressed an interest in an interim withdrawal along the Jordan River in the summer of 1979. Israel rejected this.

Palestinians and Arab states agree that Jordan would have an important role in the establishment and viability of a West Bank and Gaza Palestinian state, should one be formed. There has even been talk of a confederation between Jordan and the Palestinian state, but that would have to be in the context of Palestinian self-determination and subsequent explicit consent to Jordan's rule. A badly partitioned West Bank, with continued Israeli military presence and security settlements, excluding East Jerusalem, holds little promise for Jordan or for a solution to the Palestinian problem.

THE EBAN PROPOSAL

Among other options that have received attention in Israel is one advanced by former Labor foreign minister Abba Eban. While it is similar in some respects to the Jordanian option, particularly in terms of territory and borders, it introduces a novel and visionary element. This option calls for Israel to express its willingness to sign a peace treaty with a Palestinian nation that in turn expresses its own willingness to integrate itself into a community with Israel and Jordan. The three nations would share a network of economic, political, and defense links and be closely tied in international relations. His inspiration is the European Community, where the common interests of each state foreclose any attack upon vital interests of neighbors. The Palestinians would enjoy sovereignty over their land and have the infrastructure of a state. It could have its own flag, issue passports, etc. Jerusalem, while remaining under Israeli sovereignty, would serve as the center for institutions of the confederation.[13]

Eban's vision meets several of the key factors of Middle East reality. The plan preserves the Jewish identity of Israel by granting sovereignty to the large Arab population of the territories. It establishes boundaries similar to those of the Jordanian option and reflecting Israel's security needs. By linking Israel politically and economically to Jordan and Palestine, it would significantly integrate Israel into the political economy of the Middle East and break its isolation from other nations in the region.

From the Palestinian and Arab point of view, the proposal directly addresses Palestinian nationhood, albeit within constraints, and establishes a potentially promising basis for negotiation. While the issue of borders and security would require careful consideration by all the parties, no preconditions that are dramatically unacceptable to any party are set. The stages of transition would have to be thoughtfully planned to increase confidence at each step and the parties' sense of achieving the desired political, economic, and security goals. The potential role for international agencies or third parties in facilitating the several stages deserves further serious consideration.

AN INDEPENDENT PALESTINIAN STATE

The founding of an independent Palestinian state in the West Bank and the Gaza Strip is the other major option for solving the Palestinian problem. It is the option that has always met the stiffest resistance within Israel. Nonetheless, it has recently been a focus of serious study in Israel and has received increasing support from Palestinians.

In the wake of the 1973 war, Ahron Yariv, former chief of Israeli Military Intelligence, and Victor Shemtov, former minister of health and head of the Mapam Party, suggested in June 1974 a means for breaking the deadlocked Palestinian problem. Israel, they said, should enter negotiations with any Palestinian group that would give up terrorism as a means of achieving its political goals and that would accept United Nations Resolution 242. The Yariv-Shemtov formula, as it became known, implied reciprocal recognition between Israeli and Palestinian leadership and accepted the proposition that Israel could not decide on its own who should represent the Palestinian people.

The idea, put aside during the Camp David process and subsequent autonomy negotiations, recently has been further developed by its originators and by others. Shemtov, like many connected with the Labor alignment, prefers a "Jordanian solution"; he suggests, however, that Israel should indicate its willingness to accept Palestinian self-determination if it is designed and effected in such a way as not to jeopardize Israel's existence or security.[14] This can include the formation of an independent Palestinian state which would exist within the context of the self-interest of neighboring states such as Israel and Jordan. He believes that the Israeli military could withdraw from most of the West Bank provided that it be demilitarized and that it enter into broad economic cooperation with Israel.

General Yariv, currently director of Tel Aviv University's Center for Strategic Studies, and his associates there have directly confronted the issue of Palestinian self-determination and statehood. They fear that failure to deal satisfactorily with the Palestinian issue will bring Israel again into total confrontation with the Arab world and serve to unify the Arabs in their opposition to Israel. Further, they are concerned about the deepening international isolation of Israel, which may have the ultimate consequence of weakening it militarily. They are particularly concerned by the strained relations between Israel and the United States, and the decrease in arms supplies and financial support that may result. In addition, members of the group have pointed to the traditional concern of weakening the Jewish characteristics of the state if the large Palestinian Arab populations of the West Bank and Gaza are directly or indirectly linked to Israel. They have also noted the tensions created within Israel by having to maintain a military occupation government over a hostile population.

Many of these same points had been independently raised by the

Israeli Council for Israeli-Palestinian Peace in 1977. This council, like General Yariv and his associates, reflects the Zionist position and supports a Jewish state of Israel.

The Yariv group added explicit military security elements to their discussions. It suggested that part of the "package," including a Palestinian state, should involve Israeli integration into a U.S.-led military alliance in the Middle East. But the core of its security argument is even more direct. Yariv noted that Israel's Arab neighbors have moved away from total rejection toward a policy of "reluctant acceptance" of Israel. The strategic implications of this shift allow the development of a flexible strategy involving both military and political elements. It is this strategy which compels Israel to deal with the Palestinian question, holding promise of preventing total conflict with the Arabs and reducing international isolation, thereby improving Israel's military situation. Autonomy in this view should not be used to keep Israeli sovereignty in the territories, but rather as a means of solving the Palestinian problem. For Yariv, self-determination would come gradually; the timing would be negotiated. While he does not accept the notion of a "Jordanian Palestine" (attributed to Defense Minister Ariel Sharon and others), Yariv believes that Jordan should be involved in the process of self-determination. Jerusalem would remain the undivided capital of Israel, but Yariv would go far to seek ways of satisfying Arab interests in the city. Palestinian refugees would not be repatriated to Israel, as some Arab proposals have suggested, but would be dealt with during gradual implementation of self-determination, presumably within the Palestinian territory or in other Arab states. Security is an important issue for the proposals of the Yariv group and focuses primarily on borders and demilitarized zones that would be mutually agreed to and meet the requirements of all parties.

Yariv is uncertain, indeed pessimistic, about the willingness of the Palestine Liberation Organization to accept the proposals he advances. He also believes that it is impossible to ignore the PLO and he would welcome negotiations with Yasir Arafat should the Palestinian leader be willing. While he would not demand that the PLO recognize Israel prior to entering formal negotiations, he would insist that it find some means of annulling those clauses of the Palestinian Covenant which call for the destruction of Israel.[15]

Although he is doubtful that any of the contact that Israeli moderates and peace groups have had with the PLO has produced any results to date, Yariv believes there is room for Israeli initiatives, in private, which would permit exploration without either side committing itself.

A formulation of this sort developed by Yariv and his associates appears to run counter to the policies of the Likud-led Israeli government. The very restrictive interpretation that Begin has given to autonomy in the post-Camp David period, his encouragement of broad-scale Israeli settlements in the West Bank, and the discouragement of Arab political development in the territories have all been strengthened by claims advanced in summer 1981 by the cabinet of the new Begin government.[16] A move toward Palestinian independence would face a strong challenge from the Jewish settlers in the territories and from their political allies, especially the religious parties which hold critically important positions in the new Begin government because they provide the support that holds his tenuous coalition together.

Support for Palestinian self-determination within a Yariv-type formulation would certainly be forthcoming from the doves in Israeli politics. It could perhaps also win acceptance from the leadership of the Labor Party, if security issues were firmly enough dealt with and Labor accepted King Hussein's refusal to bring Jordan into the Labor-Party-version of the "Jordanian option" plan. Yariv's plan is based on the many concerns that Labor has had about losing the Jewishness of Israel through annexation, but whether Labor could overcome its long-standing reluctance to have dealings with the PLO is an open question. It depends to some significant degree on how the PLO would respond to the Yariv preconditions.

Support for Israel to examine seriously the question of a Palestinian state has developed within an important segment of the American Jewish leadership. Rabbi Arthur Hertzberg, a past president of the American Jewish Congress, recently has argued cogently for Israeli acceptance of the establishment of a Palestinian state on the West Bank and Gaza Strip.[17] The arguments are similar to those noted above, with particular emphasis upon the demographic factor—the potential for Arabs to outnumber Jews in an expanded Israel and for the Jewish character of the Israeli state to be lost. He also suggests that a greater danger to Israel may exist if a Jordanian solution is found and the occupied territories are partitioned and divided between the two states. In a Jordanian state of this sort, Hertzberg warns, there is a likelihood that the Palestinians would topple King Hussein, take over Jordan, and open the door fully to Palestinians from the refugee camps in Lebanon. No treaty arrangements would be in place to bring restraint and such a situation could lead to challenges to Israeli and United States interests in the region. In Rabbi Hertzberg's view, the Palestinian diaspora is the major reason for Israel to be interested in creating a Palestinian state. With each direct involvement in negotiating a Palestinian state, Israel would be in a position to insert the types of security safeguards it believes to be essential.

A formula for a negotiated creation of a Palestinian state would probably be welcomed in important sectors of the Arab world and by the PLO since it recognizes the Palestinian right to self-determination and includes, with certain reservations, the PLO as a negotiating partner. An Israeli initiative along these lines would provide an important test of the emerging Palestinian nationalist position accepting a limited Palestinian state and coexistence with Israel. Even if the PLO leadership were to meet Israeli terms, renounce terrorism, and enter negotiations on the basis of Resolution 242, would the rejectionist elements of the Palestinian movement, the Syrians, and others be able to undermine talks and compromise any solutions? The ability of PLO chairman Arafat to bring some of the reluctant guerrilla groups into the South Lebanon cease-fire in the summer of 1981 provides a positive, if not conclusive, sign. The unwillingness of the rejectionist Palestinian groups to drop their "maximalist" claims—a democratic secular state in all of Palestine—stems from at least three sources. One is the centuries-old tie to the land. A second reflects an ideological position of long standing which ties some of them to beliefs in broader revolutionary goals for the whole Arab world. The third and perhaps controlling factor is the ties that several of the rejectionist groups have to other Arab states, e.g., Syria and Iraq, which do not see a settlement with Israel to be in their national interests at this time. The rejectionists further do not believe that an acceptable Palestinian state could be achieved through negotiation and, therefore, advocate continued armed struggle. The rejectionists, however, represent a vocal minority of no more than 20 percent of the Palestinian movement. Palestinian moderates make the claim that if a state were about to be formed, the rejectionists would not want to be left out.[18]

There is, in fact, some uncertainty about the limits of Palestinian goals. Many recent Palestinian statements, while accepting the formulation of a state in the West Bank and Gaza, also include discussion of the establishment of this state as the first step in the reunification of all of Palestine. This discussion fires Israeli fears that an independent Palestine would serve as the base for later actions against Israel. Some Israeli critics claim further that a Palestinian state might serve as a base for Soviet interference in the region, particularly since the U.S.S.R. has supported Palestinian efforts and supplied a significant amount of arms. Others, however, point to the Saudi Arabian role as the major financial supporter of the PLO and argue that the Saudi's would serve a moderating and stabilizing role. In addition, the extent to which a Palestinian state, located between Israel and Jordan, would have to depend heavily on Jordan for political and economic assistance and support augurs for a further integrating influence. In any case, a Palestinian state would be militarily weaker than Israel.

These considerations focus great importance on the process through which Palestinian independence would be achieved and the use to which a transition period would be put. They weigh against a Dayan-like unilateral Israeli withdrawal and support the importance of Israel's positive involvement in finding a genuinely acceptable resolution for all parties. The potential importance of demilitarized zones and internationally guaranteed and supervised borders as part of a transition period is highlighted by these security considerations. Also important is the need to generate confidence among peoples who have been locked in conflict for generations.

Transition toward a Palestinian State

To facilitate the peace initiatives we have discussed there are several important steps which can be taken.

1. The narrow and restrictive definition of autonomy advanced by the Begin government, with its stress on continued sovereignty over the territories, must be dropped.

2. For the concept of a transition to be taken seriously, Israel must agree to refrain from building new settlements or significantly enlarging existing settlements during negotiations and during the full transition period.

3. The process of Israeli integration of the West Bank and Gaza Strip into the political economy of Israel should be stopped during the period of negotiation and transition. U.S. opposition should be made clear.

4. Arab and Palestinian peace initiatives and formulations must be developed and efforts made to gain positive responses to them. The eight-point Saudi Arabian proposal of August 1981, based largely on United Nations Resolutions 242 and 3236 and embodying gains for both Israel and the Palestinians, is an example of new initiatives and attitudes within the Arab world. The Arab nations and the PLO must be forthright in their willingness to recognize Israel.

5. To move this process forward in a realistic manner and to demonstrate its commitment to a continuation of the stalled peace process, the United States should undertake a dialogue with the PLO with the explicit aim of encouraging its full involvement in the peace process. This step would demonstrate U.S. acceptance of the role the PLO must play if the Palestinian problem is to be resolved; it would also demonstrate acceptance of the reality of the type of relations the United States has had with the PLO in evacuating U.S. citizens from Lebanon during its Civil War and more recently in arranging a cease-fire agreement in Southern Lebanon involving both the Israeli government and the PLO.

Designs of a Transition[19]

Discussions with Palestinians, including West Bank and Gaza Strip civic and political leaders, have indicated that an interim period or transition is acceptable before establishment of an independent state. Fahd Qawasmi, the deported mayor of Hebron, set the tone: "If Israel says this is the land of the Palestinians, then we can discuss security, future relations between us, how to arrive at peace, a hundred times. But the aim of negotiations must be clear from the start."[20]

West Bank Palestinians stress that it is necessary that they have assurances that the interim regime is not a step toward Israeli annexation. Instead, the transition period should prepare Palestinians and Israelis to live with separate independent states. The council to be established in the West Bank and Gaza Strip should have adequate and secure financing, including powers of taxation and the ability to receive loans and grants from abroad, from Arab countries and European and American sources. In addition the council should have authority over administrative affairs such as agriculture, commerce, customs, education, health, industry, police, postal services, social welfare, and tourism. Relationships between the council and the municipality and village bodies would need to be clarified.

Land registry, public land, and absentee lands would be administered by the council. Water and mineral resources would be regulated by the council. West Bank Palestinians are aware of the Israeli settlements' use of local water, and they see council regulation of water as a means of preventing any increase in the number or size of settlements and, ultimately, as a possible means of negotiating their removal. They express willingness, however, to negotiate for Israeli settlers who choose to remain under the jurisdiction of the local Palestinian governing council and do not claim extraterritorial status.

On questions of transport and movement, the Palestinians believe the movement of goods and people between Gaza and the West Bank on designated roads across Israel and across the Jordan River bridges could be guaranteed. The proximity of the two regions seems to make this realistic. The council should develop the Gaza port facility and have full use of Kalandia Airport north of Jerusalem. The security arrangements necessary at border crossing points could be negotiated.

Other important issues have been addressed by Palestinians examining the nature of a transition period. Security, a point of critical importance for Israelis, brings a realistic response from some Palestinian analysts. Israeli military presence limited to specific strategic sites along the Jordan River at observation posts in the central mountain ridge is acceptable during a transition period. Internal security should, however, be handled by a Palestinian police force, and Israeli troops should not be permitted to patrol city streets, enter houses at will, and arrest residents. Responsibility for the military court and prison system should be assumed by the Palestinian council. Further,

Palestinians would welcome United Nations or other international neutral forces in the territories to help assure the security needs of the Israelis and Palestinians because they believe they, too, have security needs, located as they are between Israel and Jordan.

Refugees, from the first Arab-Israeli war (1948) as well as those who fled in 1967, pose additional problems for an interim governing authority. The right of these groups to move to the West Bank and Gaza Strip would have to be established through negotiations. Their return would probably have to be phased in carefully to fit in with a broad plan for economic and social development. While identity cards would be required during transition for all residents and returning Palestinians, the issuance of passports to Palestinians remaining abroad could be deferred until later in the negotiations. Negotiations on behalf of the Palestinians would have to be carried out by the PLO. Virtually all West Bank and Gaza Strip leaders are unanimous in this view.

It is unrealistic to assume that all the Palestinians currently living in the Arab states, whether still in refugee camps or integrated into their host society, could or would want to return to a West Bank–Gaza Palestinian state. As part of a realistic transition, the Arab states should indicate their willingness fully to accept some Palestinians as permanent residents and thus make refugee camps unnecessary and relieve potential points of continued Palestinian resentment.

There are advantages for both Israel and the Palestinians in adopting current proposals for mutual recognition, negotiation, and transition to the creation of an independent Palestinian state in the West Bank and the Gaza Strip. Israel should take advantage of the increased willingness of important Arab states to exchange recognition and peaceful relations for a solution to the Palestinian problem. The proposal by Saudi Arabia (August 1981) represents the most recent manifestation of a growing willingness to accept Israel as a Middle East neighbor if it withdraws to its pre-1967 borders. The Arab states and the PLO should press ahead with realistic and just peace proposals; such proposals could not long be ignored by any Israeli administration. The international community, but especially the United States, should be prepared to aid the Israelis, Palestinians, and Arabs to take steps which they may not be able to accomplish alone.

It is not only traditional Israeli doves who dissent from the Begin government's commitment to maintain sovereignty over the occupied West Bank. General Yehoshafat Harkabi, former chief of Israeli Intelligence and a man with a hawkish reputation, believes it is in Israel's interests to leave the territories. "I am for finalizing the conflict, and you cannot do that without recognizing that the Palestinians, like any other human group, deserve self-determination. The British had to get out of India and Israel will have to get out of the West Bank." It is Harkabi's view that in spite of the former extremism of the Palestinians and lingering doubts about the PLO's readiness for peacemaking, realism requires ". . . seeing that the other side are human beings, too, with needs . . ." that must be recognized. "We have to understand the fate of the West Bank will be decided by its people, and they are overwhelmingly Arab." But he insisted: "They must also recognize that we deserve political self-determination. What I want is the final account—not leaving the door open, which is the PLO position."[21]

NOTES ON JERUSALEM

In our many conversations with Arabs, Israelis, and Palestinians, the AFSC has found the deepest and most anguishing problems centered on Jerusalem. We have also found, however, a virtually unanimous agreement that these problems should not be dealt with at the outset of negotiations. Their solution, it is held, will come as part of an agreement reached on the other central issues. When Israeli security is ensured and Palestinian statehood assured, Jerusalem may be discussed with new confidence and mutual trust. We, therefore, have chosen to discuss Jerusalem briefly in this separate note.

To Israelis and Palestinians, Jerusalem is of profound significance; it involves historical, religious, nationalist, security, and economic considerations. It is unnecessary to belabor their attachment to the city. What is important is to try to identify where the attitudes of the two sides could conceivably permit some accommodation and where the bedrock imperatives lie.

The Jerusalem issue involves almost solely the disposition of the areas occupied by Israel in 1967. Israel's possession of West Jerusalem (the part under Israeli control prior to 1967) in the context of a final peace settlement is not seriously questioned. The earlier concept of an internationalized city including both Arab and Israeli Jerusalem, set forth in the 1947 U.N. General Assembly resolution that contained the partition plan and established the state of Israel, is no longer thought to be realistic by the major parties. The areas in dispute are: the old walled city, about 1 square mile, in which are located the major Christian, Jewish, and Muslim shrines and in which communities of Israelis, Palestinians, and non-Palestinian Christians live; the modern Palestinian business and residential districts, largely north and west of the old city, into which Israel has introduced sizable Jewish housing projects and where some pre-1948 Jewish institutions have been much expanded; and outlying Palestinian communities, beyond the pre-1967 boundaries of Jerusalem, which Israel incorporated into the city after 1967.

On the major issues, the public positions of Israel and the Arabs seem far apart and irreconcilable at present. Israel insists that the city remain undivided under Israeli rule, having declared its incorporation into Israel in 1967 and formally annexed it in 1980. The Arabs demand essentially a return to the pre-1967 status, though they appear to accept the concept of a physically united city. Publicly, at least, neither side has spelled out a position in detail and probably will not, pending serious negotiations, but each no doubt has priorities which would guide its proposals.

Israeli Position

In any serious negotiations Israel would insist on continued free movement in Jerusalem. With such movement Israelis have access to their holy sites, particularly the Western Wall in the walled city, and to the university and related institutions on Mount Scopus, north of the walled city. They would also have a much higher degree of security for their own populated areas in the city than would be the case if immediately adjacent and intertwined Arab areas were closed to them. They would certainly insist that the Jewish community continue to live in its reconstructed quarter of the walled city. Moreover, Israelis would insist that freedom of movement and residence not be at the sufferance of any outside authority, whether Arab or international. Their experience of the divided city during the period of Jordanian rule (1948–1967) in East Jerusalem, when they were barred from access to the Western Wall and saw their holy sites abused, is still fresh in their minds.

If any Arab administration were to have or share authority (assuming Israel under any circumstances would agree to this as part of a peace agreement), it would be essential to Israel that it represent an Arab entity that in itself was not threatening. Since Palestinian authority in Jerusalem under any conceivable peace settlement would be exercised by the administration of the Arab areas contiguous to the city—the West Bank—the identity and acceptability of that administration would have to be established before Israel would accept an agreement involving Jerusalem. A Jerusalem agreement would ultimately have to be negotiated in the context of the West Bank solution, since the two are interrelated in so many ways. This became evident during the autonomy negotiations that flowed from the Camp David agreements, when questions arose at an early stage whether Arab Jerusalem as a geographic area was to be considered part of the autonomous area, or even if the population of Arab Jerusalem was to have some relationship to the process of establishing an autonomous authority on the West Bank. Even should it be possible to obtain Israeli agreement to some Jerusalem settlement involving the West Bank Arab authority, however, it is not conceivable that Israel would agree to the presence of Arab military forces in any part of the city.

Israel might be more flexible on the modalities of governing Jerusalem, so long as any administrative arrangement satisfied the basic requirements outlined above. The Israeli authorities have gone to great pains to make it difficult to divide Jerusalem again politically. The Jewish housing projects strategically planted among and around the Arab districts now have a population of 85,000 compared with an Arab population for the enlarged post-1967 city of about 110,000. Some of these projects, and a major settlement to the east between Jerusalem and Jericho, were designed to interrupt the contiguity of the Arab areas of Jerusalem to the adjacent West Bank. In addition to these physical barriers, Israel has taken legislative steps intended to put Israeli sovereignty over the entire city beyond any future question. In response to nationalist pressures following the Camp David accords the Knesset enacted the Basic Law on Jerusalem of July 30, 1980. Nonetheless, if a satisfactory settlement of the entire Palestinian problem depended on it, and if major Israeli priorities were provided for, it is a possibility worth working for that the current Israeli insistence on full sovereign control over the entire city would be negotiable.

Arab Position

The Arabs, for their part, have varied sets of priorities depending on who and where they are, but some priorities seem likely to be irreducible. The Palestinian population of East Jerusalem, whether Christian or Muslim, wants to be free of Israeli control and to live under Arab rule. They and other Palestinians believe that Jerusalem must be the seat of government of the Palestinian state that will be established on the West Bank in a peace settlement and that Arab Jerusalem must, therefore, not only be under Arab rule but must be linked to this wider Arab entity. Such linkage is important not only for historical-political reasons but also because Jerusalem is the logical and traditional economic and transport center for a good deal of the West Bank. Now, as in biblical times, it is Jerusalem that holds the northern and southern regions together. For Arabs other than Palestinians concerned with Jerusalem as a religious center, the primary consideration would be the ability to visit Muslim holy sites without being subject to Israeli authority.

Arab flexibility could be hoped for with respect to the precise arrangements for governing East Jerusalem (particularly the walled city), the continued residence there of Jewish communities, freedom of movement about the city, and the exact nature of the relationship between Arab Jerusalem and the adjacent Arab entity of which it would presumably be the capital. Might there also be some flexibility in demarcating the Jerusalem that was to be the Arab capital? For the Arabs, a general solution of the Palestinian problem acceptable to them—and in particular the Palestinians—would have to be in sight in order to expect compromise agreements on the knotty aspects of Jerusalem.

Potential Solutions[22]

Our suggestions about higher and lower priorities do not reflect stated official positions on either side. However, the ability to deal successfully with a few key issues will determine the success or failure of any Jerusalem negotiation:

Nature of administration of Arab Jerusalem. It will require a unique and imaginative form of administration if:

- there is to be free movement about the entire city;
- for the Israelis, this freedom is not at the sufferance of an Arab authority;
- Arab residents of East Jerusalem are under Arab, not Israeli, rule; and
- Jerusalem is to be the capital of both Israel and the West Bank Arab state.

A solution seems to become more practicable when fewer general principles, such as national sovereignty, are applied and more local considerations are used to envision the administrative system. The "borough system" proposed by some Israelis falls short of Arab requirements but might point the way to a solution. Under it, Jerusalem would be divided into sections, or boroughs, some of which would be Arab and some Jewish, and each of which would be administered by an authority of its own nationality. Such an arrangement in itself begs the question of who ultimately controls the entire city, especially in respect to security (the Israeli borough idea assumed Israel would), which cannot be avoided entirely though it can perhaps be deemphasized by joint Arab-Israeli performance of some functions and by the form of linkage between Jerusalem and the contiguous Israeli and Arab areas.

In pursuing local solutions, special treatment might be accorded the walled city, which is of such great importance to the broader communities throughout the world that it might be the one part of the city that could have an international hand in its administration in addition to basic Arab and Israeli elements.

Relationship with surrounding areas. A settlement that provided that there would be free movement throughout Jerusalem and that the city would be the capital of the respective contiguous national areas would pose the problem of establishing an effective border control between Israel and the West Bank Arab entity. Unless special steps were taken, anyone entering Jerusalem from either country would be free to cross through Jerusalem and into the other country. Again, inventive solutions would be required, the most obvious of which would involve special treatment of all traffic into and out of Jerusalem on both sides. For example, a form of such control has been applied to vehicular traffic by Israeli authorities since 1967 based on license plates. Residents of East Jerusalem have plates distinct from those of Israelis, and at times of tension they have been subject to special control on the roads into Israel.

The relationship between both countries and Jerusalem might be affected in other ways as well. Israel, for example, might well insist that military forces of an Arab West Bank entity (limited though they might be in any case) should not be brought into Jerusalem. To secure such a limitation, Israel might have to accept a similar restriction on its forces, with the effect of achieving a form of demilitarization of the city in many ways appropriate to its worldwide religious significance.

7

The Tragedy of Lebanon

Lebanon cannot wait for a solution to its searing domestic conflicts and Civil War, but Lebanon has little alternative. Lebanon's problems are its own, but they are also the problems that have kept the broader Middle East conflicts alive for more than three decades.

By the time the main battles of the Lebanese Civil War came to an end in 1976, the human toll had been severe. More than 65,000 men, women, and children were killed during the nineteen months of that war. This number takes on stark significance when compared to the 39,800 people killed in all four Arab-Israeli wars. Some 1.5 million people were uprooted from homes in cities and villages of Lebanon, and almost half that number remain displaced. One family in ten fled Lebanon during the fighting. More than 400,000 children have been victims of the warfare, wounded, displaced, abandoned, and orphaned —all in a country of 3 million people.[1]

Historically Lebanon was a place of refuge for Christian and Muslim heretics who came to hide in its rugged mountains. In the past several decades Lebanon's doors were opened to Christian Armenians and Assyrians and Muslim Kurds and Palestinians fleeing oppression and war.

The toll in the South of Lebanon, a battlefield between the Israelis and their Christian Phalangist allies against the Palestinians, has been high. The ancient port city of Tyre, which before the Civil War was a thriving center of 80,000, is now reduced to fewer than 5,000, mostly elderly and poor people with no money for relocation and nowhere to go.[2]

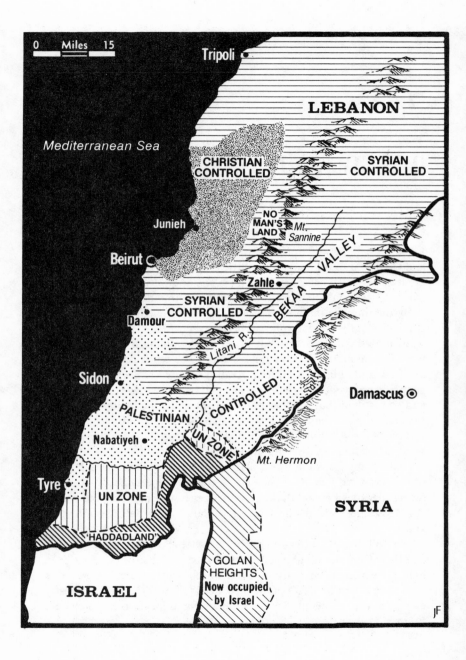

The economic toll of the Civil War was also high. Lebanese government estimates place the economic cost of the war at nearly $5 billion in property damage and lost revenue. Road, water, and electricity networks were damaged; schools, hospitals, factories, homes, and whole villages were destroyed. Beirut's commercial port, city center, and fashionable hotel district were gutted and abandoned to the militias during the fighting. Scores of foreign companies deserted the strife-torn country that had been the trading and banking center of the Arab world.

The psychological and social toll have also been great, especially among the youth who did the fighting and who now remain armed and divided among the factions of a divided society. They have been referred to as the "Kalachnikov Generation," so ever present in their lives have been the automatic rifles and the militias. Close to one-third of the young men fought in the dozen or so private militias that were active during the Civil War and the years following.

Social institutions and government, when they function at all, do so at marginal levels. During the war and often in the years since, the Lebanese Parliament could not meet because of the fighting. Garbage and rubble at the street corners are a daily reminder of the breakdown of civic services. The bombed roads and bridges of the south testify that, although the war ended, the war did not cease. The army itself collapsed during the Civil War, and its troops joined the factions or disbanded. The war was finally brought to a halt through the introduction of 30,000 Syrian troops, first battling the Muslim-Palestinian alliance as it threatened victory and then subduing the militias led by the Maronite Christian Phalangists. Syrian troops have remained in Lebanon and often find themselves in battle. Their continued presence, while in part serving a peacekeeping function by keeping the several warring factions apart, has also raised again the question of their long-term intentions. Syria has traditionally looked upon Lebanon as part of a Greater Syria.

LEBANESE ROOTS AND EXTERNAL PRESSURE

All observers, including Lebanese, agree that, at the base, the fundamental problems in Lebanon were really Lebanese—a deep internal division along religious confessional and socioeconomic lines. These divisions were made greater by a mixture of religious rivalry, nationalism, ethnocentrism, and class conflict. Lebanon had lived with the myth of a small Christian majority whose advantage had been translated into political authority and power. On top of these Lebanese issues were superimposed inter-Arab rivalries, pressures generated by the Israeli-Palestinian struggle, and the presence of armed Palestinian guerrillas in substantial numbers.[3]

The representational problems date from the National Pact of 1943, put in place as the French withdrew after twenty-three years of colonial control. They left behind a political system dominated by the Francophile Maronite Christians who had, under French rule, become a privileged class. The political arrangements of the 1943 independence divided political power by sects; the president was to be Christian, the prime minister Sunni Muslim, and the speaker of the parliament Shi'a Muslim. Christians were to enjoy a six to five advantage in legislative representation. It was inevitable that the 1943 sociopolitical status quo would collapse. While no census has been taken since 1932, Lebanese Muslims almost certainly constitute a majority of the population, with Shi'a Muslims probably the largest subgroup. The rise of Muslim political movements, seeking greater political power and representation, challenged Christian predominance in important government and commercial sectors. The left-leaning Muslim groups have often urged reform or abandonment of the confessional system of politics and governance, which gives such preeminence to the role of religious groups in the nation's politics.

The confessional system has led to a weak central government that either encouraged or tolerated factionalism and reliance on private militias even before the Civil War. Economically, the central government has had little power with only small taxation rights and consequently limited social services and little aid for development. With inflation, economic inequalities became an even more serious problem.

Confessional divisions blocked the establishment of a national identity that might have helped knit together the fragments assembled by France in the period of the 1920's to the 1940's. One Lebanese Christian scholar summed up the situation:

The Christian predominance discouraged formation of a distinctive Lebanese identity among Muslims. The Muslim mainstream was weak in both fact and perception and so many sought outside support, first from Nasser's Arab nationalism and later from the Palestinian movement. Lebanese Muslims are now disenchanted with both, but they are left without an effective identity. Lebanese Maronites, for their part, also sought outside patrons, from France to Israel, and for many of them Lebanon meant nothing more than their Christian identity.[4]

LEBANON, ISRAEL, AND THE PALESTINIANS

Tens of thousands of Palestinians fleeing Haifa and villages in the Galilee in northern Palestine in 1948 made their way across the border into Southern Lebanon. By 1952 they numbered at least 100,000 and, since they were largely Muslim, posed a special problem for Lebanon's delicate confessional balance. They were refused integration into the Lebanese political system, and being largely peasants it was difficult for them to enter Lebanon's economic system.

The 1967 war brought a new influx of Palestinian refugees from the West Bank while the Arab defeat stimulated militant Palestinian nationalism. A guerrilla campaign was launched against Israel from both Lebanon and Jordan, leading to strong Israeli reprisals to disrupt Palestinian operations and to force Lebanon and Jordan to crack down on the Palestinians. Jordan's King Hussein, with the support of a strong army, succeeded during 1970 and 1971 in halting guerrilla actions from his country and in driving the Palestinian guerrilla leadership and forces out of Jordan. Most went to Lebanon. The weak Lebanese government and army could not suppress the Palestinian forces, which had significant support from sectors of the Lebanese public and also had strong Arab backing for their attempts to persevere in Lebanon—their last political and military base.

By the mid-1970's, the Palestinian population had grown to at least 200,000, or 8 percent of Lebanon's population, and it could not be assimilated. Indeed, neither the Palestinians nor the Lebanese Christians wanted assimilation. The Palestinian movement was supported by most Muslim and many liberal and leftist Christian Lebanese but was resented and feared by the Christian right. Palestinian attacks against Israel caused Israel to intervene in Lebanon with great force, thus exacerbating sectarian and political tensions. The Palestinians, living together in full communities with a quasi-governing structure of their own, numerous local industries and social services, and a substantial armed force, became a "state within a state."

LEBANON: THE SURROGATE BATTLEFIELD

As though Lebanon had not suffered enough through civil war, it was further violated by being cast directly in the middle of the Israeli-Palestinian conflict. Lebanon became the surrogate battlefield for the intractable confrontation that has kept the Middle East in turmoil for more than three decades. As the Civil War wound down in late 1976, Israelis stepped up attacks against Palestinian refugee camps, villages, and military installations in Southern Lebanon, since Palestinian groups used it as a staging ground for attacks on Israel. But more than Palestinian forces were hurt by the fighting; Palestinian and Lebanese civilians and their property bore the brunt of the attacks. A major Israeli assault in July 1981 killed 300 civilians and wounded an additional 800 when bombs were dropped in the heavily populated Palestinian section of West Beirut which serves also as headquarters for many Palestinian organizations.

The largest and most damaging Israeli assault in Lebanon was its full-scale invasion of the South in March 1978. It came in reprisal for a terrorist attack by the PLO on the coastal highway near Tel Aviv that resulted in the killing of innocent Israeli civilians. Israel responded by sending 25,000 troops into Lebanon as far north as the Litani River, which raised fears about Israel's long-term intentions in Lebanon. An intensive air and artillery bombardment that preceded Israeli ground forces damaged 80 percent of South Lebanon's villages and destroyed some of them completely. Two hundred thousand Lebanese and sixty-five thousand Palestinian refugees fled the area, and press reports said between one and two thousand Arab civilians were killed. The March 1978 invasion confirmed what one Lebanese observer noted, that "Israel is the most powerful actor on the Lebanese stage. Syria can do nothing against it and certainly the Palestinians can't. Israel can control the Christian forces in the South and has a lot of influence on the Christian forces in the rest of the country."[5]

As Israel withdrew its forces southward after passage of U.N. Security Council Resolution 425 (March 19, 1978), it left behind an Israeli-supported Lebanese militia led by a breakaway Lebanese army major, Saad Haddad. The forces of Major Haddad control an area about 5 miles deep along most of the 60-mile Lebanese-Israeli border from the slopes of Mount Hermon in the east, to the Mediterranean coast in the west. This militia is Israeli-supplied and -paid and often engages in joint operations with Israeli troops who enter the zone on a regular basis.[6] This zone, in the southern quarter of the Lebanese border, is territory that was to be turned over after Israeli withdrawal to the control of the newly created United Nations Interim Force in Lebanon (UNIFIL). Instead, Israel, when it withdrew three months after the March invasion, turned the region over to Major Haddad.

The remainder of Lebanon is badly divided, close to de facto partition, into regions controlled by (1) the Syrian army (three-fifths of the country in the central and northern regions, especially along the Syrian border); (2) the right-wing Christian Phalange (East Beirut and the traditionally Christian Mount Lebanon highlands); (3) a smaller Christian faction led by former Lebanese president Suleiman Franjieh (confined to the north, the base of Franjieh's political and clan support); (4) the Lebanese leftists and the PLO (West Beirut, the southern coastal region from Damour to Tyre and eastward between the Zahrani and Litani Rivers); and (5) UNIFIL forces (south of the Litani River to the Haddad-Israeli enclave).

LEBANON AND INTER-ARAB RIVALRIES

The divisions which persisted in Lebanon were all too easily exploited by Arab states looking for proxies to conduct their battles, and Lebanese factions often sought outside support for their rivalries. As Hassen Sabry al-Khoul, the Arab League mediator of the Civil War, ruefully observed: "Lebanon became a hired stage with the actors completely oblivious of who had hired the stage and why."

Syria, for example, intervened at the request of the Arab League first against the left and the PLO. It then became embroiled in battles with part of the Christian right two years later, while courting one smaller Christian faction and still keeping the leftists and Palestinians under control. Saudi Arabia sent financial aid to the Christian right until the right's attacks on Muslims became too ferocious, all the while supporting Palestinian conservatives within the PLO. Egypt dispatched 1,000 regular Palestinian army troops to Lebanon to fight against the Syrians. Iraq and Libya sent arms and money to different Lebanese and Palestinian armed groups.

The Syrian-Egyptian dispute over Egypt's agreement to the Sinai II disengagement with Israel (negotiated in 1975) worsened and prolonged the Civil War. The agreement, when it was initialed on September 1, 1976, produced an immediate escalation of fighting in Lebanon. It was not possible to bring the war to an end until a Syrian-Egyptian reconciliation was arranged by Saudi Arabia in October 1976, after which the Arab states agreed to urge restraint on their respective clients in Lebanon.

IS A LEBANON SOLUTION POSSIBLE?

The social and political fabric of the country has not been reconstructed, and the government does not successfully govern. For the time being, the country remains an armed camp with no national political authority; armed local militias of the many parties maintain control over sections of the major city, Beirut, and the countryside. As one observer put it, "There are now more guns than people in Lebanon."

All parties seem agreed on one critical issue—a full internal Lebanese solution will not be possible until the Israeli-Palestinian conflict is resolved and the Palestinians have achieved a political entity of their own. An interim solution, however, may be within reach.

The Christian leadership would ultimately like to see *all* Palestinians leave Lebanon. Some Christians don't care where they go or what happens to them, but the more responsible leadership wants to see a just resolution of the Palestinian problem. Karim Pakradouni, an important member of the Phalange party's political bureau, recently said:

> To turn Lebanon into an alternative to Palestine and solve the whole problem at Lebanon's expense—that we will never accept. The real solution is a Palestinian state in Palestine. We are not ready to accept a Palestinian state on Lebanese territory.[7]

The leader of the rightist Christian National Liberal Party, former Lebanese president Camille Chamoun, in the same statement in which he declared his support for Major Haddad's "Free Lebanon," said, "I also advise the Israelis to recognize the Palestinian's rights in the West Bank and Gaza."[8]

From the point of view of the Muslim and leftist leadership, an independent Palestinian state would provide a new political focus for the Palestinians. Those Palestinians who then remained in Lebanon would no longer be stateless and displaced persons confined to camps, but would instead be expatriate citizens of a Palestinian state in which they did not necessarily live. In'am Raad, a leading figure in the leftist Lebanese National Movement, said, "We support Palestinian self-determination and don't want the Palestinians to stay in Lebanon, but neither do we want them chased to other countries. They must have a homeland."[9]

There is little expectation that even the establishment of a Palestinian state will lead to the departure of all the Palestinians from Lebanon, but it would relieve Lebanon of the pressures of the Palestinian problem, leaving it freer to rebuild its national identity and restructure the political balance. It would also be free from Israeli attacks on the Palestinian guerrillas.

But what about the immediate future? In the words of a senior Lebanese political leader, for the present the best that can be hoped for is a *modus vivendi* among the contending forces and powers presently in Lebanon. The role of the United States, this same leader said, is simple. "Yes, more aid of the material and physical sort of which some has already come, but even more importantly, real help in resolving the Palestinian-Israeli conflict and providing the Palestinians the rights and freedom of national choice and national identity."[10]

What elements should be part of a *modus vivendi,* and what steps can be taken to achieve one? In the spring of 1981, an expansion of fighting between Phalangist militiamen, attempting to establish a stronghold in the central Lebanese city of Zahle, and Syrian troops, challenging the move, reached a dangerous level. Israeli air intervention and Syrian surface-to-air missile emplacements followed. The U.S. sent veteran Middle East negotiator Philip Habib into the region to seek a limited resolution. His efforts included bringing Arab foreign ministers into negotiations. While Habib was still involved in the crisis in central Lebanon, a sharp increase in Israeli preemptive strikes, including the large-scale bombing of Beirut, and Palestinian cross-border shelling created an even more dangerous situation, threatening to ignite a broader Arab-Israeli war. The negotiating team, including Habib, the Saudi foreign minister, and U.N. officers, achieved a cease-fire between the Israelis and the Palestinians, with PLO leader Yasir Arafat taking responsibility to ensure full compliance on his side. This limited break in the fighting, as a result of diplomatic means and involving the Israeli government and the PLO leadership, suggests that if the will to seek solutions is there, the means to achieve them can be mustered. A very limited relief for Lebanon could become a model for broader resolution. It is just possible that attempts to mitigate the Lebanese tragedy can lead rather than follow resolution of the Palestine problem.

There are immediate steps that should be part of a Lebanese solution.

1. The full implementation of U.N. Security Council Resolutions 425 and 426, which were adopted in March 1978 at the time of Israel's invasion of Southern Lebanon, should receive strong international support. They provide for full Israeli withdrawal from all Lebanese territory and respect for Lebanese "territorial integrity, sovereignty and political independence . . . within its recognized boundaries."[11] The resolutions also established a U.N. Interim Force in Southern Lebanon charged with confirming withdrawal and "assisting the government of Lebanon in ensuring the return of its effective authority in the area." UNIFIL should be free to deploy to the international frontier between Lebanon and Israel and not be excluded from the strip of Lebanon controlled by Major Haddad. U.S. political and diplomatic efforts should support UNIFIL, with the clear intention of restoring full Lebanese government authority to the whole country at the earliest possible time.

2. The special relations between the PLO and Lebanon need to be reexamined in light of the Cairo agreement of 1968 and later joint accords.[12] The Lebanese view the current Palestinian presence as exceeding the limitations once agreed upon. A Palestinian scholar noted that, "A negotiated agreement with the Lebanese government that maintains the spirit and substance of the earlier ones while taking into account the new political realities on the Lebanese scene might

constitute an important gesture towards Lebanese and particularly Maronite opinion. The PLO morally owes it to all Lebanese to make some such gesture."[13] The PLO would continue to refrain from military operations across the border and would recognize UNIFIL's role, together with the Lebanese army, to seal off the Lebanese-Israeli border.

3. Achieving a *modus vivendi* should be a high priority not only for the Lebanese, but for the international community. Other nations must cease seeking to exploit Lebanese differences for their own ends. Syrian and Israeli alliances in Lebanon have been destructive of Lebanese unity and deeply harmful to the structure of Lebanese life. Lebanon will for the foreseeable future remain a pluralistic multisectarian society, and recognition of the necessity to maintain the balance of power and authority is important. Neither side—Christian nor Muslim—should need to fear the threat of being overwhelmed. At the same time, greater efforts to ensure economic, political, and social justice must be taken. A symbolic explication of this principle of equality might be to have Christians and Muslims share equally in the government. But these and other issues will best be decided by the Lebanese parties themselves. What must be assured is that Lebanese efforts at reconciliation will be aided by positive steps to resolve the Israeli-Palestinian conflict, by insulating to the greatest degree possible the fragile Lebanese political structures from other Middle East conflicts, and by international guarantees of the sovereignty and territorial integrity of Lebanon.

4. While Syrian troops entered Lebanon in an effort to end the Civil War and had the backing of the Arab League to serve as the cornerstone of an Arab Deterrent Force, their continued presence in Lebanon has become part of the problem. A resolution of the recurring crises in Lebanon almost certainly requires the pull-back of Syrian forces as part of the overall plan. Syria's intention to withdraw should be announced at once, and the withdrawal should become part of the critical series of steps involving the end of Israeli support of a surrogate army in the South, fulfillment of the UNIFIL mission as a buffer force in the South, reclarification of the Palestinian presence in Lebanon, and the effective extension of the authority of the government of Lebanon to all parts of the land.

8

Oil and Conflict

There is a second focal point of tension and potential conflict in the Middle East, geographically located around the Persian (or Arabian) Gulf and centered on oil. The politics of oil today is both separate and yet intimately connected to the Arab-Israeli conflict. The Arab oil-producing states have been a part of the thirty-five-year rivalry with Israel. Although their armies have been at most symbolically involved in the Arab-Israeli wars, their wealth and interest lie with the Arab cause. They have supported the political programs of Palestinian nationalism even while trying to shape its goals to match their own purposes or need for stability in the region. In recent years, these very wealthy and resource-rich states have used their considerable political power explicitly to try to influence the direction of Middle East events and especially the manner in which the Arab-Israeli crisis is resolved. The Arab oil-producing nations have made clear their belief that the greatest threat to stability in the Middle East, and to the unimpeded flow of oil, is the continued Arab-Israeli conflict and the failure to find a just solution to the Palestinian problem. What are the factors that place oil in a position of great political strength, but also cause it to be a center of conflict?

1. At the core is the extent to which oil is essential to modern industrialization. Ownership of oil, or unimpeded access to it, has become vital to wealth and power.

2. Nationalism in the Middle East has led to conflicts of interest between the oil-producing nations of the region and the major oil consumers in Europe, Japan, and North America.

3. The Middle East oil states and the U.S. have supported opposite sides in the Arab-Israeli conflict and the quest for Palestinian national rights.

4. Third World countries share with the oil states an interest in the worldwide redistribution of wealth and power but also find themselves economically hurt by the very factors that have brought economic success to the oil-producing nations—higher oil prices.

As a major producer and the largest consumer of oil, the United States is inescapably involved in these conflicts. Policy statements from both the Carter and Reagan administrations reveal several common assumptions (some shared in Western Europe and Japan) concerning the nature of the oil crisis. These assumptions are:

1. The supply of oil from the Middle East is vital to U.S. national security.

2. As major consumers of oil, the United States, Western Europe, and Japan should enjoy privileged access to oil.

3. If these rights of access are threatened, the United States will act to secure them by traditional diplomatic means, by political interferences in Middle East governments, and, if necessary, by direct military intervention.

4. The Soviet Union is a threat to U.S. access primarily because of its proximity and through potential "subversion" of local governments, support of revolutionary movements, or direct military means.

While we recognize the central importance of oil, we reject these U.S. assumptions and perceptions. They impede the search for solutions to the "oil problem" because they do not recognize the interests of the people of the Middle East. They are instead distorted by their overwhelming focus on U.S. national and economic interests. A balanced international view and a real goal of resource sharing hold greater promise for "solving" the "problem" of oil. We are deeply concerned about current trends and the need for new perspectives. Visionary approaches are needed that incorporate international and human values, governing attitudes toward and uses of oil.

OIL AS A PROBLEM

Oil as a focus for conflict has kept pace with its increased use by the industrial world and the subsequent loss of its control. Of the industrial users, only the United States and the Soviet Union have significant reserves of oil within their own borders and for many years both countries had surpluses which they could export. In the United States, domestic production peaked in 1971, and the last decade has seen a growth in imports to meet increased demand. The Soviet Union still remains self-sufficient and continues to export oil, largely to the European socialist bloc nations and somewhat less to Western Europe.

Early in the twentieth century, oil became an efficient source of energy, and the Middle East was discovered to have major oil reserves. Exploration for oil, ownership of these oil rights, and production and distribution of oil were, through most of the first half of the twentieth century, totally in the control of European and U.S. business enterprises. During this period, while industry in Europe and the United States was growing, the cost of energy was marginal to total production costs. In fact, the cost of oil actually dropped due to new exploration and increased production.

Sharp increases in the use of oil began in the years prior to World War II among all industrial nations, and this increase continued in the postwar years, with Japan becoming a significant additional oil consumer. A shift from coal as the basic fuel and the replacement of coal by oil for electric generation account in part for increased oil usage. Petroleum also was used in the large new petrochemical and plastics industries. Rapid postwar growth in the use of automobiles and airplanes added additional demands. Virtually every aspect of our lives in North America, Europe, and Japan depends in some way on oil, from the clothes we wear to the food we eat. Not surprisingly, many development programs in Third World countries, dependent as they have been on First World advice, aid, and technology, have also been designed to utilize cheap oil. Industrialization in many of these countries has added a new set of oil consumers with potentially very large requirements in the future.

THE CONTROL OF MIDDLE EAST OIL

In the first part of the twentieth century, prior to decolonization, the exploration and production of oil in the Middle East was controlled by large corporations owned in Western Europe and North America. A variety of local arrangements was made involving royalties paid on the number of barrels of oil produced to those who had ownership or control of the lands on which the oil was found. With the establishment of clearer political boundaries and the growth of nation states in the interwar years, the nature of the arrangements and contracts between oil-producing companies and the oil-rich nations underwent many changes.

These reflected, first, the increasing dependence on oil of the world economy and, second, the growing demands for greater shares of the income from their oil by the oil-producing nations and the impact of this added income on their own internal social structure.

The greatest changes occurred in the years following World War II. Many of the nations on whose land oil was discovered insisted on partial ownership, and commercial relationships were established which brought increasing wealth to those with political and economic control in the oil-producing states. By midcentury, very wealthy local elites, whether traditional political leaders or new local entrepreneurs, emerged. Few rules to achieve distributive equity were made, and the gap between rich and poor in the oil states grew significantly. The most substantial oil-producing states (those clustered around the Persian Gulf) were also the most traditional societies.

The most important shift in power between oil consumers and producers began in 1960 when the oil-producing states organized and coordinated their activities in an explicit attempt to gain greater political and economic control of the industry. OPEC (Organization of Petroleum Exporting Countries), made up almost entirely of Third World or nonindustrial nations, asserted the interests of these nations against those of the consuming industrialized nations that had for half a century dominated oil policy, production, and economics. OPEC represented as well an effort to find common policies to replace numerous specific national interests. With production increasing and oil prices dropping, one of OPEC's first steps was to regulate production as part of an effort to restore prices, conserve resources for future exploitation, and support more regularized economic growth. The dramatic and far-reaching change in the politics of oil that OPEC brought is clear when one remembers that in 1960, when OPEC was founded, six of its thirteen members were still colonies or protectorates and the key oil-shipping lanes—the straits of Hormuz, Aden, and Malacca—were all under European control.[1]

In shaping the world economy, the major oil companies were important actors. At the end of World War II, they controlled most of the oil available in the world. Even in the early 1970's, after the formation of OPEC but before the nationalization of oil, the seven international oil giants[2] controlled at least two-thirds of the world's proved reserves and production in the Middle East, North Africa, Canada, Latin America, Southeast Asia, and the United States. These companies controlled rates of exploration; they decided which reserves would be exploited; they refined, shipped, and sold the oil. No government, including the United States, seriously monitored their activities; nor was there any system which held them accountable for their decisions. They enjoyed huge profits.

United States government support for the oil companies goes back to the first decades of this century. Diplomatic intervention in 1943 was aimed at assuring the access of U.S. companies to Middle East oil. In 1950, the U.S. used diplomatic means in Saudi Arabia to ensure a favored position for U.S. companies. In 1953 and 1954, the United States, working together with Britain, intervened, using the CIA in covert political actions to reverse the Iranian nationalization of oil, broaden U.S. commercial access, overthrow the government of Premier Mossadegh, and restore the Shah to the throne.[3] Current pledges by U.S. government officials to protect U.S. interests in the Middle East by military intervention if necessary always include the necessity to assure access to oil at terms which the West finds suitable. The statement by President Reagan in October 1981 that the U.S. would not permit Saudi Arabia to become another Iran, suggests a growing U.S. commitment to intervene militarily in the Middle East to prevent internal political revolt.

THE ARAB OIL EMBARGO

Nineteen seventy-three represents a significant turning point in the relations between the oil-exporting nations and Europe and the United States. Three things occurred: the October war between Israel and the Arab states, the embargo on oil shipments to the United States and Western Europe by a number of the Arab oil-producing countries, and the OPEC decision to increase the price of oil. The increase was not caused solely by the Arab-Israeli war, nor was it supported only in the political context. OPEC already had planned a 70 percent price increase. Even the Shah of Iran, on friendly terms with Israel and the United States, had worked hard in 1973 to gain a significant oil price increase. But the cutback in production, the embargo, and the accompanying scare brought a 400 percent increase over pre-1973 prices.[4] Each of these events built the self-confidence of the Arab oil-producing nations. The war was interpreted by many in the Middle East as an "Arab victory," redressing the sense of technological and military inferiority. The embargo on oil shipments was a clear indication that oil could be used as a political "weapon." The Arab states objected to the U.S. resupply of Israel during the war and in response cut oil production 25 percent. The price increases accelerated a trend already under way, bringing a massive transfer of wealth from the Western industrial world to previously poor nations. The extent to which the economies of the industrial West could be affected by changes in oil policy became clear.

EFFECTS ON THE UNITED STATES

The United States is the most significant user of the total world's oil output. Representing approximately 6 percent of the population of the world, the U.S. uses approximately 30 percent of the oil produced.[5] During the 1970's the United States consumed petroleum at a 50 percent greater per capita rate than the next highest users—Germany, Switzerland, and Sweden—while the United States' per capita income was below that of these European states. The growth in U.S. oil imports and costs during the decade of the 1970's is striking. In 1970, 3.5 million barrels per day were imported at an average cost of about

$2 per barrel. This represented one-quarter of U.S. oil needs. By 1979 the United States was importing 8.5 million barrels per day, at $30 per barrel, to meet one-half of its oil use.[6]

This increased dependence on imported oil and the rise in the cost of this oil have fueled inflation and helped to undermine the preeminent position of the United States in the world economy. Nevertheless, the major oil companies have, if anything, grown stronger as a result of these developments. While there are attempts among some of the oil-producing nations to develop their own refineries and to participate more actively in decisions concerning distribution by entering into nation-to-nation contracts for the delivery of their oil, the major oil companies continue to play the central role in exploration, refining, shipping, and marketing of oil in the Middle East and in much of the rest of the world. They are still able to influence supply and demand, and thereby defend price levels and insure profits. With each rise in the price set by the oil-producing nations, the major oil companies have been able to increase their own profits. They have been able to drive many smaller competitors out of business, and to invest heavily in alternative energy sources, ensuring their own continued profitability.

In the months following the embargo and price increase in 1974, hints or threats that the United States might intervene militarily to secure access to oil in the Middle East were common. The history of direct U.S. governmental involvement in aid of the oil companies, noted previously, meant that the possibility of U.S. intervention could not be taken lightly.

PROBLEMS IN THE OIL-PRODUCING NATIONS

The whole range of economic, political, and military strains that exist in other parts of the world is also evident within the oil-producing nations. While none has a social or economic infrastructure which permits comprehensive distribution and sharing of the oil income (though some of the states have adopted the ideology of social distribution), in all of the states there has been some significant improvement in economic status of the entire population.

The Persian Gulf and Arabian peninsula oil-producing states have come to rely heavily on expatriate labor drawn from other parts of the Middle East, North Africa, and Asia. In countries like Saudi Arabia and Kuwait, the contract labor force (and others with limited residence permission) ranges from one-third to one-half or more of the total population. In the explicitly industrial and oil-producing sectors, as well as in the service sector, noncitizen labor makes up an even higher proportion of the total. Eighty-five percent of the work force of the United Arab Emirates are expatriate laborers, and only five percent of the labor force in Dubai are nationals.[7] There are two primary reasons for the large importation of labor. These states have small indigenous populations from which to draw to support their growing economic activity, and they retain social and religious traditions which limit participation in industrial activities. The noncitizen laborers do not enjoy many of the benefits of increased national wealth that are available to citizens of the Middle East states.

The rise in oil prices has far outstripped the cost of oil production, allowing the accumulation of very large sums of money. Extensive efforts have been undertaken in many of the oil-producing nations to begin processes of large-scale development, but social and economic infrastructures have not been developed sufficiently to absorb the resulting funds. Thus, tremendous sums have been invested overseas, primarily in Europe and North America. These investments have in turn been weakened through inflationary pressures in the industrial world caused by the oil price increases. As Europe and North America have been negatively affected by increased prices and diminishing supplies of oil, many Third World nations undertaking early steps in industrialization have been more dramatically hurt. The oil-producing states have recognized the hardships produced in other Third World non-oil-producing and poor nations. OPEC nations, the Arab states as a group, and many of the individual oil producers have established new funds for development aid, specifically aimed at non-oil-producing Third World nations. The proportion of gross national product (GNP) given as aid on an annual basis in recent years by the major oil-producing states is significantly higher than the proportion of GNP given as aid by any of the major industrial states.[8]

The new wealth produced by oil has created a new politics in the Middle East. Calls for sharing of the newfound wealth among the

Arab states have been frequent, and to some extent such sharing has occurred. But the sharing of wealth and the giving of aid has sometimes had a direct political rather than humanitarian purpose. A major aim of the conservative oil-producing states has been to preserve or to achieve stability in the Middle East and Southwest Asia and to undermine threats of insurrection or challenges to their political leadership. Nevertheless, the very real tensions arising from the existence of great wealth amid enormous poverty are not easily overcome and they portend continued instability.

The oil-producing states of the Middle East directly or indirectly reveal their vulnerability. Some fear internal insurrection; others fear challenge from neighboring states. The most striking reversal of power in the Middle East was in Iran (see Chapter 10). Its 1979 revolution leaves few Middle East leaders feeling secure. The Iranian revolutionary government sharply curtailed oil production both through dislocations and through the adoption of a policy of resource conservation aimed at national needs, not international commerce. The cutback in world supplies was serious, since Iran had been second to Saudi Arabia as oil exporter from the Middle East. Many of the Shah's critics judged the extraordinarily high oil revenues to be a destabilizing factor in his regime, as were his overrapid modernization program (at the expense of the agricultural sector) and unwise acquisition of highly sophisticated armaments.

Further, vulnerability arises from the tensions brought about as new wealth is turned toward the introduction of new technologies, new industries, new cities, new patterns of residence; and all the direct or implied challenges of industrialization and modernization to older traditions may be seen as both part of the problem and part of the solution.

THE SOVIET UNION AND MIDDLE EAST OIL

The Soviet Union's potential need for Middle East oil has been identified by U.S. analysts as a possible source of conflict between the Soviet Union on the one hand and the United States, Western Europe, and Japan on the other. The perception that the United States' and its allies' national interests are linked to Middle East oil makes potential Soviet claims to its use seem illegitimate and threatening. At this time the Soviet Union remains the largest single producer of oil in the world and an oil-exporting nation. Because Soviet use of oil is increasing, however, some people suggest that a turnaround point is approaching when the Soviets will need to extend their influence into the Middle East in order to gain oil. Estimates vary regarding Soviet oil productivity, the size and strength of its reserves, and the growth of its consumption. The most pessimistic assessments have been "leaked" from Central Intelligence Agency reports through partial publication of these documents and citation of them in speeches by members of the Carter and Reagan administrations. More optimistic assessments are produced by scholars such as Marshall Goldman, author of a thorough study of Soviet oil policy, and others. Recently, CIA estimates of Soviet oil reserves have been revised upward, suggesting that the low estimates might have been politically motivated to raise the specter of a Soviet threat and to justify new levels of U.S. military and political involvement.[9]

Soviet intent in the Persian Gulf was questioned immediately after the invasion of Afghanistan. President Jimmy Carter and members of his administration identified this Soviet move as the first step toward the Persian Gulf and saw it as part of a challenge to the United States and European presence in the Gulf. They claimed that the Soviet aim was either to gain Middle East oil for its own use or to thwart the West. When we discussed this issue with leaders in the Middle East, however, one conservative foreign minister from the Persian Gulf countered, "Why won't the Soviets, if and when they need oil, buy it from the Gulf states? They bought natural gas from the Shah of Iran; they can simply purchase what they need, and they have done so in the past."

This view represents an outlook which is worthy of serious consideration. It questions the assumption that the only way to interpret the role of oil in the Middle East is to reduce it to terms of bipolar contention between the United States and the Soviet Union or between East and West. After all, this view holds, the oil is owned by third parties who reject hegemony over their resources of either the United States or the Soviet Union. When President Carter in his state of the union address in January 1980 announced that the United

States would place the oil states of the Middle East under a U.S. military umbrella as a means of protecting what he called U.S. "vital interests," leaders in the Persian Gulf greeted the announcement warily. Moves to establish a rapid deployment force for military intervention in the region and attempts to secure U.S. military bases in the area are likewise greeted skeptically.

The Soviet Union is by no means seen as a friend by the conservative states of the Persian Gulf and the Arabian peninsula. Nonetheless, Saudi, Kuwaiti, and other local leaders judge the Soviet "threat" to be significantly less important than the primary threat of instability arising from the continued Israeli-Arab conflict and the failure to resolve the Palestinian problem. In this context, the United States is seen by Arab leaders as a partisan of the wrong side.[10] Its stress on a Soviet threat is seen as irrelevant. Further, the oil-producing technologies are fragile. Oil experts have indicated that while one side in a conflict could deny the use of oil to the other side by destroying the production facilities, neither side would be able to defend its own facilities from destruction. The complex technologies of oil production are not, they say, militarily defensible.

But can oil, which has become so critical an element in the productive systems of all industrial nations, be removed as a locus of conflict, thereby reducing one critical facet of tensions and fear in the Middle East?

THE NEED FOR NEW PERSPECTIVES

Even a brief survey of the problem of oil shows the need to develop new perspectives. We call for a new sanity which reflects human needs and human responsibility. Too many of the "solutions" being discussed in Washington and European capitals are almost totally reflective of narrow self-interest. They largely ignore the interest of the Middle East states and are silent on the needs and interests of people of the Middle East. Among the new approaches needed to construct an appropriate context within which to deal with oil, we propose the following:

Oil is a resource like many others—metals, minerals, water, etc. Even as we identify the critical importance of oil for the industrial nations, we must also note the importance of technology and food to less developed and hungry nations. In other words, resources—such as water, food, oil—are vital for survival in *all* societies, and oil should be seen in this broader context.

It is imperative that the nations of the world adopt an ethic based on humane, just, and rational use of resources—an ethic of sharing in which resources are utilized for the widest human benefit and not seized for narrower interests by whoever is strong enough. Nor, in the longer run, is unilateral control by the nation where a resource is found sufficient guarantee of humane world use. Integration into an equitable world system of distribution, including the developing nations as well as the oil producers and consumers, is essential.

Control of resources through military strength and coercion must be abandoned. The militarily powerful have no right, on the basis of their military strength, to enjoy special access to the world's resources. Conversely, the producers have the responsibility not to use resources for narrow national needs alone.

Decisions affecting production and price can be made for other than market reasons. They can reflect national, political, and social goals as demonstrated in such countries as Norway, Britain, and Mexico. These decisions should come to reflect broader international needs, such as Third World development and international wealth, technology, and resource sharing.

Plans for oil production levels which reflect the longer-term economic interests of the oil-producing countries and their people for ordered economic growth and development must replace the plans proposed largely to meet the needs of the U.S. and others currently consuming oil at wasteful levels.[11]

Support should be given to principles of democratization in the oil-producing states, encouraging both political participation and greater economic distributive justice. Interests should be identified with the people and their well-being, rather than solely with the flow of oil. But this does not mean the use of external interference to "put" a democratic government in place. There is an important balance to be maintained between encouragement and interference. Recent history has made abundantly clear that stability sought by outsiders through a policy of supporting regimes against the will of their own people is neither workable nor effective in the long run.

Energy and oil conservation in the U.S. should be adopted as part of a long-term movement for more equitable sharing of the earth's resources, not in narrow terms of self-interest, using some of the same underlying principles that are at the basis of the projected Law of the Sea agreements.

Efforts for international planning, through conferences and the establishment of truly international agencies, to develop cooperative use and sharing of natural resources should be encouraged. The forum and agencies must explicitly include the producers of the resource as well as *all* the users—U.S., Western Europe, developing nations, and the Soviet Union and its allies.

The U.S., a nation which has threatened military intervention to secure oil supplies, should renounce any resort to military force and direct political intervention and join with other consuming nations to assure nonintervention. This means abandoning the bipolar policy the U.S. has taken in the region. All nations should recognize the explicit calls made by the Middle East oil-producing states to respect and recognize their independence, nonalignment, and need to achieve local and regional security arrangements.

Many of these suggestions are visionary. They call for far-reaching changes in the economic and political lives of both oil-producing and oil-consuming countries. We do not believe that they will be easily achieved. Realism, however, demands that we see the possibility of genuine and lasting peace in the long run, built upon immediate steps to alter the institutional or political circumstances which perpetuate conflicts and erode peace.

9

The Arms Race

The Middle East today is the largest importer of arms in the world, buying well over one-third of all the world's arms exports at an annual rate approaching $10 billion per year. Arms have been the fastest growing sector of the economies of most states in the region. While the total military budget of the region lags behind North America, Europe, and East Asia, the Middle East is spending more than $30 billion per year on its armed forces, has the highest per capita military expenditure and the highest rate of arms growth, more than three and one-half times since the 1967 war. Eight of the ten leading arms importing countries are located in the Middle East.[1] Arms are no longer a symptom alone; they have become the problem.

The Middle East arms race has taken on a life of its own, even while it is spurred by a variety of causes: local rivalries and the perceived need to obtain ever more sophisticated weaponry; the long-standing, unresolved Arab-Israeli conflict and the military support the contestants have won from their superpower sponsors; the desire of the superpowers to "play out" their conflict in the Middle East by arming and securing allies through arms transfer agreements; the desire of the Western industrial nations to recycle through arms sales the petrodollars created by their reliance on imported oil, especially with the steep increases in oil prices; and, ironically enough, the Egyptian-Israeli peace treaty, which called for massive new arms supplies from the U.S. to both nations.

The leading arms exporters are the United States, the Soviet Union, Great Britain, France, and Germany (in that order). In the following discussion, it should be kept in mind that the arms-manufacturing nations bear *the* primary responsibility for arms buildups throughout the world. During the last decade, the U.S. alone sold $47.7 billion worth of arms to the Middle East, according to the conservative estimates of the Defense Department. This accounted for 57 percent of all U.S. military sales abroad during these years.[2] The U.S. Arms Control and Disarmament Agency in its most recent summary report indicates that for the years 1974–1978 (immediately following the October 1973 war), during which time $29 billion of arms were sent to the Middle East, 48 percent were supplied by the U.S. (ten recipients), 26 percent by the Soviet Union (seven recipients), 7 percent by Great Britain (twelve recipients), 6 percent by France (thirteen recipients), and 3 percent by West Germany (eight recipients). The top three U.S. recipients, in that period (Iran, Israel, and Saudi Arabia), received $12.8 billion, or 93 percent, of all U.S. arms exported to the Middle East, and two Soviet arms recipients (Syria and Iraq) account for $8.6 billion, or 84 percent, of Soviet arms sent to the region.[3] The figures for the years since 1978 will register several changes, most notably the halt of all U.S. arms shipments to Iran. But the U.S. total to the region will still remain very high since the loss of sales to Iran has largely been taken up by the significant commitments made to Egypt, through agreements surrounding the peace treaty, coupled with marked increases in arms committed to Saudi Arabia and Israel. The Soviet Union during this same period has halted all shipments to Egypt, but increased its sales to Libya and maintained its shipments to Syria and Iraq.

The economies of a number of the key countries in the region have been severely strained and subjected to inflationary pressure by their military budgets and arms imports; Israel in 1980 suffered an astounding 130 percent inflation, with other countries trailing but still sharply affected. Major problems for the Shah of Iran in his final few years arose directly from his massive and expensive arms acquisitions program. Weapons are purchased largely at the expense of reduced spending on social and economic development. The effect of huge military expenditures takes other tolls on social structure and balance. The creation of military sectors of the society; the growth of elite officers' groups, often sent to other countries for training by superpower sponsors; and the wide-scale spread of training in the use of arms have had destabilizing effects on societies in the Middle East as elsewhere. There is no single pattern, but it would be irresponsible to ignore the extent to which military regimes have emerged in many Middle Eastern countries.

The arms race in the Middle East involves a number of critically important factors. The magnitude and rate of growth already noted has been until recently the most obvious. In both operational jet combat aircraft and main battle tanks, the numbers available today in the Middle East are almost equal with the total NATO forces in Europe.[4] In addition to the issue of the volume of weapons transferred, there is the issue of their sophistication. Middle Eastern countries have obtained from the U.S., Europe, and the Soviet Union successive generations of new conventional weapons just as rapidly as they have been developed. The latest Soviet MiG-23 fighter planes and the newest U.S. F-15 fighters are already in use, and agreements are in place for delivery of the new-generation Soviet MiG-25's and MiG-27's and U.S. F-16's. The 1981 U.S. decision to sell to Saudi Arabia five AWAC highly sophisticated advance-warning radar and control planes previously used only by U.S. forces is a further indication of the trend toward acquisition of the latest, and often most expensive and complicated, weapons systems by Middle East nations. The situation is the same in other conventional weapons systems such as tanks, T-V and laser-guided missiles, electronic countermeasure systems, helicopters, tankers for aerial refueling of combat aircraft, etc. A recent SIPRI survey concluded that in conventional weapons, Middle East arsenals are among the most up-to-date in the world. These arms have significantly increased destructive power. New wars in the region (and portents of them can be seen in Lebanon and the conflicts between Iran and Iraq) will prove significantly more devastating of civilian populations as well as more destructive of both civilian and military physical facilities.

The pattern of weapons distribution is also changing. There is an ever-spreading arena of conflict that is associated with the loosely defined Middle East. In the 1950's, the flow of arms to the region was more or less confined to Israel and the Arab states confronting it; thirty years later, the Middle East arms race had widened to include both the Persian Gulf region and North Africa. In the 1980's, Middle East problems have spilled over into the Horn of Africa (Ethiopia and Somalia) and Southwest Asia (Afghanistan and Pakistan). Conflicts are piled one on top of another, with the result that local crises and conflicts often assume international stature out of proportion to the issues involved.

One striking feature of arms transfer agreements has been their fluidity. With the exception of the long-term relationship between Israel and the U.S., other arrangements have shifted during the past three decades, usually back and forth between the U.S. and the Soviet Union, though some arms importers have received weapons simultaneously from both superpowers. Until 1975 Egypt received the bulk of its military equipment from the Soviet Union, but since then the U.S. has supplied Egypt and currently is supplying upward of $1 billion per year in weaponry and associated military needs. Until 1979 Iran was the largest importer of arms in the Middle East. The major Mideast arms importer now is Saudi Arabia and in actual arms purchases has been the leading world customer for U.S. arms since 1975.[5] Somalia, on the Horn of Africa directly across from the Arabian peninsula, has been a recipient of Soviet arms aid, and had allowed the Soviets to construct a deep-water harbor and airstrip for the use of Soviet military forces. Today it receives its arms aid largely from the U.S. and has negotiated U.S. use of the harbor and airport built by the Soviets. Ethiopia, its enemy, now receives Soviet arms. Almost any war now fought in the region, and especially another Arab-Israeli war, will find U.S.-supplied weapons and technologies on both sides of the battle. This pattern of shifting and insecure alliances will continue because it primarily reflects local and regional interests in spite of superpower attempts to impose bipolar East-West divisions.

Indigenous production of arms in the Middle East is growing, with Israel as the leader. It produces all but the most sophisticated and heavy weapons for its own armed forces and now exports an advanced fighter/bomber and a tactical missile system as well as a wide variety of small arms. In 1981, arms exports from Israel reached the level of $1 billion.[6]

Iran, during the period prior to 1979, had included in virtually all of its weapons-procurement deals agreements to establish facilities for maintenance and repair of hardware and for training of personnel in needed skills. It was also negotiating agreements to produce weapons under license.

Although far behind Israel, other Middle Eastern and Southwest Asian countries, notably Egypt and Pakistan, are also acquiring an important indigenous capability to manufacture major armaments. For example, part of the far-reaching agreement between the United States and Egypt in the wake of the Camp David treaty calls for U.S. assistance to develop Egypt's arms industry.

The decision on the part of several Middle East countries to create military capabilities is further evident in their large-scale projects to build military infrastructure. Israel had obviously undertaken such an effort early in its national existence. More recently, Iran and now Saudi Arabia are spending large sums of money on air, land, and sea bases, on training centers, communications networks, headquarters and command centers. In Saudi Arabia, for example, the U.S. Army Corps of Engineers is under contract for approximately $24 billion.[7]

An analysis of arms transfers shows some important trends. From 1950 to 1966, the countries directly involved in the Arab-Israeli conflict and the Persian Gulf countries (including Iran) imported arms at approximately the same rate. In the period 1966 to 1972, the nations directly involved in the 1967 war accelerated their arms procurements, and the Persian Gulf states lagged behind, reaccelerating their imports in 1973. The cumulative value of arms imported by the nations involved in the Arab-Israeli conflict still remains greater, but it is worth noting that significant arms acquisitions by the Persian Gulf states predates the 1973 oil embargo and price increases, though expenditures since 1973 have risen. The Arab-Israeli confrontation, therefore, while certainly one major cause for the Middle East arms race, is not the only one. Other factors, other fears, sometimes related but often separate from the focal conflict between the Arab states and Israel, have also fueled the process of massive arms acquisitions by nations in the Middle East.

ARMS EXPORT AND ACQUISITION POLICIES

Why have the United States, the Soviet Union, and Western Europe supplied arms on such massive scale to Middle Eastern states? What rationale has guided the nations of the Middle East in their extraordinary acquisition of arms?

The Soviet Union

Soviet policy through the Stalin period accepted a rigid division of the world into capitalist and socialist camps, and ideology dictated that only socialist countries could be given tangible assistance. After Stalin, the Soviet leadership began a reassessment of its foreign policy, deemphasized ideological purity, and became more pragmatic.

With respect to the Third World, the Soviets perceived the existence of a group of nations motivated by nationalist forces "uncommitted" to either the capitalist or socialist camps. By cooperating with these nations, many of which had only recently won their independence from colonial rule, the Soviet Union hoped to enlist them into the pro-Soviet camp.

This change in Soviet policy was possibly motivated by its perceptions of the policies being pursued by the United States in Europe and in the Third World. The post-World War II U.S. doctrine of containment led to the construction of a series of regional alliances along the periphery of the Soviet Union explicitly to prevent the expansion of Soviet influence. Using the tools of economic and military aid, successive U.S. administrations built NATO in Europe, SEATO in Southeast Asia, and the Baghdad Pact in the Middle East. Thwarting these encircling alliances became a major Soviet preoccupation.

The Middle East was an obvious focus for the new Soviet policy. First, the proximity of the region to Soviet borders brought their response. Domination of the region by an adversary was perceived as a threat to Soviet security, a perception which, it should be pointed out, was shared by the Soviet's Czarist predecessors. The second factor was the Western world's growing dependence on oil from the Middle East. Any weakening of the pro-Western alliance in the region would weaken the West's access to a vital resource. Third, the region presented the Soviet Union with many targets of opportunity because of the resentment against the traditional Western colonial powers, France and Great Britain.

These three reasons led to the 1955 Soviet decision to extend military aid, for the first time, to a Third World country, Egypt. For its part, Egypt turned to the Soviet Union out of anger at Western support for the new state of Israel and lack of similar support for Egyptian economic and military development.[8] Similar motives underlay subsequent Syrian and Iraqi ties with the Soviets. All three states had only recently thrown off traditional monarchies and established forms of "Arab socialism." Eventually the Soviet Union extended military aid to liberation movements in the region, including the PLO.[9] Throughout the history of Soviet arms exports to the Middle East, the central rationale has been to sell or give arms to any regime or movement that weakened the perceived anti-Soviet alliance and undermined Western hegemony in the Middle East. The Soviet Union, like the U.S., adopted a policy of selling and transferring military arms as a means of buying and winning political friends.

Also, as is true for the U.S., Soviet arms exports to this region constitute the bulk of Soviet arms transfers to the Third World. They account for 50 to 60 percent of total Soviet arms exports in any year. In another parallel to U.S. arms-transfer policies, Soviet exports have increased greatly since the 1973 Arab-Israeli war. CIA estimates show that Soviet arms exports were five times as great in the 1974–1979 period as in the interwar years of 1967–1973.[10]

After 1974, the Soviet Union adopted a policy of supplying up-to-date versions of its fighters, tanks, and missiles and no longer selling outmoded, reconditioned equipment. At the same time it considerably tightened the financial terms on which such exports were negotiated. Sales of the new MiG-25 and MiG-27 jet fighters, IL-76 transports, SA-9 surface-to-air missile systems, and T-72 tanks were made for hard Western currencies. This Soviet policy of demanding economic gain for its arms arises from the same economic pressures that have clearly spurred the West to try to recoup petro-dollars. In addition, it provides the Soviets with Western currencies for purchasing technologies from Europe and the United States.

Four Arab countries account for more than 70 percent of Soviet arms exports to the region, with Iraq and Syria far in the lead. The Soviet Union has provided jet aircraft, light and medium tanks, armored personnel carriers, and naval craft to Iraq, and many of these items are among the most modern Soviet military equipment ever supplied to a Third World country.

Syria, the second largest recipient of Soviet arms, predates Iraq as a Soviet client and, now that Egypt has dropped its Soviet ties, is the oldest Middle East recipient of military supplies from the Soviet Union. Syria signed a "Treaty of Friendship and Cooperation" with the Kremlin in late 1980 to remove the last obstacle to the receipt by Syria of the Soviet Union's latest and best weaponry. Unlike Iraq and Libya, however, Syria has no oil wealth with which to purchase Soviet arms.

In addition to the transfer of arms from the Soviet Union, a large number of Middle East nationals are given military training in the Soviet Union, and sizeable Soviet military units are in various Middle East countries to help operate and maintain Soviet equipment. In addition, the Soviets built and use a large naval facility in the People's Democratic Republic of Yemen (South).

Western Europe

The European rationale for arms exports to the Middle East has been less ideological than that of the United States and the Soviet Union. Rather than being tied to unchanging strategic policies, European exports have been motivated principally by economic considerations. Because arms supplies have not been linked to a grand strategy, European suppliers have found themselves simultaneously selling to both sides of a conflict, the most recent example being the war between Iraq and Iran.

During the decades of the 1950's and 1960's, the three main European suppliers (Britain, France, and West Germany) played a small role. Germany, of course, as a defeated Axis power was not yet a significant arms exporter. While Britain and France were important suppliers of armaments to their former colonies (for example, Great Britain to Jordan and Iraq), an all-out conventional arms race was prevented by a 1950 arms-limitation agreement negotiated by the foreign ministers of Britain, France, and the United States.[11] This tripartite commitment, growing out of the truce which followed the 1948 war, stipulated that supplier countries would not stimulate an arms race between Israel and the Arab countries.

Arms exports from Europe were further limited by contemporary political disputes. Egypt's support for the Algerian revolution and

Nasser's overthrow of King Farouk, for example, made Britain and France loath to supply the Nasser regime. Of even greater significance was the ill-fated seizure of the Suez Canal by the Europeans in 1956, which chilled bilateral relations between the Europeans and nearly every Arab country. As a consequence, Israel, which had cooperated in the canal seizure and·the invasion of Egypt, became the leading recipient of European weapons—a situation that lasted until the June 1967 war.

Between 1969 and 1971, Britain's policy shifted and it withdrew all its troops from east of the Suez. The United States, which ordinarily would have supplanted the British, was already stretched to the limit by its commitments in Indochina and to NATO. The consequent search for a regional power to protect Western interests focused on Iran. Iran then sought arms from all manufacturers of modern military weapons, including Britain, France, and for the first time, Germany. Iran's increased oil wealth made this possible, and the Shah of Iran came to value modern weapons as a symbol of power.

The European countries entered this growing Middle Eastern market in the 1970's. As the research, development, and production costs of their arms industries grew, a major justification for such extravagant industries was the profit to be realized by selling sophisticated weapons to the Third World. The oil-rich nations were prime customers.

The oil embargo imposed by the Arab producers in 1973 affected European arms sales to the Middle East. Oil was costlier, and the stability of its supply was in question. Arms exports were needed to help pay the bill for costly imported oil and often were considered "sweeteners" for oil supply agreements.

Eight years later (1981), the economic motivations still predominate, but new elements have emerged. Arab oil producers have become wary of depending too much on the United States and have shown their dissatisfaction at continuing U.S. support for Israel. They have negotiated agreements that virtually barter sophisticated armaments in return for guaranteed oil supplies, access to Arab markets, and Arab investment in European industry. European governments are willing to negotiate on these terms because they, too, are worried about the continuing stalemate over the Palestinian issue and its potential effect on the stability of oil supplies.

The United States

The twofold justification for U.S. arms exports to the Middle East has been remarkably consistent since 1950. The prime objective has been to strengthen any government in the region that is friendly to U.S. political, strategic, and economic interests because the Middle East is perceived, in the words of the State Department, as "the greatest strategic prize." A parallel objective has been to deny influence in the region to the Soviet Union, the one power deemed capable of supplanting the United States' hegemony. In addition to this strategic rationale, a tradition of special aid to Israel developed as a permanent part of U.S. Middle East policy.

Initially, the U.S. government, recognizing the volatility of the region, opted for arms restraint. The Truman administration persuaded Britain and France to go along with the 1950 tripartite declaration to limit an arms race between the Israelis and the Arab states. But this policy was undercut during the Eisenhower years because the U.S. refused to treat the Soviet Union as a country whose interests had to be taken seriously in the Middle East. Egypt's anger at the West's refusal to support its army against Israel, however, led the new Egyptian leader Gamel Nasser to turn to the Soviet Union for military aid, thus dooming attempts at conventional arms restraint in the region.

Early in the 1950's the United States began actively pushing the same formula that had worked in Europe and the Far East, namely, establishment of a regional alliance among pro-Western countries, held together by U.S. economic and military aid. The Baghdad Pact of 1955 stretched across the Middle East as far as Pakistan, but in contrast to NATO or SEATO, it was essentially a theoretical alliance. The complex and constantly shifting alignments within the region obviated its unity and stability.

Early U.S. arms exports to the Middle East were actually modest and limited. The presence of British troops stationed at critical points throughout the region made them unnecessary. There were American bases as well, including Wheelus Air Force Base in Libya, which in the early post-World War II years was the largest foreign air base operated by the United States. Until 1965 the United States refrained from supplying Israel with significant amounts of weaponry, and

Britain and France served as the Israelis' chief suppliers. This arrangement was preferred by the United States since it did not want to disturb relations with the oil-producing Arab states. Lastly, of course, throughout the 1950's and 1960's the United States focused its military attention on the Korean and Indochinese wars.

But the pace of U.S. exports accelerated dramatically when Britain announced its intention to withdraw all its troops from bases east of the Suez Canal by the early 1970's. Since U.S. forces were already stretched to the limit by the Indochina war and NATO commitments, American troops could not supplant the British forces. It was then that the Nixon administration sought in Iran a reliable, regional policeman for Western interests in the region. This represented a departure from the regional grouping heretofore sought by U.S. policymakers.

In an unprecedented step, Henry Kissinger and the White House told the State and Defense Departments to accede to any weapons request the Shah might make, disregarding, if need be, their own analysts in the process. This decision marked the beginning of one of the most rapid and massive militarizations of a region the world has ever seen.

The 1970's also strengthened the role of economic factors in U.S. arms exports. U.S. arms manufacturers and the Pentagon, like their European counterparts, were plagued by cost overruns, increasing research and development costs, and inflated production costs. The Vietnam war had created a war-based economy that, even as that war wound down, had little incentive to retool and adjust itself to civilian production. The result was a built-in lobby for U.S. conventional arms sales in key congressional districts throughout the country. The export of arms protected jobs, maintained the Pentagon budget, and assured corporate profits. And arms sales helped recoup dollars being spent on petroleum. The 1973 embargo and OPEC price increase, as we have seen, increased the pressure to sell arms. The Middle East arms race was fueled by both "push" and "pull" factors.

The fall of the Shah in January–February 1979 brought about an immediate reassessment in the United States of the wisdom of relying on a Third World country to protect Western interests. Direct U.S. military involvement in the region has been renewed. At the same time, the amount of U.S. arms being exported to the region has remained high. Indeed, under the Reagan administration, the U.S. seems to be accelerating efforts to forge a regional strategic alliance, however unnatural and unreliable; the U.S. is attempting to put down threatening revolts and secure the region against Soviet influence. Current U.S. concern stretches from Morocco to Pakistan and includes Egypt, Israel, Jordan, and Saudi Arabia.

In addition, the U.S. has moved to secure major bases in Egypt, Kenya, Somalia, Oman, and the Indian Ocean island of Diego Garcia. As part of its new military involvement in the region, the U.S. is developing a rapid deployment force which would be dispatched to deal with perceived threats (internal or external) to the stability of countries in the region. This 200,000-troop force represents a significant escalation of U.S. military commitment in the region.

The most significant transfers of U.S. arms and military assistance to the Middle East have occurred since the 1973 Arab-Israeli war. Among the three countries receiving the most—Israel, Saudi Arabia, and Egypt—there are some differences. Saudi Arabia's total is extraordinarily large because of the $24 billion construction program conducted by the U.S. Army Corps of Engineers. The U.S., in serving as the contract coordinator, is building the entire Saudi military infrastructure, including army, air force, and naval bases, providing training for personnel, as well as shipping large amounts of late-model, highly sophisticated weaponry. Israel, which ranks as the third largest arms recipient, contrasts with the Saudis in the nature of the materials bought. Virtually every Israeli purchase is hardware, the most up-to-date electronic gear, F-15 fighters, tanks, missiles, etc. This means that in a genuine sense the immediate military value of Israel's $8.9 billion in purchases is greater than the comparable $39.5 billion spent by Saudi Arabia. Further, Israel's purchases are largely financed by Foreign Military Sales (FMS) credits, unlike the Saudis' which are direct sales. For example, Israel received more than $11 billion in credits to finance its FMS agreements as well as its commercial sales. A further important indication of Israel's special relationship with the U.S. is that it alone among all the recipients of FMS credits has been forgiven payment on about 50 percent of these credits each year. This means that, in effect, there has been a grant by the U.S. of $5.5 billion in arms exports to Israel.[12]

Egypt, the fourth largest customer of U.S. arms exports, is also a large recipient of FMS credits. As the Shah was being overthrown in Iran (1979), Egypt was signing the Camp David accords, making it eligible to receive more than $4.6 billion in arms in just over four years. Some observers estimate that Egypt will ask for a total of $10 billion in arms over the next five years, as it strives to replace Iran as the guarantor of U.S. and Western interests in the region.

The U.S. pattern of ever-enlarging military involvement in the Middle East involves elements of internal conflict and contradiction. First, as noted above, the U.S. is now a significant supplier to Arab states and to Israel. Jordan, next to Egypt as a recipient of U.S. arms exports (albeit considerably fewer), has a long common border with Israel and has fought alongside the other Arab states in wars against Israel. Ironically, Jordan has aided the transport of Soviet-supplied weapons across its territory from the port of Aqaba to Iraq during the latter's war with Iran. Saudi Arabia considers itself closely tied to the other Arab states in their ongoing confrontation with Israel and has been a major financial supporter of the Arab efforts. Egypt, until it concluded its peace treaty with Israel in 1980, was the major belligerent power on the Arab side and had supplied the most forces in each Arab-Israeli war. It is surely one of the weaknesses of the peace treaty that it has triggered a massive rearmament of Egypt comparable in scale and rate to the arming of Iran begun in 1969.

Israel's arms-acquisitions policy has followed from its judgment that it must maintain an undisputed military superiority in the whole region. Each U.S. sale of arms to Arab states (or the acquisition of arms from the Soviet Union) has been coupled with new supplies for Israel. This direct linkage was evident during the U.S. sales negotiations with Saudi Arabia for F-15 fighters (and improvements for them) and AWAC aerial reconnaissance aircraft. Even arms sales to Egypt following the peace treaty were interpreted by Israel as threatening, requiring additional assurances and supplies for Israel. Thus U.S. policy has not been able to achieve even its stated goals. As noted above, the U.S. attempts to gain security and stability have fueled insecurity and instability. Each addition of arms to Israel's arsenal has given Israel a greater sense of independence from the U.S. and has tempted Israel to fend for itself in its relations with its Arab neighbors. This sense of military superiority and the need to maintain it may help explain Israel's raid on the Iraqi nuclear reactor in the summer of 1981.

It is hard to see the interests of any party or nation being truly served by the current arms race in the Middle East. Insecurity remains high; for the wealthy states in the region, military expenditures represent a diversion of resources from social and economic development; in the poorer states, arms purchases prompt cruelly high inflation rates and distorted economies; the superpowers pursue increased military involvement and commitment in a volatile area and gain continued uncertainty of how long allies will remain allied; for the people of the region, the arms race means that each new conflict—or continuing conflict—exacts a heavier toll in devastation and destruction.

The arms race in the Middle East is out of control. The notion of avoiding conflict by maintaining a dynamic military balance between conflicting parties has failed. This failure is demonstrated by repeated Arab-Israeli wars, the Lebanese civil war and Syrian intervention, and the Iran-Iraq war. The arms race itself has become an increasing source of tension and even of provocation. Even peace agreements have led to new levels of armament. The one slim chance for slowing and limiting the spiral of arms acquisition lies with the arms-supplying countries—U.S., U.S.S.R., France, Britain, and West Germany.

NUCLEAR WEAPONS IN THE MIDDLE EAST

In June 1981, Israel used a preemptive air attack to destroy an experimental nuclear reactor in Baghdad, Iraq. This brought the issue of nuclear weapons in the Middle East sharply to the public attention. Although there are many unanswered questions about nuclear capabilities in the region, some things are known. Several Middle East nations have active nuclear reactor programs. Not all those countries with advanced nuclear development have committed themselves *not* to undertake nuclear-weapons building by signing the nonproliferation treaty and permitting regular inspection by the International Atomic Energy Agency.[13] Europe and the U.S., as suppliers of reactor components, fuels, and technical advice, have not always insisted on full commitments by the recipients to nonproliferation and effective inspections.[14]

Israel is the Middle Eastern country with the most advanced nuclear program and is widely thought to have either a small stockpile of nuclear weapons or the capacity to construct bombs on very short notice. While the Israeli government has maintained silence on its weapons capacity and has said it would not be the first nation to introduce nuclear weapons in the Middle East, it has refused to sign the nuclear nonproliferation treaty and has not allowed international inspection at its nuclear facilities. The Central Intelligence Agency issued a five-page memorandum as early as September 1974, asserting its belief that Israel already had produced nuclear weapons. It based its assessment on its belief that Israel had been involved in clandestine acquisition of large amounts of uranium. There has been recent discussion in Israel concerning the potential necessity of adopting a nuclear-weapons strategy to deal with the shifting military balance in the Middle East. One such study, whose director is Israel's former chief of army intelligence General Ahron Yariv, is currently under way at the Center for Strategic Studies at Tel Aviv University.

The most startling confirmation of Israel's nuclear capacity came from General Moshe Dayan, who served as both minister of defense and foreign minister in recent Israeli governments. Just after Israel's raid on the Baghdad reactor, Dayan announced that although Israel did not have an atomic bomb now, it had the capacity to construct one rapidly should the Arabs move in that direction.[15] Of the nations in the Middle East, Israel certainly possesses the most advanced technological capacity and the most significant pool of trained scientists. In addition, its overall nuclear facilities are the most developed.

The only other country in the region with a serious nuclear reactor program is Iraq.[16] Its program is far behind Israel's, and its pool of technical skills is lower. The destruction of its Osirak reactor represents a significant setback. Was Iraq building nuclear weapons or developing the capacity to build nuclear weapons? Iraq, unlike Israel, was an early signer of the nonproliferation treaty and had regularly permitted its facilities to be inspected by the IAEA. As recently as January 1981, the inspectors were satisfied that Iraq was not diverting materials for bombs use and that Iraq was abiding by the terms of the treaty. But it is also possible that the technologies of the reactor program undertaken by Iraq could have been altered for use in weapons construction. The type of reactor under construction and the nature of fuels Iraq had received had raised doubts in the minds of some international nuclear experts.

Egypt and Libya, the two other Middle East states with a nuclear program, are at such early stages of their development that there seems to be no real threat in the near future of nuclear weapons development. Both countries are also signatories to the nonproliferation treaty. Egypt ratified the treaty in 1980 and at the same time called for creating a nuclear-free zone in the Middle East.

Pakistan, a country with a rapidly moving nuclear program, is a potential source of an "Islamic bomb." Some fear that Pakistan, in return for financial support from oil-rich Arab states for its nuclear program, will share nuclear weapons with them. Pakistan is not a signatory to the nonproliferation treaty and is widely believed to be eager to match the nuclear weapons capacity of its long-time rival India. Pakistan in the past has received its nuclear technologies and fuels from Europe and the United States. Recently it has negotiated with the Reagan administration for the U.S. to resume fuel shipments that had been stopped because of U.S. fears regarding Pakistan's weapons construction.

The Middle East may be poised on the edge of a full-scale nuclear arms race—perhaps exacerbated by the Israeli raid on the Iraqi reactor. The Middle East poses a critical test of the nonproliferation treaty, the International Atomic Energy Agency, and civilian nuclear development, and of the depth of commitment of the nuclear technology and fuel-supplying nations to the principle and practice of nonproliferation. The addition of nuclear weapons to the massive conventional arsenals in the volatile and war-prone Middle East is deeply frightening.

Efforts must be made to curtail the proliferation of conventional and nuclear weapons in the Middle East. As we have demonstrated, such an arms race will contribute to the further destabilization and insecurity of the region and to the potential for superpower confrontation. Therefore, we offer the following recommendations.

RECOMMENDATIONS ON CONVENTIONAL WEAPONS

The key to breaking the cycle of the Middle East arms race lies with the supplier nations, the United States, the U.S.S.R., France, the United Kingdom, and West Germany. We call upon the conscience of these nations and urge them to take strong and immediate actions to stop and, ultimately, reverse the massive buildup of arms in the Middle East.

A comprehensive peace will provide the long-term basis for arms reductions in the Middle East, but since high levels of sophisticated arms have become part of the problem, reductions in arms cannot await the peace agreements. In the interim it is essential that an arms-transfer limitation agreement be achieved. In the current context of conflict in the region, it is unrealistic to expect the Middle East states by themselves to negotiate an arms agreement. A major moratorium by the arms suppliers on the shipment of new weapons to the Middle East is an achievable life-saving step which the suppliers can undertake. We call upon the leaders of our nation to take the initiative in entering an arms transfer moratorium and calling for full involvement of the other major suppliers. Such a moratorium could provide the framework for the longer-term, fuller agreements on Middle East arms limitations and significant arms reductions.

As a means of starting the arms control process a standing committee on arms control might be established among the arms-supplying nations and involving the purchasing nations. Their first task might be to set restrictions both on arms sales to the confrontation states and the nonconfrontation states and on transfers among them. As an intermediate step a Middle East arms limitation treaty might first reduce the armed forces of all nations in the Middle East to purely defensive low-fire-power weapons and ban all high-fire-power arms, particularly those that are destructive of civilian populations. This might mean that interim security needs will be met in part, at least, by United Nations or other international forces.

Tacit agreements among the suppliers to restrict the types of arms transferred could be entered into and enforced by the suppliers. In the past, both the U.S. and the Soviet Union have been reluctant to supply the most advanced weapons systems. The U.S., for example, refused Israel's requests for Pershing I ballistic missiles armed with conventional warheads. The Soviet Union has refrained until recently from supplying its most advanced fighters and surface-to-air missiles. Both countries have recently reversed this policy of restraint and have been responsible for agreements transferring the most sophisticated new weapons systems. If arms limitations and reductions are to be pursued, this policy must be reversed. Some strong and visible efforts must be undertaken.

The recipient nations have in the past accepted restrictions on the use of sophisticated weaponry. During the 1973 war both Egypt and Israel were deterred from using surface-to-surface missiles against each other's cities and entered into a tacit agreement negotiated by the International Committee of the Red Cross toward this end. The U.S. has included use restrictions on weapons it has sold to Israel and Saudi Arabia. Each of these represents a limited form of arms control, albeit often in the context of weapons expansion, and albeit sometimes stretched or violated. Multinational agreements, particularly initiated by the suppliers, are not only possible but could serve as an important constraining element. Beginning at once, new restrictions should be enacted to limit arms use.

CREATING A NUCLEAR-WEAPONS-FREE MIDDLE EAST

Although nuclear reactor technologies are widespread in the region and one state (Israel) has the admitted capability for rapidly assembling a small number of nuclear weapons, it is not too late to create a nuclear-weapons-free zone in the Middle East. None of the Middle East nations has adopted a nuclear weapons strategy and leaders in several key countries, including Egypt, Kuwait, and Israel, have in the past indicated serious interest in a nonnuclear Middle East.

Extraordinary steps must be taken to make the Middle East a

nuclear-weapons-free zone. Included in our concern regarding the proliferation of nuclear weapons is our concern about the role of civilian nuclear power. We question the short-term gains—economic or political—to be had through the export and development of nuclear reactor technologies. We believe that those are thoroughly outweighed by the possibility that these technologies will be used to proliferate nuclear weapons in the region.

There are immediate steps that can be taken to create a nuclear-weapons-free Middle East:

1. All nations in the region not already signatories to the nuclear nonproliferation treaty should sign and ratify the treaty. Egypt, Iraq, and Libya *are* signatories. Israel and Pakistan are not.

Middle East nations, as required by the treaty, should open their nuclear facilities to regular inspection by the International Atomic Energy Agency (IAEA).

The IAEA safeguards should be improved to enhance confidence in them. This is especially important for dealing with sensitive materials, such as highly enriched uranium and plutonium and the facilities for handling them. It may be necessary, for example, to increase the number of inspections and the ability of IAEA inspectors to make "surprise" visits.

The supplier nations should also make stronger commitments to the nuclear nonproliferation treaty and to IAEA requirements, through their bilateral agreements and by broadening the powers of the IAEA or other international agencies to enforce this.

2. Israel, as the only Middle East nation with a nuclear weapons capability, should, as an important confidence-building action, rapidly accept, sign, and ratify the nuclear nonproliferation treaty and work within the community of nonnuclear-weapons states to increase the credibility of the IAEA and improve its system for safeguards.

Israel should open its own nuclear facilities to inspections by the IAEA. As part of this step, Israel should demonstrate its commitment to a nonnuclear Middle East by dismantling the components, or weapons prototypes, that currently exist.

The Arab states, as a confidence-building and reciprocal step, should sign the nuclear nonproliferation treaty if they are not already signatories. Or they should reinforce their commitment to the treaty and make explicit their direct desire for a nuclear-weapons-free Middle East.

3. The U.S. and other nations supplying nuclear fuel and technology should immediately announce their refusal to export nuclear fuels or technologies to nonsignatories of the nuclear nonproliferation treaty. Further, they should tighten their own bilateral safeguards as part of nuclear export agreements.

The U.S. can immediately take a lead in these two areas by rigorously following them in relations with Pakistan and Israel.

4. To indicate a seriousness of commitment to halt nuclear weapons proliferation, the U.S. and U.S.S.R. should take immediate steps to achieve control and reduction of their own nuclear weapons. At the very least this requires a freeze on nuclear weapons deployment, testing, and production. It also calls for the acceptance of SALT II and rapid movement to negotiate SALT III including significant nuclear arms reduction.

5. The U.S., U.S.S.R., and other states possessing nuclear weapons should announce their agreement to make the Middle East a nuclear-weapons-free zone and join the nations in the region to achieve this end. There already exists a model for this in the Tlatelolco Treaty covering Latin America. They should pledge to keep their own nuclear weapons out of the region.

10

Iran

Events in Iran during the past three years cast their shadow over the whole Middle East. On February 11, 1979, Shahpour Bakhtiar, the last prime minister appointed by the Shah, fled Iran. The collapse of his government came only twenty-six days after the Shah, Mohammed Reza Pahlavi, had himself left Tehran for an "extended vacation." The fall of the Shah was precipitated mostly by peaceful methods, such as general strikes and massive street demonstrations, that rendered the Shah's sophisticated 400,000-person army—the fifth largest military force in the world—ineffective.

This chapter will survey the background and some of the major developments leading to the Iranian revolution. It will conclude with an overview of the role of the Shah and Iran in U.S. foreign policy and a discussion of the implications of Iranian events for the Middle East.

Iran's first serious attempt at government reform occurred at the turn of the century. The Constitutional Movement (1905–1911) reflected a growing discontent with corruption in government and with foreign (primarily British and Russian) economic control. The reform movement, like the government itself, was weak and ineffective. This period of constitutional experimentation ended when Reza Khan (father of the last Shah), then the leader of the Cossack brigade, seized power in a British-assisted coup d'état in 1921.

Initially, Reza Khan, the founder of the Pahlavi dynasty, sought the support of the clergy. However, his accommodation policies soon became secondary to his far-reaching program of Westernization, modernization, and centralization of governmental power. His policies produced a major upheaval in the traditional social order. As his reign progressed, Reza Shah became increasingly despotic and he supressed political parties, trade unions, and the press. In 1941, Britain and the U.S.S.R. demanded that Reza Shah expel the large number of Germans from Iran. Upon his refusal, Soviet and British troops entered Iran and forced Reza Shah to abdicate. His son, Mohammed Reza Pahlavi, became the new Shah. Britain, the Soviet Union, and later the United States stationed troops in Iran for the duration of World War II.

In 1945, the communist Tudeh Party, working closely with the Soviet Union, overthrew the central government in the Azerbáyjan and Kurdistan regions of Iran. The young Shah's gendarmerie, assisted by U.S. military advisors, effectively crushed this leftist uprising in 1946. This was the beginning of a long and intimate relationship between the Shah and U.S. military advisors and assistance.

On February 4, 1949, a lone gunman tried to assassinate the Shah. Although no evidence ever linked him to a political party, the Shah responded by outlawing the Tudeh Party and proclaiming martial law. The monarch also banned newspapers deemed too critical of his policies or his family and ordered the arrest of many opposition politicians, including Mohammed Mossadegh.

Responding to this show of force, a group of prominent liberal politicians, headed by Mossadegh, a circle of religious leaders (most notably representing the middle-class bazaar merchants), and various secular and nationalistic parties all allied to form the National Front. Their demands included free elections, a free press, an end to martial law, and nationalization of the British-owned oil industry. Within months, support for the National Front was evident in many well-attended mass demonstrations.

Shaken by these mass rallies and a general strike in the oil industry organized by the outlawed Tudeh Party, the Shah appointed Mossadegh prime minister in May 1951. Mossadegh immediately enacted an oil nationalization law and appropriated the Anglo-Iranian oil company installations.

In July 1952 Mossadegh called for civilian control of the military. The Shah refused, later changed his mind in the face of public demonstrations, and eventually left Iran. Mossadegh continued his policies of reform. But the National Front began to disintegrate. The nationalization of the oil industry and the victories over the Shah had removed the focal points around which the National Front had been united.[1]

Iranian army officers, heartened by the National Front's fragmentation and directly assisted financially and logistically by the CIA took the offensive. Military troops occupied government offices and arrested Mossadegh while crowds of CIA-paid demonstrators marched through Tehran to create the image of popular support for the Shah and against Mossadegh. The Shah returned to Iran, accompanied personally by Allen Dulles, the Director of the CIA, and Kermit Roosevelt, the agent who masterminded the successful coup d'état to return him.[2]

The Shah moved quickly to consolidate his power. He outlawed the National Front, arrested most of its leaders, and dismantled the Tudeh Party.

The 1954 CIA-assisted coup was something of a watershed. It effectively ended Iran's second attempt at constitutional politics. It also marked the beginning of close cooperation between the Shah and the U.S. in intelligence, economic, and military matters. Bolstered by rapidly increasing oil revenues, the monarch began to build a massive military establishment. The army grew slowly from 1953 to 1968 and more rapidly thereafter, eventually going from 120,000 troops in 1953 to more than 400,000 in 1976.

In 1957, with the aid of the CIA and the Israeli MOSSAD, the National Security Organization (SAVAK) of Iran was formed. Much has been written about its brutal tactics, especially during the 1970's. Torture victims, former agents, and periodic reports by Amnesty International and the International Red Cross paint a grim picture of SAVAK's efforts to assure Iran's "security" against its domestic opponents. The Shah's policies of political repression were central in pushing the Iranian people toward revolution. In the popular perception, the CIA was working hand-in-glove with the SAVAK.[3] Despite SAVAK's tactics, in the period between 1957 and 1963 opposition to the Shah continued to mount. Bricklayers, teachers, cabdrivers, and oil-field workers went out on strike. Responding to the pressure, and with the encouragement of the U.S., which feared the instability, the

Shah launched the so-called "White Revolution" or "revolution from above" in the early 1960's with the stated purpose of improving the lot of the Iranian citizenry. Some critics assailed the program for having as its real goals the increasing power of the Shah and the enhancement of his role as gendarme of the Middle East.

The Shah's White Revolution did generate certain improvements in health services, education, literacy, and the standard of living. Also, the program broke up large landholdings and redistributed some of the arable land. But for the majority of Iranians the Shah's policies failed to produce their stated aims. While many families in Tehran gained access to modern apartments and were able to buy consumer goods, shanty towns proliferated, and urban crowding and inflation worsened. By the late 1970's, over 40 percent of the four million residents of Tehran lived in inadequate housing, there was still no sewer system, and public transportation was minimal. The Shah's policies produced uneven results in the countryside. Certain poor families received land in the redistribution, but it was almost impossible for them to make a living without adequate credit, which was not available. Many of them sold their farms and moved to Tehran. In certain sectors of Iran large farms were established for mechanized cash cropping; however, many of them ran into financial and organizational difficulties. With tempting urban salaries drawing people off the countryside, and a lack of appropriate government interest, Iran's agricultural production began to decline. When Mohammed Reza Pahlavi assumed the throne in 1941, Iran was self-sufficient in agriculture. By 1976, the country imported 76 percent of the food products it consumed.

One insight into the Shah's approach to agriculture is reflected in his autobiography, *Mission for My Country,* where he boasts about the tobacco monopoly:

> The government operates a very lucrative tobacco industry, practically doubled in capacity through a big plant expansion completed in 1960. Every working day we now turn out about 50 million cigarettes—enough to keep even quite a few chain-smokers busy—plus about 10 tons of pipe tobacco. In any Persian village you can see farmers smoking inexpensive cigarettes from our government factories. Lately we have followed the Western trend by starting the manufacture of filter-tip cigarettes, and now

we are opening up a new market by embellishing the boxes with lavish Arabian scenes and sending them to the Persian Gulf sheikdoms.[4]

While one section of the Shah's government was engaged in expanding cigarette sales, 87 percent of Iran's roughly 50,000 villages still had no schools, only 1 percent had medical facilities, and a national literacy rate of 15 percent was seldom approached outside the large towns.

The failures in the implementation of the White Revolution served to refresh and broaden the ranks of the opposition. There were mass demonstrations by teachers, clergy, students, and bazaar merchants. In early June 1963, Ayatollah Khomeini raised the banner of revolt by openly denouncing the Shah and his policies. Bazaars throughout the country closed in support of this leading cleric. Then, in a swift move, the armed forces struck at peaceful demonstrations in Qom, Tehran, Tabriz, and Isfahan. Thousands were killed, and Khomeini was arrested and exiled to Iraq.

In putting down the successive rebellions in 1946, 1953, and 1963, the Shah alienated an ever larger number of groups within Iran. During the period from 1963 to 1979, public resentment smoldered under the surface. Many individuals, like Mehdi Bazargan[5] and Ali Shariati[6], and influential groups, like the Marxist Fedayeen and the Islamic leftist Mujahidin al-Khalq, emerged as leaders of the opposition. The Fedayeen and Mujahidin al-Khalq are today major factors in the struggle against the Khomeini-led government in Iran.

While inflation crippled most of Iran, the Shah pursued a policy of enlarging and modernizing the army and thereby aggravating inflation even further by diverting large sums for military expenditures. This was spurred by the Nixon doctrine. Between 1973 and 1978 he spent some $18 billion on armaments in the U.S., making him at that time the single largest customer for U.S. arms sales abroad.

By 1978 some 500 U.S. firms were operating in Iran. In addition to a large contingent of military advisors, between 40,000 and 50,000 American expatriates were living and working in Iran, many of them enjoying privileges usually reserved for diplomats. For the most part, these people were paid salaries of $40,000 to $80,000 a year because Iran was considered a "hardship post" and the local cost of living was high. At the same time, the average Iranian's annual income was between $2,500 and $3,000.

Mohammed Reza Pahlavi had no substantial fortune when he became the Shah, although he had inherited certain lands from his father, some of which he donated to the state. He later reconfiscated this land and sold it for a very high price, establishing the beginning of his vast family fortune. Within two decades the Shah and his family joined the ranks of the wealthiest people in the world; his twin sister, Ashraf, had twelve palaces in various parts of the world, while his brother-in-law was found guilty of accepting multimillion-dollar payoffs for help with contracts from the Textron Corporation. Devout Muslims as well as many of Iran's poor were angered by the lavish parties of the Pahlavi family, by their "jet-set" image, and by the drug trafficking of the Shah's sister, Shams, who, in 1976, was apprehended in Switzerland with $20 million worth of heroin in her car.[7]

The Shah attacked many aspects of Iranian culture, restricted freedom of speech, and censored the press. The Iranian calendar, historically based on Islamic events, was changed to the monarchical calendar. Religious activities were limited and in some instances prohibited. University students were monitored by SAVAK agents in the classroom in Iran and also on campuses in the U.S. During the 1970's, the activities carried out by the SAVAK intensified. Accurate figures are hard to obtain. However, Amnesty International charged the Shah with one of the worst records of human rights violations in the world. While the 1976 Amnesty International annual report said the number of political prisoners in Iran was uncertain and estimated several thousand, other estimates ranged as high as 50,000. In the same year, the International Commission of Jurists reported, "there can be no doubt that torture has been systematically practiced over a number of years against recalcitrant suspects under interrogation by the SAVAK."[8]

The precise number of people who died under torture or who disappeared is not known. Estimates range as high as 100,000 plus. During the last two years of the revolution, 60,000 to 80,000 died.

An acute economic crisis between 1975 and 1977 touched off large-scale strikes and demonstrations which characterized the final two years of the Shah's rule. By this time, most segments of society—from the intelligentsia and the educated middle class to the powerful religious establishment and the bazaar merchants fearing the damaging expansion of multinational corporations—were determined to limit and finally to end the monarchy.

In view of the widespread resentments simmering beneath the surface in Iran, the words of President Carter's 1978 New Year's toast as he and Mrs. Carter celebrated the holiday with the Shah and his wife, are poignant in their irony:

> Iran under the great leadership of the Shah is an island of stability in one of the most troubled areas in the world. This is a great tribute to you, Your Majesty, and to your leadership and to the respect, admiration and love which your people give to you.

These words suggest how out of touch with Iranian reality U.S. leadership had become; within one year the Shah was deposed from his throne.

THE ROLE OF ISLAM IN THE IRANIAN REVOLUTION

Although much of the anger of the Iranian people against the Shah stemmed from specific complaints against him or his family's cruelty, profiteering, and corruption, the forms in which the Iranian people's anger was expressed reflected certain Islamic components—components which have often remained incomprehensible to Western observers. From the days when the Prophet Muhammad was both secular and spiritual ruler of Medina and Mecca, orthodox Muslims have expected their secular leaders to maintain high standards of ethical and spiritual behavior, to live austerely and incorruptibly, and to observe behavior appropriate for a Muslim, one who "submits" to the will of God (referred to as Allah). Furthermore, from the days of the *Qur'an* (Koran)[9] Muslims have been enjoined to view the lands of the world as divided into two categories: (1) The lands of Islam *(dar al-Islam),* where the name of Allah is invoked in public, the call to worship is heard five times a day, Friday is the weekly holy day, Ramadan (the annual month of fasting) is observed, and *imams, mullahs,* and other religious leaders are respected. (2) The lands of struggle *(dar al-harb)* in which unbelievers predominate, where Muslim observances must be followed privately or, perhaps, even clandestinely, and where Muslims must struggle to establish a *dar al-Islam.*

By the 1970's the Shah and his family were seen by more and more Iranians to have abandoned the austere and incorruptible model of a Muslim leader in a *dar al-Islam* and to have adopted the decadence and luxury of the *dar al-harb,* non-Islamic West. As public demonstrations against the Shah escalated, Islamic elements emerged. The struggle was called a *jihad* (sometimes translated as "holy war")—a term used throughout the Muslim world to connote a holy struggle to achieve an ideal. Citizens who were imprisoned, tortured, or killed were identified as martyrs. The tradition of martyrdom is strong among all Muslims. In the *Qur'an,* martyrs are promised a direct path to paradise, or heaven. The tradition of martyrdom has played a particularly important role among the Shi'ites, the branch of Islam which comprises the bulk of Iran's population. Every year on the tenth day of the month of Muharram, Shi'ites commemorate the death of Hussein, the Prophet Muhammad's martyred grandson, and accompanied by such memorabilia as bloodstained banners and an arrow-pierced waterbag, processions of Shi'ites cut themselves with knives and other instruments to the accompaniment of chants and prayer. The bloodstained clothes of mourners symbolize the blood-soaked clothes of the martyred Hussein.[10] During the months of anti-Shah demonstrations, when police and helicopters fired into crowds, the victims' bloodstained clothes were held aloft by the crowd in a manner reminiscent of the tenth of Muharram Shi'ite processions, and during this period, visitors to Iran were regularly shown the graves of the martyrs of the holy struggle against the Shah.[11]

When the Shah finally yielded to public pressure and departed from Iran, he left behind as his appointed prime minister Shahpour Bakhtiar. Few people were surprised that the Iranian public rejected Bakhtiar. What puzzled the world was the person the public chose to replace him—the Ayatollah Ruhollah Khomeini, an elderly Muslim theologian who had once dominated the religious life in Qom (Iran's most holy city), whom the Shah had exiled from Iran in 1963, and who from his exiled base in Paris had issued continuing public denunciations of the Shah and appeals for the establishment of an Islamic state. Large pictures of the Ayatollah Khomeini had been carried as anti-Shah symbols in countless street demonstrations, and his name had become a household word throughout Iran.

The concept of an Islamic state dates back to the time of the prophet Muhammad. Under his leadership and that of the first four Caliphs, the precedent for Islamic government was set in Mecca and Medina. Since then, there have been numerous attempts to use that government as a model. Following World War II, several predominantly Muslim countries, upon achieving independence from colonial powers, declared themselves to be Islamic states, Pakistan being the best known.

What *is* an Islamic state? The answer varies as widely as the answer to the question: "What is a Christian state?" and "What is a Jewish state?" In Pakistan, which declared itself an Islamic state in 1947, the question remains unanswered, as constitution replaces constitution, martial edict replaces martial edict, and as orthodox *mullahs* vie with socialist intellectuals and internationally trained lawyers to provide a "correct" explanation of what an Islamic state should be. For some, an Islamic state requires the implementation of the strict eye-for-an-eye penal code contained in the *Qur'an*. For others, an Islamic state requires the establishment of an elected legislative assembly committed to public service and the general welfare. For still others, an Islamic state requires the socialization of the means of production and the distribution of goods and services to all people on the basis of their needs.

In post-1980 Iran, the definition of an Islamic state was provided by the Ayatollah Khomeini. Within the Shi'ite tradition, a complex hierarchical system among the clergy has developed over the centuries, with the highest rank that of Ayatollah. A cleric emerges as an Ayatollah when it is the consensus of his fellow Muslims that he possesses vast knowledge of the *Qur'an* and Islamic jurisprudence. To these qualifications the Ayatollah Khomeini added his long years of exile by the Shah, and his participation both in Iran and from France in the final popular struggle to rid his country of the Shah. The Ayatollah Khomeini, upon his return from exile, became the de facto political center of the country, and all decisions affecting elections, presidents, budgets, petroleum production, inflation, and foreign policy had little force unless and until they had been approved by the Ayatollah himself.

U.S. RESPONSE TO THE IRANIAN REVOLUTION

The U.S. government has been consistently critical of the Iranian revolution. Former secretary of state Henry Kissinger called the "loss" of Iran "the greatest single blow to U.S. foreign policy interests since World War Two," and the then national security advisor, Zbigniew Brzezinski, discussed with his military advisors the possibility of dislodging the Khomeini-led government by military force.

The focal point for crisis came in October 1979, eight months after the former Shah fled Iran, when President Carter allowed the exiled monarch to enter the U.S.—ostensibly for medical care at a New York City hospital. This act, combined with the fact that the U.S. government had not formally recognized the new government in Tehran, shocked people throughout Iran, and for two weeks there were peaceful demonstrations and protests in Iran calling for the removal of Mohammed Reza Pahlavi from the U.S. Iranians knew well the history of CIA involvement in the 1953 coup d'état, and there was widespread fear that another coup was being planned.

On November 4, 1979, a well-organized group of some 400 Iranian students stormed the U.S. embassy compound and seized American hostages, beginning the drama which dominated the attention of the U.S. media for 444 days. The behavior of both governments during the hostage stalemate removed any chance for improved relations between the U.S. and Iran.

Initially, the seizure of the U.S. embassy received widespread support among Iranians. Symbolically, tiny Iran had brought the great American giant to its knees. Soon, however, the whole affair became hopelessly enmeshed in internal political struggles, and as the standoff continued, Iran became increasingly crippled by the political and economic costs of continuing to hold the Americans.

Throughout the ordeal, the U.S. media selectively described the Iranian government's vacillations, "feudal" policies, and executions. Political cartoonists and commentators were harsh in their portrayal of the Ayatollah Khomeini. At times, resentment toward the Iranians and the Ayatollah spilled over into acts of retaliation against Iranians in America and remarks of general hostility against all Muslims anywhere in the world.

Declarations from the government in Washington reflected an inability to see Iran as anything but a source of oil and a strategically located military base. This distorted view has continued under the Reagan administration, and on October 1, 1981, the President stated: "We will not allow Saudi Arabia to become another Iran . . . as long as Saudi Arabia and the OPEC nations—and Saudi Arabia's the most important—provide the bulk of the energy that is needed to turn the wheels of industry in the Western world, there is no way we could stand by and see that taken over by anyone that would shut off that oil."[12]

The Iranian revolution has had other repercussions. Iran's neighbors (including Iraq, Saudi Arabia, and other Gulf countries) have become anxious lest the model of a successful Islamic uprising against an unpopular ruler be imitated within their own borders. Their desire to prevent such uprisings has been reflected in sharp increases in arms purchases, defended as providing security against Iran, the Soviet Union, and Israel, but which may also be used against their own people should they attempt popular uprisings.

In Afghanistan, the possibility of one, or several, indigenous *mullahs* patterning themselves after the Ayatollah Khomeini and becoming politically powerful at the expense of Afghanistan's indigenous Marxists was among the factors in the Soviet Union's decision to invade Afghanistan. The war in Afghanistan has already been labeled a *jihad* by the anti-Soviet Afghans and has brought support from other Muslim states. The desire to restore Islam to a position of prominence is one of the common goals binding together the otherwise disparate bands of armed Afghan guerrillas.

Iraq's invasion of Iran was also a response to the Iranian revolution. Apparently hoping that Iran's internal disarray might prevent effective military resistance, irritated at the Ayatollah Khomeini's call to the Shi'ites in Iraq to join the revolution, and perhaps also hoping that the Arab-descended Sunnis[13] in neighboring Khusistan province might abandon Shi'ite Iran in support of Sunni Iraq, Iraq's President Sadam Hussein ordered his troops in September 1980 across the

Shatt-al-Arab waterway into the Khusistan section of Iran. This border had been an irritant to Iraq ever since 1975 when the Shah, holding superior power, pushed the border from the Iranian shore to the middle of the waterway. The period of revolutionary turmoil seemed like a good time for Iraq to try to restore the old border and perhaps annex portions of Khusistan. Events did not bear out President Hussein's hopes, and the ensuing war has been indecisive, exacting a heavy toll, not only in human terms but also on the material resources of both Iran and Iraq.

SOME CONSEQUENCES OF THE IRANIAN REVOLUTION

The downfall of the Shah and his replacement by the Ayatollah Khomeini and an Islamic government have posed a series of problems for the United States. Following World War II, the British had maintained a military presence in the Gulf area to police its vital oil supplies and to see that its lanes remained open to international shipping. When, in 1968, the British announced their withdrawal from the Gulf, the Shah of Iran stepped into the void left by the British. The U.S., happy to see the Shah as a surrogate force in the region, supplied him with virtually any sophisticated weapons he wanted, believing that the more overwhelming the military might of the Shah, the less likely were political disturbances in the Gulf area. This policy appeared to pay off, and for the next decade the Shah maintained a generally evenhanded stance between Israel and the Arab nations, and Iranian oil supplies continued to flow to the rest of the world with hardly an interruption, albeit commencing in 1973 at greatly increased prices.

Then, in early 1979, the Shah was gone, and with him the policeman of the Gulf. Before 1979 ended, two other events occurred in the Middle East that affected U.S. foreign and domestic policy. In November 1979 Iranian militants took as hostages the U.S. personnel in the Tehran embassy, and in December Soviet troops entered Afghanistan. In the wake of these two events, President Carter, in his 1980 state of the union message, announced a new doctrine which, in addition to its retaliatory measures against the Soviet Union, put the world on notice that the U.S. would henceforth depend on no one else to defend its national interests. From then on it would use its *own* troops and its *own* weapons to police the Gulf and any other sectors of the globe where it felt its interests threatened. A U.S. rapid deployment force was to be quickly strengthened as one part of America's replacement for the missing Shah.[14]

Upon assuming office in 1981, President Reagan extended the Carter Doctrine. In addition to authorizing more sophisticated and expensive weapons, he moved to include U.S. military units in the Sinai peacekeeping forces between Israel and Egypt and to establish additional U.S. bases in North Africa, the Middle East, and the Indian Ocean.[15] The rapid deployment force is being enlarged and trained for Middle East actions. Stationing U.S. military personnel near international flashpoints raises the probability that U.S. troops will be drawn into military confrontations. U.S. allies in Europe have expressed serious uneasiness with these moves and have initiated their own policies toward the Middle East.

A comparison between the U.S. "loss" of China in the late 1940's and the U.S. "loss" of Iran in the late 1970's may be instructive. Within the United States the "fall" of China in the late 1940's was seen to stem from an international communist conspiracy to which misguided and leftist Americans had contributed. It fueled Joseph McCarthy's attacks on individuals and groups within the United States identified as communists or soft on communism. It led to the John Foster Dulles doctrine of encircling the Soviet Union with a chain of military alliances: NATO, CENTO, SEATO, and various bilateral treaties.

The "fall" of Iran does not fit any such neat formulation. Within the United States, many saw it as an expression of xenophobic Iranian nationalism combined with Islamic fundamentalism. No major groups within the United States (except some Iranian students) supported Iran. The only "blame" that could be pinned on any American was blame for not doing *something* to free the hostages. For U.S. policy, the "fall" of Iran brought the new militarism of the Carter and Reagan administrations. Through a complex chain of events and U.S. interpretations of those events, the Iranian revolution escalated the danger of U.S. military action in the Middle East and of U.S.-Soviet confrontation.

ASSESSMENT OF THE IRANIAN REVOLUTION

The Iranian revolution stands as one of the more remarkable political events of recent history. Millions of Iranians using primarily nonviolent collective action rendered ineffective the most powerful and well-armed military force in the Middle East. A broad-based coalition peacefully deposed the Shah, while he still enjoyed the full support of his own secret-police apparatus as well as the full backing of the United States.

After the Shah's departure, elements of this coalition fragmented into numerous internal groups struggling for power. Censorship, arrests, and firing squads reemerged as techniques to settle old scores, eliminate political alternatives, and suppress such minorities as women, Jews, Christians, Bahais, Kurds, Turks, Baluchis, and tribals. Amnesty International reports more executions in the past year in Iran than in the rest of the world combined. For those who were sympathetic to the courage and commitment of the Iranian people and to their largely nonviolent overthrow of the regime of the Shah, the current severe violations of human rights and the resort to assassination, murder, and execution to challenge power and to hold it brings deep sorrow.

11

Afghanistan

The Soviet invasion of Afghanistan (in December 1979) and the strong U.S. military response in the Indian Ocean, the Persian Gulf, and the Arabian peninsula thrust Afghanistan into the politics of the Middle East.

The overwhelming majority of Afghanistan's population are Sunni Muslims; its two major languages, Dari (Afghan Farsi) and Pashtu, are both written with a modified Arabic script; and Muslim pilgrims make the *hajj* to Mecca every year. But aside from these cultural links, for the past 150 years Afghanistan has appeared to have few ties to the Middle East. During that period the Mohammadzai dynasty dominated Afghan politics; its major wars were with Russia (in the north) and Britain (based in British India to the southeast), and during the past thirty years, Afghanistan's most persistent international problem has concerned the political loyalties of the Pashtu-speaking tribes which occupy the rugged terrain along Afghanistan's southeastern border with Pakistan.

In 1964, under the direction of King Mohammad Zahir, an Afghanistan constitution was drawn up, and national elections were held in 1965 and 1969. But the "partyless democracy" envisioned in the constitution failed to take root. In 1973, Daoud Khan, first cousin and brother-in-law of the king (and prime minister of Afghanistan from 1953 to 1963), staged a coup while the king was abroad, declared Afghanistan a republic, and presented himself as the new president and prime minister. In 1978 another specially convened *Loya Jirgah* (gathering of leaders) approved a second constitution, this one of the Republic of Afghanistan, and elected Daoud Khan the first president.

The constitutional and personnel changes in Afghanistan's political hierarchy had little effect on Afghanistan's domestic and international policies. Internationally, Afghanistan chose a nonaligned stance, which left it free to accept aid from any source, and the U.S.A. and the U.S.S.R. were quick to provide such aid in the form of special development projects, advisors, and loans. U.S. assistance produced such benefits as the Hilmand Valley project and Ariana Afghan Airlines, while Soviet assistance produced the Darunta hydroelectric project and the improved north-south road to Kabul, including the 3-kilometer-long Salang Tunnel.

Domestically, Afghanistan pursued a policy of modified, centralized economic planning based on a series of five-year plans. These were carried out with assistance from the United Nations, China, West Germany, Yugoslavia, Czechoslovakia, France, Japan, and India—although the greatest amount of aid came from the U.S.S.R. and the United States. Socially, Afghanistan's leaders followed a policy of cautious reform, including voluntary removal of women's veils and the establishment of more women's facilities for higher education. Politically, the emphasis on constitutional government of these decades accompanied the development of political parties. Frequently, however, political organizers were imprisoned, and newspapers printing politically critical stories were forcibly closed.

On January 1, 1965, a leftist party known as Khalq (Masses) was formed under the leadership, among others, of Nur Mohammad Taraki. In June 1967 a second leftist party known as Parcham (Banner or Flag) was formed under the leadership of Babrak Karmal, at least in part as a result of personality and policy clashes between Karmal and Taraki. The Khalq party tended to be more oriented toward Pashtu-speaking Afghans and to concentrate its organizing efforts among members of the military and civil services, while the Parcham party was more oriented to the Dari-speaking Afghans and concentrated its efforts on the intellectuals and urban middle classes.[1]

1978 SAUR REVOLUTION

On April 27, 1978, leaders of the combined Khalq and Parcham parties launched a coup, and to the surprise of many, the coup succeeded. President Daoud Khan and a group of his close supporters were killed, and the combined Khalq-Parcham leadership announced the establishment of a Democratic Republic of Afghanistan. In their first public statement, the leaders of the "Saur Revolution" (because it occurred during the month of Saur) declared that they were not communists and that their policies would be based on Afghan nationalism, respect for Islam, a continuing commitment to a nonaligned foreign policy, and economic and social justice.

Between the end of April and November 1978, the Democratic Republic of Afghanistan (DRA), under the leadership of Khalq Party leader Taraki and a revolutionary council initially composed about half-and-half of Khalqis and Parchamis, issued eight decrees, including the abolition of usury, the granting of equal rights to women, a prohibition against forced marriages, a regularization of dowry and marriage expenses, and the introduction of land reforms. Lofty in principle, these decrees were largely the product of urban-based intellectuals, with little appreciation for the rural resistance such decrees would generate.

As the urban-based intellectuals began to try to enforce their decrees, they triggered two responses: armed resistance in the countryside and the flight of Afghan refugees, primarily across the border into Pakistan but also across the border into Iran. Armed resistance in the countryside met armed enforcement by the DRA authorities, and within a few months Afghanistan was embroiled in a running civil war.

The complexities of the civil war were aggravated by an increasingly open rift between the Khalqis and the Parchamis. Prime Minister Taraki and his Khalqi supporters arrested an increasing number of Parchamis, charging them with plotting to overthrow the government, extorting "confessions" from them, and broadcasting the "confessions" over Radio Afghanistan. Parcham leaders such as Babrak Karmal went into hiding or fled the country, and their supporters, and those afraid of being denounced as their supporters, augmented the flow of refugees across Afghanistan's borders. Within this context of a deteriorating domestic situation, Taraki went to Moscow and, with Leonid Brezhnev, signed on December 5, 1978, a "Treaty of Friendship and Cooperation" which stipulated that Afghanistan and the Soviet Union would consult each other on all major issues affecting both parties.

By the spring of 1979, armed revolts, largely uncoordinated and under the direction of local landlords and *mullahs,* had erupted in all of Afghanistan's provinces. Soviet military advisors played a role in directing DRA military units in their warfare against the rebelling countryside. The DRA military units, composed largely of conscripts, faced problems of morale and desertion. By mid-August 1979, approximately 165,000 refugees had fled from Afghanistan into Pakistan, and Radio Afghanistan had begun accusing Pakistan and Iran (and eventually China, the U.S., Israel, and Egypt) of arming and training the men in the refugee camps and assisting them in their guerrilla raids back into Afghanistan. All of these countries denied the accusations.

Troubles within the DRA high command continued. In September 1979, a shoot-out between DRA President Taraki and DRA Prime Minister Hafizullah Amin resulted in Taraki's death and a takeover by Amin.[3] But under Amin's direction, the instabilities in the countryside continued, as did the threats of arrests in those locations under Kabul's control. By December 1979 the DRA controlled only the major cities and their link roads—and those only by day. By night, virtually the entire countryside, as well as sections of the major cities, reverted to the control of the Afghan opposition. That opposition also was plagued by internal dissension and lack of coordination. The opposition members were united only in their deep sense of Afghan nationalism and their commitment to carry out their *jihad* (holy struggle) against the DRA leadership in Kabul.

1979 SOVIET INVASION OF AFGHANISTAN

The full details of the Soviet invasion will probably never be known. The U.S.S.R. maintains that the Afghanistan Revolutionary Council, without the knowledge of Amin, invited in the Soviet troops to help restore order in Afghanistan and thereby allow the formation of a new government committed to the welfare of all Afghans. The Revolutionary Council, with its loyal troops, then overwhelmed and killed Amin and replaced him with Babrak Karmal, long-time leader of the Parchamis, who had been living outside the country since 1978. According to the U.S.S.R., Soviet troops arrived in Kabul with a clear and limited objective; they would return to the Soviet Union as soon as they had achieved that objective.

Critics of the Soviet Union maintain that the Soviet troop invasion was initiated by Moscow, and the almost immediate death of Amin following the troop arrivals casts doubts upon any Afghan invitation for the Soviet troops. These critics claim also that the arrival of Babrak Karmal as Afghanistan's *new* ruler reflects all too clearly the imposition of a Soviet-backed puppet government on the people of Afghanistan.

Regardless of which interpretation is closer to the truth, on the night of December 27, 1979, after hearing the constant drone of military planes for several days and nights followed by outbursts of shooting in various sectors of Kabul, thousands of Afghans heard a broadcast by Babrak Karmal announcing that Hafizullah Amin, "that treacherous foe of God . . . the CIA agent and scheming spy of American imperialism," was dead.[3] Karmal's only reference to the Soviet troops was his mention of the "observation of the Treaty of Friendship and Cooperation of December 5, 1978, with the Soviet Union." Karmal announced that his policies would include the release of political prisoners, the abolition of arbitrary arrests, respect for Islam, a nonaligned foreign policy, and loyalty to the United Nations.

Within a few weeks of December 27, 1979, Soviet troop levels reached between 85,000 and 90,000, where they have remained. Another 30,000 troops are in the Soviet Union just north of the Afghanistan border.[4] The DRA army strength, despite calls for a more rigorous conscription system, has declined from about 70,000 at the time of the Soviet invasion to about 25,000 to 30,000 in May 1981. The mujahadin, as the DRA opponents call themselves, have waged ongoing guerrilla warfare, moving with relative freedom around the countryside. The DRA and Soviet military units have typically fought from within armored vehicles and helicopter gunships. But at night they have returned to well-guarded military bases adjoining airfields.

Although Babrak Karmal made initial conciliatory moves to bring together his Parcham faction and the Khalq faction, the passing months witnessed a steady deterioration of interfaction unity. The U.S.S.R. had placed its support behind Babrak Karmal and his Parchamis. From time to time Soviet troops saw action against DRA troops loyal to the Khalq faction. There was widespread agreement that, if the Soviet troops withdrew, the Babrak Karmal government would collapse. This observation itself made it difficult for Babrak Karmal to establish the legitimacy of his government.

REFUGEES AND MUJAHADIN

By October 1981, about 2.3 million Afghan refugees had fled from Afghanistan (out of a population of about 15 million).[5] An undetermined number of men among these refugees used the refugee camps as staging bases for raids back into Afghanistan. Their weapons consisted largely of traditional, handmade mountaineer rifles, captured Soviet weapons (or weapons brought over by defectors), and an assortment of more modern weapons such as Egyptian-made Kalashnikov and Chinese recoilless rifles. The leaders of various mujahadin groups that were concentrated in the Peshawar (Pakistan) region constantly squabbled among themselves. No single leader or group of leaders appeared able to unite the disparate tribal, regional, political, or sectarian groups into a unified military or political force. Support for the refugees came from the government of Pakistan and the U.N. High Commission for Refugees, as well as from numerous church relief agencies and the Red Crescent agency. Sources for the support of the mujahadin guerrillas were harder to identify. The DRA and the Soviet Union continued to accuse the United States, China, Pakistan, Iran, Egypt, and Israel of providing military assistance to the mujahadin. While most of those countries denied the accusations, there was general agreement that the Arab world was giving considerable financial support for the Afghan refugees, and Egyptian President Sadat openly claimed to be supplying arms.

WORLD RESPONSE

The world response to the Soviet invasion of Afghanistan was consistent. On January 15, 1980, the U.N. General Assembly condemned the Soviet invasion of Afghanistan and called for the immediate withdrawal of Soviet troops. In late January, the Conference of Islamic States, which included representation from the PLO and Iraq, condemned the U.S.S.R. for its invasion of Afghanistan, suspended Afghanistan as a member of the conference, and called for the immediate withdrawal of Soviet troops. At a subsequent meeting in May 1980, the Conference of Islamic States again condemned the Soviet invasion and appointed a special committee composed of the foreign ministers of Pakistan and Iran and the secretary general of the conference to seek a political solution to the Afghan problem. In Iran the Ayatollah Khomeini publicly condemned the Soviet intervention in Afghanistan. In September 1980, the sixteen-nation Asian and Pacific Commonwealth Nations conference in New Delhi also called for the withdrawal of Soviet troops from Afghanistan.

In the face of these many international criticisms, the Soviet Union and the government of Babrak Karmal have maintained that the Soviet Union did not "invade" Afghanistan but, instead, responded to a legitimate request from Afghanistan based on the December 5, 1978, Treaty of Friendship and Cooperation. Furthermore, both the Soviet Union and Babrak Karmal have stated that a precondition for Soviet troops leaving Afghanistan will be political stability in Afghanistan and the cessation of outside assistance to the rebels fighting against the Kabul government.

UNITED STATES RESPONSE

The U.S. response to the presence of Soviet troops in Afghanistan has been more severe than that of most of the rest of the world. On January 4, 1980, President Carter announced a grain embargo against the Soviet Union, banned exports to the U.S.S.R. of certain sophisticated technology, limited certain Soviet fishing privileges in U.S. waters, and suggested a possible boycott of the 1980 Olympic Games, scheduled to be held in Moscow. In his state of the union message later in January, President Carter declared that the implications of the Soviet invasion of Afghanistan "pose a serious threat to peace," marking the first time since World War II that the U.S.S.R. had moved its forces into a nation outside its direct sphere of influence.[6] In a similar vein he enunciated the Carter Doctrine that threats to the Gulf region challenged vital interests of the U.S. which the U.S. would be prepared to meet with force. He requested from Congress the authority to revive registration for the draft, increase the U.S. military budget by at least 5 percent above inflation during the next five years, loosen controls over the CIA for covert operations, offer increased military aid to Pakistan, and expand the U.S. military presence in northeast Africa, the Gulf, and the Indian Ocean. In May 1980, a special meeting of NATO foreign and defense ministers declared they were bolstering their strike capabilities in response to the Soviet Union's continued occupation of Afghanistan. In August 1980, the United States, Canada, Japan, and West Germany were among the nations boycotting the XXII Summer Olympic Games in Moscow to protest the continued Soviet presence in Afghanistan, and in November 1980, the Western delegates to the Madrid conference reviewing the Helsinki human rights accords again criticized the Soviet Union's refusal to withdraw its troops from Afghanistan.

The Reagan administration has continued many of the Carter policies aimed at strengthening U.S. capabilities in the Gulf area. These have included:

1. Developing a rapid deployment force of combat troops to move quickly into the world's trouble spots to protect U.S. interests, with primary focus on the Middle East.

2. Acquiring access to ports and airfields throughout the greater Gulf area for logistical support for the rapid deployment force. The Reagan administration's interest in including U.S. troops in the Sinai peacekeeping force between Egypt and Israel has also been linked to the increase of U.S. military personnel in the general Gulf area.

3. Providing Pakistan with substantial new military support. In September 1981, the U.S. was negotiating a $3.2 billion economic aid and military sales package to Pakistan to be spread over a six-year period. The package included forty F-16 advanced fighter aircraft.

Pakistan had also requested a Pakistan-U.S. security treaty that would assure U.S. assistance to Pakistan in the event of any actual combat, whether with the Soviet Union, India, or any other of Pakistan's neighbors.[7]

4. Developing a "security consensus" extending from Egypt to Pakistan that local troops (i.e., Egyptian, Pakistani, etc.) would be available initially to block any Soviet moves or local revolts until the U.S. could bring in its rapid deployment force.

SOVIET RESPONSE

The Soviet Union has also been actively strengthening its position in the greater Gulf area. The Shindand base in Afghanistan puts Soviet aircraft within striking range of the Gulf, and a Soviet-built airbase in South Yemen is nearing completion. The Soviets are reported to be building a naval base in the Dhalak archipelago in the Red Sea, and, in addition, the Soviet Union has more than thirty divisions, with air support, on the Iranian and Afghanistan borders.[8] The U.S.S.R. has also increased the strength of its naval presence in the Indian Ocean.

GULF NATIONS RESPONSE

Nations within the greater Gulf area have expressed alarm at the increasing likelihood of a United States-Soviet Union confrontation or intervention in the Middle East. The Arab Gulf Council for Cooperation (including Saudi Arabia, Kuwait, Bahrain, Qatar, Oman, and the United Arab Emirates) held its first meeting in March 1981 and discussed establishing its own collective military capacity. Although they reached no consensus on this point, the Gulf nations unanimously opposed the permanent presence of any superpower (Soviet or U.S.) military force in the Gulf. India has expressed strong criticism of the U.S. proposal to provide Pakistan with substantial new arms support since in both its 1965 and 1971 wars with Pakistan, India found itself fighting Pakistanis who were using military matériel supplied by the U.S. for the avowed purpose of halting Soviet expansion.

CONCLUSIONS

There are several ways in which events in the Middle East and events in Afghanistan have impinged upon each other in recent years:

1. Events in the Middle East (as well as in Western Europe and the United States) may have contributed to the international climate in which the Soviet Union decided to send troops into Afghanistan. The steady deterioration of detente, beginning in the summer of 1979, as well as the political events in Iran may have weighed significantly in the minds of the Soviet leaders as they decided how to respond to the deteriorating situation in Afghanistan. A "worst possible scenario" of the collapse of the Democratic Republic of Afghanistan, multiple Islamic leaders emerging in different sectors of Afghanistan, and an anti-Soviet foreign policy that might have brought U.S. missiles into the northern regions of Afghanistan on the Soviet border might have strengthened the hands of the hawks within the Kremlin who wanted to send Soviet troops into Afghanistan.

2. The Soviet troop movements into Afghanistan introduced into U.S. discussions of the Middle East the possibility of further Soviet military expansion into the region. After all, if Soviet troops invaded Afghanistan in 1979, what would prevent their invading Iran in 1981 or Pakistan in 1982? Soviet actions in Afghanistan have strengthened the arguments of U.S. hawks that the U.S.S.R. is bent on territorial expansion.

3. The continued presence of Soviet troops in Afghanistan and their involvement in military operations up to the border of Pakistan have provided the U.S. with reasons for significantly escalating its arms supplies to Pakistan.

4. The continued presence of Soviet troops in Afghanistan has provided the U.S. with the major excuse for increasing its own military presence in the Middle East.

5. The Soviet Union's maintenance and rotation of military personnel in Afghanistan may have inhibited the Soviet Union's willingness to assign troops to military duty elsewhere in the world. Analysts have speculated that the Soviet Union's decision not to invade Poland in the spring and summer of 1981 was related in part to the Soviet Union's ongoing military activities in Afghanistan.

6. The Soviet Union's invasion of Afghanistan has deprived the Soviet Union of considerable goodwill from the Arab world as well as from much of the rest of the Third World. In the past, the Third World has frequently condemned U.S. economic and military interventions into the affairs of Third World countries. They now have what they feel is an equally clear illustration of Soviet willingness to intervene militarily into the affairs of a Third World country when it seems to serve the purposes of the Soviet Union.

AFGHANISTAN IN PERSPECTIVE

The Soviet invasion has been deeply disturbing; it dramatically illustrates the interrelatedness of the countries in the Middle East and the greater Gulf area. Events in one country or between two countries can have far-reaching effects on neighboring countries. Soviet troops entered Afghanistan; the U.S. responded by increasing its arms supplies to Pakistan and the Middle East; this in turn aggravated tensions throughout the area. An alternative response to the Soviet invasion might have involved immediate assistance to the refugees, attempts to facilitate avenues of dialogue between Afghans within and Afghans outside of Afghanistan, and direct discussions with the Soviet Union regarding their agenda for troop withdrawal. In the Middle East and Gulf areas, each policy undertaken must be carefully weighed, for its ramifications may extend far and any miscalculations may have disastrous and far-reaching consequences.

12

The Soviet Union

Interpretation of events in the Middle East is as important as the events themselves. U.S. interpretations have focused on an "arc of crisis." According to this view, the Soviet Union has been actively encouraging, or actually precipitating, crises in an "arc" of nations stretching from Ethiopia and Yemen in the west to Afghanistan and Bangladesh in the east. OPEC price increases, the fall of the Shah, the invasion of Afghanistan, the continuing crisis between Arabs and Israelis, and the Iraq-Iran war are all seen as fitting into a master plan of the Kremlin, with the ultimate goal of winning territory and/or support for the Soviet Union. In this context the Carter Doctrine was enunciated and the massive arms buildup, continued by Reagan's administration, was launched.

Within the framework of this interpretation, factual errors about the Soviet Union have crept into U.S. discussions. Iran is sometimes said to have come under Soviet influence, despite the Ayatollah Khomeini's fierce dislike of Marxism and his continuing attacks on Iranian communists. Iraq is named as a Soviet client, despite Iraq's execution of pro-Soviet communists in 1978–1979 and open denunciation of Soviet policies in Afghanistan, South Yemen, and Ethiopia. The Arabs are seen as being backed by the Soviet Union, despite the conservative nature of many Arab states and in the face of the Soviet's own recognition of Israel and their insistence that the Arabs recognize Israel's right to exist. The Soviet Union has grudgingly permitted the Jews—including Jewish scientists—to migrate to, and thereby strengthen, Israel, a fact much criticized in the Arab world. The

Soviet Union's influence in the Middle East has been defined as expanding, despite the loss of Soviet influence in such countries as Egypt, Somalia, and the Sudan, and the weakening of its position in Algeria. The Soviet Union is seen as committed to acquiring a warmwater port in the Middle East, despite its current possession of several warm-water ports and the declining relevance of warm-water ports in a day of air transportation and ICBM's. The Soviet Union is seen as aggravating tensions in the Middle East, despite its moderating influences during the Ethiopia-Somalia, Iraq-Iran, and South Yemen-North Yemen disputes. And the PLO is seen as a client of the Soviet Union, despite Moscow's denunciations of hijackings and the Soviet refusal to recognize the PLO as the sole representative of the Palestinians.

The Soviet Union does have a series of ongoing interests in the Middle East. It does have an agenda which it appears to be trying to pursue. The Soviet Union has made agreements and established treaties with several Arab states covering economic and technical aid, military assistance and training, arms transfers, military basing rights and ports of call, and "friendship." But the interests it is pursuing and the agenda it has constructed are often at variance with the official U.S. interpretation of the Soviet role in the Middle East.

The Soviet Union and the Middle East share a common border of over 1,200 miles. With the Soviet-Finnish and Soviet-Norwegian borders, this represents to the Soviet Union a major border with the noncommunist world. Various religious and ethnic groups straddle the Soviet-Middle East border: Muslims, Jews, Christians and Armenians, Turkomans, Uzbeks, Tajiks, and Khirgiz. The Middle East impinges on the Soviet economy more than does any other Third World area. Of ten major noncommunist recipients of Soviet aid between 1954 and 1976, seven were in the Middle East, including Turkey, Afghanistan, Egypt, Algeria, Iran, Iraq, and Syria.[1] Egypt severed its military ties in 1974 and relations with Iran are strained since the overthrow of the Shah.

The central issue in Middle East politics continues to be the Arab-Israeli dispute, and here the Soviet Union is in a difficult position. When the U.N. partition plan was approved in 1947, the Soviet Union supported partition and rushed to recognize the newly formed state of Israel. These positions were denounced by the Palestinian Arabs and the neighboring Arab states. Even though the Soviet Union broke diplomatic relations with Israel following the 1967 Arab-Israeli war, the Soviet Union has never denied Israel's right to exist. Furthermore, the Soviet Union has never wavered in its support for U.N. Security Council Resolution 242 (calling on Israel to withdraw to its pre-1967 borders and guaranteeing secure borders for all states in the region) and Resolution 338 (establishing the 1973 cease-fire), even though the Soviet Union has been unable to persuade any Arab states formally to agree. Partly as a result of this Soviet stance, conservative Arab nations have periodically charged the Soviet Union with participating in a Zionist-communist conspiracy. As proof of the fluidity of the region's politics, Soviet foreign minister Gromyko and his Israeli counterpart, Yitzhak Shamir, met for talks in October 1981. On the other hand, as the U.S. has supplied arms to Israel, so the Soviet Union has supplied arms to the Arabs, including, in recent years, the PLO. The Soviet Union, as well as most Arab states, has been hostile to the Camp David agreements. This has been interpreted by many in the United States as a sign of the Soviet's desire to keep the Middle East in turmoil, but the Soviet position is more complicated. From the start the Soviet Union has opposed step-by-step diplomacy in the Middle East, believing it will not work because it will not solve the Palestinian problem. Furthermore, the Soviet Union believes that solutions to the Arab-Israeli conflict should be developed jointly by the U.S. and the U.S.S.R. (as were the cease-fires in 1967 and 1973) and that it should be included in any peace negotiations.[2] The Soviet Union was distressed when the October 1977 U.S.-Soviet joint statement on the Middle East and the "legitimate rights of the Palestinian people" was weakened by the subsequent Vance-Dayan statement and superseded by the Camp David meetings which effectively excluded Soviet participation. The highly publicized agreement concluded in 1979 between Egypt and Israel, for which President Carter and the United States received considerable credit, added to this distress.

Elsewhere in the Middle East (except Afghanistan), the Soviet role has been cautious. In Iran the Soviet Union played no significant role. In South Yemen the Soviet Union has tried to sustain a government that was ostracized by the Arab world and that turned to the Soviet

Union for support. A major Soviet naval base has since been built in South Yemen. The Soviets were not involved in the popular movement that overthrew the Emperor of Ethiopia in 1974 but became involved two and a half years later, after the eruption of conflict between Ethiopia and Somalia. To this day there continue to be differences between Ethiopia and the Soviet Union on such issues as the right of Eritrea to independence, party building, and economic matters. The large-scale deployment of Soviet troops into Afghanistan, an invasion, has been the most destabilizing Soviet move in Middle East-Southwest Asia in recent years. This move has brought denunciation of the Soviet Union by the international community and especially the Arab world, including Iraq and the PLO. The Islamic states were deeply concerned by this Soviet move against a Muslim people. Economically, the Soviet policies in Ethiopia and Afghanistan have proved costly as well. The Soviet Union spends the equivalent of several million dollars a day to sustain its forces in Afghanistan and has dispatched a billion dollars worth of weapons to Ethiopia with no assurance that Ethiopia will pay for them.[3]

The Soviet Union possesses a great deal more military capacity now than it did twenty years ago, but it seems unlikely that it would use that power actually to invade the Middle East. In the last twenty years the Soviet Union has not had substantial economic gains from the Middle East (although it has gained "hard currencies" through its large arms sales to Iraq and Libya), and it has not been able to establish a stable relationship with any of the Arab states.

While the Soviet Union is quite willing to challenge the West politically in the region, its primary concern in the Middle East remains the security of its own southern frontiers. No issue specific to the Middle East is sufficient to divert the Soviet Union from its overall global stance. The U.S.S.R. shares the U.S. concern about Middle East regional stability; from their side, they know that instability can provide opportunities for anticommunist forces to gain local advantages. In search of stability, the Soviet Union has been willing to reach an accommodation with any stable government in the Middle East, whether socialist or monarchy. The Soviet Union, for example, bought natural gas from the Shah of Iran, transported to the U.S.S.R. through jointly maintained pipelines. While giving lip service to liberation struggles generally, the Soviets have opposed specific struggles in the Middle East, such as that of the Kurds in 1972 and the Eritreans in 1978. Indeed, in its willingness to support stable governments in the Middle East, the Soviet Union has sometimes supported those governments' more repressive characteristics. The Soviet Union's concerns about its own global strategies have forced local communist parties in the Middle East to follow what, from their perspectives, have often been the zigzags of Moscow policy.[4] This has led to such anomalies as the Soviet Union backing governments that are imprisoning and executing members of local communist parties, as in Iraq today and Iran in the past.

We do not know the full meaning of President Brezhnev's call in 1980 (in the wake of the Afghanistan invasion) for a zone of peace in the Indian Ocean, but do know that it was given a positive reception in India (where Brezhnev made his idea public) and several other countries in the region. The brusque rebuff of the proposal by the U.S. gave little room to probe its intent and discover whether it had within it elements worthy of support. Could the U.S., working jointly with the Soviet Union and nations bordering the Indian Ocean, have turned the proposal to one safeguarding the interests of all parties by reducing the flow of arms to the region and the threat of superpower intervention?

The "arc of crisis" interpretation of events in the Middle East has little credibility. There have been a number of political upheavals in the Middle East in the 1970's which ended or modified the preexisting order, but, under examination, there is no firm evidence to support the view that the Soviet Union masterminded or engineered those events. To the contrary, the overall position of the Soviet Union in the Middle East seems weaker now than it did one or two decades ago. Based as they have been on a flawed "arc of crisis" interpretation, U.S. policies toward the Soviet Union, at best, fail to follow up possible initiatives for peace in the Middle East and, at worst, enhance the dangers of a global war. These policies cause the U.S. to ignore important local conditions and problems that have led to open conflict and war and to substitute the supplying of arms and the seeking of military alliances for the urgently needed political and diplomatic support for peacemaking.

13

United States Policy

United States policy in the Middle East has been dominated by three sometimes contradictory concerns since the end of World War II:

- Unrestricted access to the region's vast oil reserves
- The strategic location of the region both as a bridge between Europe and Asia and as a critical place to contain the Soviet Union
- Support for Israel and its security among hostile neighbors

United States policy has largely ignored the domestic political, social, and human needs of the countries in the region; the growing force of Arab nationalism was consistently underestimated and too often cast in the mold of U.S.-Soviet confrontation; political challenges to conservative regimes were regularly interpreted as threats to stability. These facts have given rise to the distortions and in some cases negative impact of the U.S. role in the area. A major thread running through U.S. policy, and the focus of the U.S. public's concern, has been the Arab-Israeli conflict.

Israel's stunning victory in the June 1967 war did nothing to solve any of the outstanding problems between Israel and its Arab neighbors, indeed it significantly increased some of them. In addition to leaving Israel occupying territories belonging to Syria, Jordan, and Egypt, the intensity of the conflict between Israel and the Palestinians was sharply increased as close to a million Palestinians came under Israeli occupation.

The war brought U.S. policy in the region under great strain. The attempts to keep apart the three strands of U.S. interests—especially support for Israel and strategic control over access to Arab oil supplies—failed. This failure reached its climax several years later when the Arab oil-producing states imposed a partial oil embargo in the wake of the October 1973 war. It is against this background that new dimensions of U.S. involvement emerged.

Since the war of June 1967, the United States government has been actively involved in efforts to promote a peace settlement among the parties to the Arab-Israeli dispute, as a means of achieving regional stability and protecting its conception of U.S. interests. During the same period it was Israel's major arms supplier and became engaged in arms sales to other parties. The official American concept of peace as well as that of a peace process has changed, as the Middle East situation and the attitudes of the conflicting parties have evolved. The nature of the American role also has swung between that of providing good offices and the more involved one of active mediator. Similarly, the avenues and tactics have varied widely. But the policy considerations that have compelled this degree of commitment at high governmental levels have remained fairly constant in at least five administrations. They may be summarized:

- A commitment to Israel's survival.
- An awareness that Arab-Israeli polarization and conflict jeopardize U.S. relations with the Arab countries and put at risk U.S. relations with strategic allies in much of the Middle East.
- A parallel assumption that confrontation and conflict provide opportunities for the Soviet Union to increase its influence in the area.
- Concern that outbreaks of active conflict could prompt U.S.-Soviet confrontation, threatening a larger war.
- In recent years, concern that U.S. access to Middle East oil is insecure in the absence of a peace settlement. (Prior to 1973 this was not a serious consideration, and even after that it was a consideration that led to only slight modification of policies already in place, except in the case of arms sales to conservative Arab states.)

From the point of view of U.S. policy, the period 1967–1981 can be divided roughly into four phases: from 1967 to the 1973 war; from 1973 to Sadat's Jerusalem trip in November 1977; 1977 to 1980; and the beginning of the Reagan administration.

FIRST PHASE, 1967–1973

The United States was one of the key architects of U.N. Security Council Resolution 242 that established the basis for peace efforts in the wake of the 1967 war. The resolution also was endorsed by the U.S.S.R. The resolution set up a bargain: withdrawal of Israel from occupied territories in exchange for assured security of "every State in the area" within its prewar boundaries. In the U.S. view, achieving this bargain required negotiations between the Arabs and Israel, and much of the diplomatic activity of the ensuing years involved a search for agreement on the terms of this resolution. Israel favored direct negotiations, because if the Arab states would agree to these *ipso facto,* they would be recognizing the reality of Israel. The Arab states, however, including even those that accepted the resolution, refused to bargain for territory they considered rightfully theirs, calling instead for implementation of the resolution's terms—Israeli withdrawal. The U.S. at first supported the efforts of the U.N. special representative, Ambassador Gunnar Jarring, to promote agreement on the basis of Resolution 242. When Jarring gave up, the U.S. became more directly active, although initially it refrained from offering its own proposals for peace terms.

In April 1969, the U.S. joined Britain, France, and the U.S.S.R. in quadripartite talks under the aegis of the United Nations. In addition, the U.S. entered bilateral discussions with the Soviets in Washington and Moscow in which they sought a formula that might provide a basis for negotiation among the parties. In the course of these two sets of talks, the U.S. presented its own proposals for guidelines for agreements between Israel and Egypt and Israel and Jordan. In December 1969 Secretary of State William Rogers spelled out the basic elements of these proposals, which became known as the Rogers Plan. Rogers, confirming the necessity of a negotiated settlement, said that "any changes in the pre-existing lines should not reflect the weight of conquest and should be confined to insubstantial alterations required for mutual security . . . We do not support expansionism." Jerusalem, he said, should be a "unified city" in which both Jordan and Israel would have roles "in the civic, economic, and religious life of the city."[1] Israel vigorously objected, neither the Palestinians nor the Arab states reacted favorably, and the U.S. did not press the proposals. In fact, the U.S., while commenting negatively on Israeli settlement policy in the West Bank and Gaza, has continued to give Israel strong general support.

The major U.S. negotiating effort during this phase came to relate less and less to the basic issues of a Middle East settlement and focused instead on frictions between Egypt and Israel in the Sinai. In 1969 the Egyptians, concerned that the highly unfavorable status quo might become generally accepted over time, commenced a campaign of artillery bombardment across the Suez Canal. Israel responded with more and more devastating air strikes over Egypt, and a serious exchange developed. History has recorded the fighting as the War of Attrition. The U.S. proposed a plan for a cease-fire which allowed both sides to find a way out of an increasingly costly conflict; it was accepted by both in August 1970.

SECOND PHASE, 1973–1977

All plans for further initiatives in the search for a peace settlement were interrupted by the October 1973 war.

It was in this war that the confrontation between oil and Israel came to a head as conservative and radical Arab oil-producing states jointly imposed their selective oil embargo in retaliation for the massive airlift of U.S. supplies to Israel, during the war, when Israel appeared threatened. In the wake of the war, circumstances in the Middle East were sufficiently altered—politically and psychologically —that expanded opportunities for peacemaking seemed available. In particular, the deadlock arising from a general Arab unwillingness to negotiate that had characterized the prewar period ceased to be a factor. U.N. Security Council Resolution 338 ending the 1973 war called explicitly for negotiations, and it was accepted both by the Arab states that were principally concerned and by Israel.

In turn U.S. efforts to seek a settlement between Israel and its immediate neighbors were intensified, in part because only the U.S. seemed in position both to serve as an intermediary and to "deliver" Israel to the negotiating table. The Soviet Union having broken relations with Israel in 1967 and having refused to substantially resupply its Arab clients with arms sufficient to match U.S. supplies to Israel did not have effective influence or credit with either side.

In its first effort the United States collaborated with the Soviet Union in establishing a forum for the negotiations called for in Resolution 338. Under their joint chairmanship, the Geneva Peace Conference was convened December 21, 1973. The U.S., however, while it considered the conference framework important for the negotiations, doubted that progress could be made at that point by tackling the Arab-Israeli conflict as a whole. It also believed the large formal conference (which Syria, in fact, did not attend) to be an inappropriate forum for serious progress. Several issues lay behind this judgment. The U.S., while recognizing the value of Soviet involvement to give legitimacy to the process, did not really consider Moscow a useful participant in serious negotiations and was in any case not anxious to see the Soviets actively involved in Middle East affairs.

The next U.S. efforts were designed to exclude them. Secretary of State Henry Kissinger undertook an intensive two-year mission to achieve limited agreements between Israel on the one hand and Egypt and Syria on the other. Through what became known as "shuttle diplomacy," Kissinger hoped to win a series of agreements that would ultimately create an atmosphere in which it would be possible to defuse the Palestinian problem. By this point the U.S. government had come to realize that a Palestinian solution lay at the heart of any long-term Arab-Israeli settlement. Kissinger's efforts at step-by-step diplomacy culminated in the Sinai II agreement between Israel and Egypt.[2] One of the "secret" elements leading to this agreement was a U.S. commitment to have no negotiations with the PLO until it recognized Israel.

In addition the U.S. promised to supply Israel with new and sophisticated weapons in order to fully secure it a substantial military superiority over its Arab foes. The Soviet Union, which had previously been reticent to supply its most sophisticated weaponry to its clients, quickly followed suit, significantly upgrading the military potential of Libya, Syria, and Iraq. A new phase of the Middle East arms race was under way and all signs of restraint were lost. The Lebanese Civil War, which broke out as the Sinai II agreement was being signed, and the U.S. election campaign prevented a useful U.S. role during 1976, and the Democratic election victory that year brought an end to the step-by-step process.

The Carter administration took office with a commitment to seek a Middle East settlement that was at least as great as that of the preceding leadership. It differed in its approach in three important respects, however: (1) It considered that the step-by-step method of putting together a peace in the area had run its course and that the time had come for a comprehensive settlement; (2) It was far more ready than its predecessor had been to accept the need for a Palestinian entity on the West Bank. Following President Carter's early call for a Palestinian "homeland," the administration had a less reserved attitude toward the Palestinians and the PLO, although it never put into effect this greater openness; (3) It believed that in return for withdrawing from the occupied territories Israel should receive from the Arab states a full peace rather than only the nonbelligerency provided for in Resolution 242. Thus, within a few months of his inauguration, President Carter had laid down three key elements of what he conceived to be a just settlement: a homeland for the Palestinians, Israeli withdrawal to borders essentially those of 1967, and a full peace.

After an unsuccessful attempt to get Arab and Israeli agreement on a more detailed and precise basis for negotiation than was contained in Resolution 242, the U.S. turned, in the late summer of 1977, to an all-out effort to reconvene the Geneva conference by the end of the year in order to set in motion the negotiation of a comprehensive settlement. During the early weeks of the U.N. General Assembly meeting, Secretary of State Cyrus Vance carried on separate talks with high-level officials of Israel, Egypt, Syria, and Jordan in an attempt to get agreement on the form of the conference and participation in it. He was particularly concerned with how to invite the Palestinians. A major, though not the only, stumbling block was the question of whether all Arab participants would negotiate all aspects of the peace, as it affected all Arabs, or whether each Arab state would negotiate with Israel separately about its own front. The Syrian suspicion that Egypt planned a separate peace led Damascus to insist that all Arab states participate in each negotiation. The Syrians wanted negotiations focused not on fronts but on elements of a settlement such as borders, security measures, etc. The Egyptians rejected this approach and no agreement was reached. Furthermore, the Israelis strenuously objected to any explicit inclusion of the PLO. These issues and the general level of Arab-Israeli distrust frustrated the negotiations and by the end of October the sessions had reached an impasse.

Two other U.S. initiatives during this period bear mention. Seeing merit in some form of contact with the PLO, the U.S. sought a formula whereby the PLO could accept Resolution 242 while at the same time reserving its position on the resolution's inadequate treatment of Palestinians. This would allow the U.S. to overcome the restrictions earlier promised to Israel. During Secretary Vance's trip to the Middle East in the summer of 1977, a proposed formula was forwarded to the PLO through Arab governments. Ultimately, the PLO rejected it and instead substituted a demand for a guaranteed role in the negotiation of Arab-Israeli peace. It subsequently appeared that inter-Arab rivalries and Syrian reservations about direct U.S.-PLO contacts had as much to do with the rejection as PLO reaction to the merits of the proposal.

Secondly, on September 30, 1977, the U.S. and the Soviet Union issued a joint communiqué setting out an agreed-upon basis for Middle East peace negotiations. In the perception of the U.S., the language of the communiqué did not differ importantly from positions it had already taken, and a joint U.S.-Soviet statement at this time was unexceptional in view of the expectation that the two countries, as co-chairs, would shortly reconvene the Geneva conference. The U.S., it turned out, was alone in expecting that this interpretation of the joint statement would be widely accepted. The Israelis were furious, and the Egyptians were as upset. The PLO, on the other hand, was gratified and has subsequently pointed to the statement as one it could accept as a basis for negotiations. Largely because of Israeli pressure, the U.S. government promptly issued a second statement that had the effect of negating the communiqué.

THIRD PHASE, 1977–1980

Following the breakdown of the efforts to reconvene the Geneva conference by the end of 1977, and with the aim of again excluding Soviet involvement, President Sadat drastically altered Middle East dynamics by traveling to Jerusalem in November. Sadat clearly caught everyone off balance, including the U.S. Convinced that a comprehensive negotiation of all aspects of a settlement was the most viable course and engaged in mounting a new effort in this direction, Washington was initially concerned that Sadat's move would lead inevitably to a bilateral treaty. This was still considered undesirable. As so often happens in the Middle East, however, the main directions are set by the local states. Washington had no choice, if it wished to play a role, but to follow Sadat's lead, and it did so. While the U.S. may have wished to link the bilateral process between Israel and Egypt to a comprehensive peace and a settlement of the Palestinian problem, the manner in which negotiations proceeded and the very restrictive Israeli definition of the Palestinian problem foreclosed this possibility.

During the months that followed Sadat's Jerusalem trip, it became increasingly clear that the impetus provided by that extraordinary breakthrough would not suffice to bring about an Israeli-Egyptian peace or a broad Middle East settlement. The negative reaction of other Arab states and the PLO, coupled with Israel's reluctance to reciprocate the spirit of Sadat's step, gradually slowed the momentum and soured the atmosphere. With Egyptian-Israeli relations stalemated and the Arabs far too bitterly divided to permit a return to a comprehensive negotiation, there seemed little opportunity for forward movement.

In these circumstances, in the summer of 1978, President Carter invited Prime Minister Begin and President Sadat to Camp David to negotiate a peace between them. The President, by extending the invitation, and the Israeli and Egyptian leaders, by accepting it, greatly increased the stakes involved in reaching a peace agreement. The resulting pressure, in the unique environment of the prolonged and isolated summit negotiation, produced a complex set of agreements later interpreted differently by each party. The one subject of agreement was that of a bilateral Egyptian-Israeli peace and the treaty to embody them.

The complexity and subsequent differences lay in the establishment of a process for dealing with the Palestinian problem. The three leaders agreed to a process whereby Jordan would be invited to join Israel and Egypt in negotiating procedures for establishing an elected self-governing authority on the West Bank and in the Gaza Strip. It provided that Israeli military government and civilian administrations would be withdrawn from these areas upon the election of a self-governing authority. At the same time, a transitional period of five years was conceived by the end of which the final status of the West Bank and Gaza would have been negotiated and a final Israeli-Jordanian peace concluded. Elected representatives of the West Bank and Gaza were to participate in the negotiation of these two outcomes. As Sadat pointed out in his public remarks following Camp David, it was significant for a broader settlement that the U.S. was at the heart of the process projected by the agreement.

The other Arab parties, including Jordan, reacted with dismay. They interpreted the accords as an Egyptian sellout, stage-managed by the U.S. The Palestinians, focusing on the autonomy provisions for the West Bank and Gaza, saw these as giving Israel continued control over all the issues of importance to them—land use, water rights, and political self-determination—thereby foreclosing the possibility of independence. The U.S. negotiators, while aware they would encounter problems in obtaining Arab cooperation for the West Bank-Gaza process, seem to have seriously underestimated them. They apparently also underestimated Israel's reluctance to give the process any substance.

American diplomacy turned almost at once to the task of persuading Jordan and the Palestinians that if they committed themselves to the autonomy talks and the subsequent negotiations for the long-term disposition of the West Bank and Gaza, the provisions could be made to work for them. In addition the U.S. hoped that Saudi Arabia, among the most pro-Western nations in the region, could be drawn into the process. The Arabs were intensely distrustful of a prolonged open-ended process, over which Israel, with military and political control on the ground, could exercise such a high degree of influence, and in which their only guarantor was the United States. Almost at once, beginning on the night the Camp David results were announced, Israeli policy had the effect of demonstrating that Arab suspicions were well founded and that American goodwill was not to be credited. In particular, the narrow Israeli interpretation of autonomy that was revealed as the Egyptian-Israeli-U.S. talks proceeded was disturbing. The subsequent repeated Israeli assertion that Israel would remain sovereign on the West Bank after the transition period convinced the Arabs that the so-called self-governing authority on the West Bank and Gaza was intended by Israel to be nothing more than an agency of Israel's continued occupation.

By the end of the Carter administration, the Arab-Israeli conflict had hardened and other events in the Persian Gulf and Iran were claiming priority. U.S. diplomacy faced a problem of several dimensions. The U.S. sought to preserve the gains it believed had been made at Camp David, in terms of both Israeli-Egyptian peace and U.S.-Egyptian relations. It also accepted involvement in supporting Sadat's legitimacy and the policy he stood for in Egypt, through completion of the phased peace terms and Israeli Sinai withdrawal. But the issue that remained unresolved was the Palestinian question. More clearly than ever, solving that issue was vital to the stability of the Egyptian-Israeli treaty as well as for a lasting comprehensive settlement.

Iran proved to be another site where the contradictions in basic U.S. policy became dramatically apparent. By continually emphasizing external threats and ignoring the extent to which crises in domestic Iranian policies—political repression, skewed development, overemphasis on military spending, etc.—would catalyze decisive internal opposition to the rule of the Shah, the U.S. helped pave the way for his downfall. The Iranian revolution, with its strong Islamic orientation, and its markedly anti-Western values, added a new dimension to the revolutionary politics of the Middle East. It demonstrated as well that a ruler and his policies could be rejected when they were perceived by the people to be largely serving external interests and opposing the interests of their own country.

For the U.S. the loss of the Shah and his armies was a setback to the Nixon doctrine of using surrogate forces to protect U.S. interests abroad. But it also halted the lucrative flow of U.S. arms to Iran, at the time the world's largest importer of weapons. The Shah's demise also challenged the image that sophisticated arms, rapid Western-oriented development, and alliance with the U.S. would provide the rocks of stability. No wonder that Henry Kissinger, architect of America's Iran policy for the Nixon administration, called the overthrow of the Shah the worst setback to U.S. policy since World War II, greater even than the debacle in Indochina.

In the wake of the Iranian revolution the U.S. began to redesign a policy that would not shy away from securing U.S. interests through direct military intervention if it should prove necessary. The Carter administration, even prior to the Soviet invasion of Afghanistan, began to take the steps—upgrading the Indian Ocean naval base at Diego Garcia, seeking additional bases near the Gulf region, further developing the rapid deployment force—that became the basic elements of the Carter Doctrine in January 1980. The destabilizing Soviet entry into Afghanistan served to dramatically punctuate the Carter efforts.

FOURTH PHASE: THE REAGAN ADMINISTRATION

The Reagan administration took office with the hope that it could downgrade the Arab-Israeli conflict, put aside the Palestinian problem, and focus instead on its own Middle East agenda. It placed priority on three concerns:

1. Its perception of a Soviet threat in the Middle East and the problem of protecting the oil-rich Persian Gulf

2. The need to build an anti-Soviet strategic consensus in the region and enlist allies such as Egypt, Israel, and Saudi Arabia because of the bases and facilities they might provide

3. To strengthen its military potential in the Persian Gulf/Indian Ocean region significantly through acquiring basing rights, building a rapid deployment force, and providing sophisticated arms to Middle East allies

The Middle East, the Reagan government seems to believe, can best be understood through the lens of worldwide U.S.-U.S.S.R. confrontation. Regional disputes and local problems in this new formulation are secondary to the need to deal with what they see as a worldwide Soviet military advantage.

The President entered office naming Israel as "a major strategic asset to America." Aid to Israel was not a case of charity but an investment in U.S. security. Reagan has expressed his belief that Israel's West Bank-Gaza settlements are legal. He has been flatly opposed to an independent Palestinian state, and he consistently objects to including the PLO in any peace negotiations, calling them a "terrorist organization."[3] His attitude toward the Camp David process has been lukewarm, and while he seems to favor a Jordanian solution to the Palestine problem, his overall view is to oppose an activist U.S. role in the peace process.

But the Middle East has not behaved according to Reagan's hopes. The new administration began its elaboration of a Middle East policy when it gave approval to an enlargement of the supply of sophisticated aircraft to Saudi Arabia. Within two months of taking office, the Reagan government found itself in the middle of the predictably volatile Arab-Israeli conflict.

The spring/summer of 1981 will probably be seen historically as a turning point in relations between Israel and the U.S. Several significant events propelled Reagan administration reevaluations in U.S. Middle East policy. The first of these was the sharp escalation in fighting in Lebanon in March and April, culminating in direct Israeli intervention in central Lebanon on behalf of the Phalangist forces and the Syrian countermove introducing into Lebanon sophisticated Soviet-manufactured surface-to-air missiles. Second, the Israeli air attack and destruction of the Osirak nuclear reactor near Baghdad in June raised new issues in the Middle East. Third, the renewed cross-border warfare in Southern Lebanon and the large-scale Israeli air raid in June on the Palestinian section of West Beirut that killed over 300 and wounded 800, primarily civilians. Lastly, the Saudi Arabian peace proposal announced in August became an additional source of Israeli-U.S. contention. All this meant that the Reagan administration could not avoid the central Israeli-Palestinian issue.

The U.S. did respond in each instance since it judged that U.S. interests would be negatively affected by heightened conflict in the region. Further, because U.S.-supplied aircraft and ordnance were used in both the Osirak and Beirut raids, perhaps in violation of the terms on which they were supplied, many people called for governmental review of arms sales to Israel. The first clear signs that members of the Reagan administration saw a potential divergence between U.S. Middle East interests and Israeli policies and actions appeared.

The flare-up of actual fighting in Lebanon and escalation of Israeli and Syrian involvement caused the U.S. to recall from retirement Philip Habib, a veteran State Department Middle East diplomat. His aim was to help the parties back away from confrontation. To do so, he found it necessary to deal with the heightened tension in Israel caused by Syria's introduction into Lebanon of very accurate surface-to-air missiles and with the smoldering civil war in Lebanon that had pitted the Phalange militias, largely Maronite Christian, against a mix of Lebanese Muslim groups, the PLO, and the Syrian forces. Habib encouraged the Saudi Arabians to join other Arab state diplomats to seek through diplomacy an end to the renewed fighting, a withdrawal of the Syrian missiles and a reduction in Israeli military involvement. The U.S. had a political stake in Habib's success and communicated this to Israel to postpone threatened Israeli air attacks on the Syrian missiles.

The Israeli bombing of the Iraqi nuclear reactor on June 8, 1981, occurred just three weeks before Israeli elections and during the joint U.S.-Arab diplomatic efforts in Lebanon. The attack carried out by U.S.-supplied aircraft involved crossing the airspace of Jordan and Saudi Arabia, both U.S. Middle East friends. The Israeli venture was successful on technical grounds and demonstrated that Israel maintains military dominance in the region. The political ramifications of the attack, however, were not positive for Israel.

The timing of the attack brought the criticism from Prime Minister Begin's opponents within Israel that it was motivated by the forthcoming elections. In the international community, questions were raised about the legitimacy and legality of bombing a nuclear facility. Critics of Israel's raid noted that the Iraqi reactor was not yet operational and that Iraq was an early signatory of the nuclear nonproliferation treaty, thereby formally signifying its intent not to build nuclear weapons. Iraq had regularly opened its facility to international inspections in accordance with the treaty. Critics further noted Israel's refusal to sign the nonproliferation treaty and the high probability that Israel has produced nuclear weapons itself. The Arab countries reacted with anger at the Israeli attack across national borders and frustration at being unable to offer any significant response. The U.S. reacted by immediately placing under embargo a small shipment of F-16 fighter-bombers destined for Israel while it examined whether Israel had broken the prohibition against use of U.S.-supplied weapons for anything but defensive purposes. Although the examination led to no firm conclusion and the planes were subsequently shipped, this represented one of the few times that the U.S. had expressed such strong disapproval of an Israeli action. Diplomatically, the U.S. moved to an unfamiliar position of supporting in the U.N. Security Council a resolution written by Iraq in consultation with the U.S.[4] While it was clear that Israel had embarrassed the U.S. by the timing of its Iraqi raid, coming as it did in the midst of diplomatic efforts, it seemed unlikely that deeper shifts in the U.S. policy toward Israel would follow.

The Israelis argued, in justification of their raid, that the nonproliferation treaty and the inspections by the International Atomic Energy Agency were inadequate to detect the diversion of materials from the reactor. They claimed that the type of reactor Iraq was building is not needed for the research purposes specified and that the enriched fuels Iraq was securing supported Israeli judgments about Iraq's intent to build a bomb. They justified their unilateral action by claiming that no one else really cares about Israel's security or is in a position to judge what is essential to guarantee it.

Even as this argument was being pursued, Israel launched a series of preemptive attacks against a strong PLO military build-up in Southern Lebanon, culminating in the large-scale raid on West Beirut on July 18. The Israeli attacks were followed immediately by heavy shelling of Israeli border settlements by the PLO. Prime Minister Begin claimed that Israel's intent was to attack PLO headquarters and thus prevent their attacks on northern Israel. Further, he said that Israel would not refrain from bombing civilian sectors if the PLO headquarters was located among them, even though he regretted the loss of civilian lives. It is doubtful that Israel expected the level of international condemnation that followed or the degree of anger it met from Washington. The Reagan administration immediately suspended the delivery of an additional shipment of F-16's and again sent Ambassador Habib to seek a cease-fire. With Saudi diplomatic help, the guns were silenced along the Lebanese-Israeli border. The world watched as Israel and the PLO, operating through intermediaries, negotiated the terms of a cease-fire. Yasir Arafat enforced the cease-fire on the Palestinian side by disciplining hard-line Palestinian guerrilla groups.

The import of this negotiated cease-fire underlines the fact that, if peace is to come in the long Arab-Israeli conflict, the Palestinian problem must be solved and the PLO must be a partner to the solution. Israel's traditional unwillingness to deal with the PLO and the unwillingness of the PLO to deal with Israel have always stood in the way of any resolution. The rapidity with which the PLO assented to the cease-fire put extra pressure on Israel.

The peace process can proceed successfully only with the direct involvement of the Palestinians and the PLO. For the U.S., the question of Israel's restriction on U.S. diplomatic contact with the PLO becomes central. The Reagan administration recently has shown some willingness to alter its previous dismissal of the PLO and an openness to engage the PLO in dialogue. Movement of this sort requires care and perseverance as well as aid from others, such as concerned Arab parties and the Europeans who are in contact with the Palestinian movement.

It is also clear that a U.S. move for Palestinian discussions would have numerous other ramifications. Israel will surely react negatively, at least at first, seeing its preeminence in shaping U.S. Middle East policy eroded. Arab states, across the political spectrum, would perceive this move as a more even-handed and more responsive U.S. policy. An openness, long missing in the Middle East conflict, might be introduced.

The Reagan administration faces a challenge and an opportunity in restructuring U.S. relations with Israel and the Arab world. To develop an effective peace strategy, the Reagan administration will have to recognize the subtlety and nuance of problems and recognize the fundamental political dimensions of the conflict. To treat the Middle East as a military and strategic problem, related only to U.S.-U.S.S.R.

power struggles, will not address or resolve the underlying conflicts and may well exacerbate them. Exclusion of the Soviet Union from any peace process and engagement with them solely on military terms will almost certainly increase tension and instability in the Middle East. The aim should be to build on common interests rather than polarize the region, because to do so is in the interests of the U.S. and of the people of the Middle East.

That a U.S. policy shift on the Middle East was under way during the fall of 1981 is clear to all viewers. The directions of that shift, however, and the forces guiding it are less clear. The Reagan administration, by making the sale to Saudi Arabia of sophisticated fighter planes and airborne surveillance systems (AWACS) the first test of its new policy, has further underscored the widely held belief that the new administration has little foreign policy beyond arms transfers. It has had the further effect of confronting Israel (and its U.S. supporters) on the most sensitive ground, security, and will almost certainly lead to a new and more costly round of arms purchases. While the Saudi arms agreement surely has as one aim greater Saudi involvement in U.S.-oriented Middle East peacemaking, it will have to be matched with a strong and coherent commitment by the U.S. to help resolve the Palestinian question. Will the Reagan administration demonstrate its interest in the peacemaking side of the Saudi agreement by taking seriously the proposals elaborated by Saudi Prince Fahd and vigorously encouraging an Arab-based peace initiative, one which includes Palestinian self-determination alongside recognition of and security for Israel?

The contradictions in American Middle East policy have once again emerged with some clarity. Since the assassination of Egyptian President Sadat, the Reagan administration is being advised to forego its goal of achieving an anti-Soviet "strategic consensus" until there is much greater progress toward a comprehensive Arab-Israeli agreement and substantial resolution of the Palestinian problem. Only then, the argument goes, will the pro-Western Arab states, Jordan and Saudi Arabia, be willing to openly join a U.S.-led coalition. Such a policy runs counter to the current very strong expressions of Israel and its supporters who offer contrasting advice—that Israel as the strongest and most reliable military power in the region should be regarded as the major military asset in the region and thus given basic support. But this tension as perceived by U.S. policymakers is flawed by the degree to which it reduces the problems of the Middle East to those primarily of strategic considerations in the perceived confrontation with the Soviet Union. But history and compassion should compel the U.S. to place its basic concerns on the needs and interests of the people in the Middle East, to seek peace because it will serve those who suffer from war and conflict, and to aid political and economic change because it will relieve the burdens of oppression and poverty. Out of these considerations will the true interests of the people of the U.S. be served and a faithful policy for the U.S. be constructed.

14

Conclusions

Our report treats what have often appeared to be intractable problems. As we examine the numerous issues of conflict and the many layers of apparently contradictory interests, we can sympathize with the sense of despair that often overcomes those engaged in the problems of the Middle East. We can understand why emotion runs so strong and why effective discourse can be so hard to achieve.

Our own ability to continue without despair to deal with these issues has gained strength from the numerous personal contacts that the AFSC has developed over the years with people in the Middle East who are deeply involved in and committed to one or another issue or side in the conflicts there. We are realistic about the seriousness and depth of the problems in the Middle East but we are still, as we said at the outset, cautiously optimistic.

As we neared the completion of writing this report, we shared it with individuals whom we know represent deeply held positions in the various Middle East conflicts. We have been impressed by the seriousness and helpfulness of their often critical responses, and we have incorporated many of their perspectives and considerations into this document. More important, these responses supported our view that there does exist within the Middle East a reservoir of will and ability to face squarely and seek resolution for the most difficult problems.

Our criticisms, suggestions, and proposals are spread through the volume in the contexts in which they arose. We bring them together here to show relationships among the problems and among solutions to them. We hope that they can serve as guideposts to new perspectives and new policies.

THE ARAB-ISRAELI CONFLICT

The core of any solution to the Arab-Israeli conflict is the resolution of the Palestinian problem. It is clear that major initiatives must be taken by the countries and peoples of the Middle East. It is equally certain that there are crucial efforts that can be taken by the United Nations, the U.S., U.S.S.R., and the nations of Europe. The outlines for most of the needed steps can be found in resolutions of the United Nations Security Council and General Assembly. What is required now is the will to break out of the continuing stalemate.

We believe that the solution of the Palestinian problem will involve compromises of positions currently held by both the Israelis and the Palestinians. We believe that to conclude a just peace which provides for the security of all nations, the basic provisions of U.N. Security Council Resolution 242 should be carried out. In addition, we believe that Palestinian self-determination should set the terms for the ultimate decision about the West Bank and Gaza Strip and that an independent Palestinian state on these territories should be supported if it is the chosen option of the Palestinian people. In turn, Palestinian recognition of Israel and its right to a secure and peaceful existence within the pre-1967 borders must be unequivocally given. All parties must renounce terrorism. We believe that this solution provides a measure of justice for both parties who have contested the same lands. It will bring a long-awaited peace to both and promise a greater degree of security for Israel than continued occupation and primary reliance on military force promises.

To unblock the continued impasse, each side must be willing to undertake bold actions. The PLO is in a position to make a proposal that no Israeli political leadership could long resist. It would recognize Israel as a state and make peace with it in return for Israel's recognition of the right of Palestinian self-determination in the West Bank and Gaza Strip. The PLO leadership has often talked of recognition as the "trump card" to be held onto until negotiations are nearly complete. The step of recognition need not be viewed as the final step but may be more effectively used to initiate serious peace negotiations. The PLO must be willing to take political risks if the goal of a Palestinian state is to be realized. Discussion of any future reunification of all of Palestine, the "dream" which some Palestinians talk of, must explicitly renounce the use of force and be cast in terms of mutual desires and negotiated agreements.

For a PLO proposal to have full credibility it must be supported by the Arab states who have made the resolution of the Palestinian problem a key element in ending the Arab-Israeli conflict. Serious proposals of the sort advanced by Saudi Arabia in August 1981 can demonstrate Arab intent and strengthen the will to peace among all the parties. But to be successful a proposal must be diplomatically and politically pursued so as to overcome the fears and rigidities that mark the Middle East today. Such proposals should be recognized as the beginning of a process and not necessarily the final outcome. A PLO-Arab peace initiative would have important reverberations, not only throughout the Middle East but in the policies of the United States, the Soviet Union, Europe, and elsewhere.

For Israel's commitment to peace to be fully appreciated, Israel must drop its claim to extended sovereignty over the West Bank and Gaza and deal openly and positively with Palestinian desires for self-determination and statehood. Israel should be generous in its interpretation of U.N. Security Council Resolution 242 and, in return for withdrawal to the approximate pre-1967 borders and recognition of Palestinian nationalism, require Palestinian and Arab recognition of Israel's legitimate right to live peacefully within secure borders. Israel's desire for security and a long-term peace is compromised by the policy of broad-scale settlements in the West Bank and Gaza. For Israel, the choice is between peace or occupation. If continued steps to integrate the occupied territories into the political economy of Israel are taken, a future agreement with the Palestinians and Arabs is all but foreclosed. As part of any negotiated peace, Israel must either withdraw its settlements or negotiate terms for the population to live under Palestinian sovereignty. Just as Israel insists on its right to determine its national leadership, realism dictates that Israel will have to negotiate agreements with the leadership whom the Palestinians and Arab states recognize—the PLO. All present evidence indicates that the Israeli government is deeply reluctant to consider proposals of this sort. Therefore, we believe that Israelis, American Jews, and others who care about Israel's democratic traditions, its Jewish character, and its responsible role in the world of nations must undertake vigorous action to bring a change in Israeli government policies concerning the Palestinian problem.

All parties, Israeli and Palestinian, should stop the cycle of violence and terror that has held the area in its grip and instead rely solely on political, diplomatic, and other nonviolent means to resolve conflict and achieve agreements.

We hope for more than an end to conflict and seek more than a mere coexistence of two states sharing a nervously guarded border. Important as these are, their very achievement should be used to propel Israelis and Palestinians toward a new relationship with each other. These two peoples who have common histories of persecution and dispersion will, we hope, come to respect—and support—each other's quests for self-determination and self-identity.

The United States cannot alone bring peace to the Middle East, but it can aid the process in important ways. As the primary economic supporter of Israel and supplier of armaments, the U.S. is in a position to reassure Israel of continued concern for its security and to encourage strongly the adoption of policies which can effectively resolve the Palestinian problem. The United States government must strengthen its opposition to land expropriation, settlements, seizure of water resources, deportations of civic leaders, and other moves aimed to insure long-term Israeli control of the West Bank and Gaza Strip. The U.S. must use more than words to indicate its belief that the current occupation and settlements policies are harmful to the peace process. In its genuine support for Israel, the U.S. must not by default support these policies. To reduce U.S. aid to Israel in direct proportion to the amount Israel uses on settlements would be an effective symbolic action.

The U.S. has an additional important role to play in bringing all parties into the peace process. It should, therefore, become involved in direct dialogue with the PLO. The aim should be vigorously to encourage the PLO's involvement in the political and diplomatic efforts seeking to establish a just peace between Israelis and Palestinians.

The U.S. commitment to a just peace should include both its belief in Israel's right to live at peace and in security and the right of the Palestinians to create an independent nation alongside Israel.

We are aware that the adoption of these policies will require changes in currently held views of the Reagan administration. We believe that these changes are in the best interests of both the Israeli and Palestinian peoples and the U.S., and we urge thoughtful and vigorous support for them.

LEBANON

The survival of Lebanon and the well-being of the Lebanese people depend upon the nations of the Middle East and the support of the international community. Although the long-term solution depends upon resolving the Israeli-Palestinian conflict and lifting the pressures it has put upon Lebanon, there are immediate steps that can be taken which will save lives and preserve order within Lebanon.

U.N. Security Council Resolutions 425 and 426, providing for U.N. troop supervision of the border between Lebanon and Israel, should be fully implemented, and the section of the border now controlled by the Israeli-backed militia should be brought under U.N. supervision and Lebanese government authority. United Nations and U.S. diplomatic efforts are urgently required to make this happen.

The diplomatic efforts led by Arab foreign ministers to seek interim agreements among the feuding parties within Lebanon should be given all the support possible from the international community. The large-scale flow of arms to the various militias coming from many directions should be cut by the suppliers and by international efforts, thus giving the Lebanese government a greater chance to regain authority and secure civil order.

The special relations between the PLO and Lebanon need to be reclarified. The PLO should refrain from cross-border military operations and fully recognize UNIFIL's charge, together with the Lebanese army, to seal off the Lebanese-Israeli border.

The Syrian military presence in Lebanon under Arab League auspices, though originally provided to secure an end to civil war, has become itself a factor in the conflict. Withdrawal of these Syrian military forces and reestablishment of the authority of the Lebanese government are important steps toward achieving peace in Lebanon. This withdrawal will be linked in Syrian policy to the resolution of its conflict with Israel, particularly in the Golan Heights, as part of the broader Arab states' initiatives (discussed above) for rapprochement with Israel.

It is important for all parties—Lebanese, Israeli, Palestinian, and Syrian—to show true compassion for the war-battered civilian population and to refrain from any further violence.

MIDDLE EAST OIL

Our conclusions and recommendations regarding oil have two main components. One centers on our call for a broad reassessment of oil as a resource that, while owned by some, has international consequences of political as well as economic nature. We note the importance of establishing just systems of access and distribution for this resource, not only as a long-term vision but, in our oil-scarce world, as an urgent necessity.

The second aspect of our concern centers on U.S. policy toward the oil-producing nations. We are alarmed by the repeated expressions of the U.S. government of a willingness and a right to intervene militarily in the Middle East to protect its access to the resource, oil. We are disturbed by the tendency to support repressive regimes such as that of the Shah of Iran as a means of retaining preferential access to oil. The U.S. must renounce its intentions to resort to military force and political intervention in the area and, instead, respect and recognize the nonalignment of the oil-producing states and their need to establish regional security arrangements.

THE ARMS RACE

The major supplier nations should declare a moratorium on the shipment of all new weapons and halt all current arms transfer agreements. The U.S., as the largest supplier, can take a crucial lead in freezing the arms race in the Middle East. During a moratorium, it can work with the other supplier nations and the recipients to develop strong long-term agreements on Middle East arms limitations.

The Middle East should be declared a nuclear-weapons-free zone, and the suppliers and users of nuclear technologies should work quickly to secure full agreement by all states in the region to the nuclear nonproliferation treaty. Nuclear technology supplier states should refuse to ship nuclear fuels or technologies to states not in compliance with the treaty. They should also tighten their own bilateral safeguards as part of nuclear export agreements. In order to indicate the seriousness of their commitments to halt nuclear weapons proliferation, the U.S. and U.S.S.R. should undertake immediate steps to achieve control and reduction of their own nuclear weapons. This would require acceptance of the SALT II agreement and additional steps to provide for significant nuclear arms reduction.

Israel, as the technologically most advanced nation in the region and the one state with a nuclear weapons capacity, has the potential either to stop or to encourage a Middle East nuclear arms race. If it takes the crucial steps of signing the nonproliferation treaty, dismantling its weapons capability, and opening its facilities to international inspection, Israel can go far to block the nuclear arms race and secure a Middle East free from nuclear weapons.

IRAN AND AFGHANISTAN

Recent events in Iran and Afghanistan have been interpreted by U.S. policymakers as proof that the Middle East/Gulf region is, first and foremost, an area of U.S.-U.S.S.R. confrontation. This interpretation oversimplifies or ignores local realities and the concerns of the peoples of the region. Following the overthrow of the Shah and the resultant loss of its strong regional ally, the U.S. has been unable to find an appropriate alternative to whom it may assign its policing functions for the area. In its place, the U.S. has moved to increase its own military presence in the region with the establishment of a string of military bases spanning the region and the development of the rapid deployment force. It, further, supplies increasingly sophisticated weapons to more and more parties in the area, extending as far east as Pakistan. Each arms sale brings a new need for another sale to maintain balanced relationships among the parties and, in the case of Israel, to assure military superiority. Emphasizing the view that the U.S. is engaged in an East-West contest in the Middle East and substantially increasing arms supplies to potential allies significantly increases the prospects that localized conflicts will be escalated to larger, more encompassing wars.

The U.S. must accept the fact that local concerns and political realities are the governing factors in the Middle East/Gulf area and that a policy seeking superpower nonintervention agreements will more clearly serve the interests of the people of the Middle East and the cause of peace, regionally and internationally.

There are real issues that emerge from the conflicts and crises and from the daily lives of people and governments in the Middle East. They are not on the agendas of either the U.S. or the Soviet Union. They focus instead both on the much more proximate problems— employment, hunger, political liberty, human rights—and on the less tangible questions of national self-identity and political-economic modernization, on Westernization and traditional religious values. It is America's ability to understand and to respond to these issues that will govern our real contribution to the Middle East and permit us to render real aid in the amelioration of conflicts that do occur in the region. The rush to arms, alliances, and grand strategic designs exacerbates tensions and makes the U.S. more surely part of the problem, rather than the solution.

We believe that peace, security, and justice are possible in the Middle East. The area of the world from which the religious prophetic traditions of Judaism, Christianity, and Islam have come may rediscover the faithfulness of these traditions to justice and peace. If war continues in the area, it will be because the contenders and the rest of us do not truly believe that peace is possible. If peace comes it will be because one or more of those countries and peoples involved will have believed and, believing, will have acted daringly and faithfully in that belief.

Notes

1 INTRODUCTION

1. American Friends Service Committee, *Search for Peace in the Middle East* (New York: Fawcett Publications, Inc.; 1970).

2 ISRAEL

1. American Friends Service Committee, op. cit., p. 79.
2. Arie Eliav, *Shalom: Peace in Jewish Tradition* (Israel: Massadah, 1977), p. 1.
3. American Jewish Committee, "The Resurgence of Islam and the Jewish Communities of the Middle East and North Africa," AJC information packet, April 1981, p. 3.
4. Albert Stern, "A Cautious Visit with Syrian Jews," *Cleveland Jewish News,* January 11, 1980, p. 15. For further information on the treatment of Jews in Arab lands, see: Sachar, op. cit., p. 395.
5. For a thorough examination of the Israeli economy, see: Ann Crittenden, "Israel's Economic Plight," *Foreign Affairs,* Vol. 57, No. 5, Summer 1979, pp. 1006–16.
6. Howard M. Sachar, *A History of Israel* (New York: Alfred A. Knopf, 1979), pp. 833–4.
7. For the changing Middle East arms balance see: Stockholm International Peace Research Institute, *Yearbook,* 1981, and *The Military Balance,* (1981–1982), International Institute of Strategic Studies, London.
8. Drew Middleton, "Israel's Might: Are the Arabs Catching Up?" *New York Times,* October 15, 1981; a more recent Israeli assessment is Yehoshua Raviv, "Arab Israel: Military Balance," *Jerusalem Quarterly* 18, 1981, pp. 121–44.
9. Jacob Talmon, "The Homeland Is in the Diaspora: An Open Letter to

Menachem Begin," trans. Arthur Samuelson, *Dissent,* Vol. 27, No. 4, Fall 1980, pp. 444 –5.

10. Ibid., p. 449.

11. For an interesting analysis of the 1981 Israeli election, see: Robert Shaplen, "Letter from Israel," *The New Yorker,* July 27, 1981.

12. Mark Heller, "Begin's False Autonomy," *Foreign Policy,* Winter 1979–1980, pp. 111–32.

13. "Speech by Prime Minister Begin of Israel to the Knesset on the Occasion of the Visit to Israel of President Sadat of Egypt, Jerusalem, November 20, 1977," *International Documents on Palestine* (Beirut: Institute for Palestine Studies, 1979), pp. 275–9.

14. Sachar, op. cit., p. 668.

15. Ian Lustick, "Kill the Autonomy Talks," *Foreign Policy,* No. 41, Winter 1980–1981, p. 25; and *Jerusalem Post,* April 6–7, 1981. Other good references on Israeli settlements in the West Bank and Gaza include: William W. Harris, *Taking Root: Israeli Settlement in the West Bank, the Golan, and Gaza-Sinai 1967–1981* (Chichester: Research Studies Press, 1980); and testimony of Ann Mosely Lesch and Paul Quiring in: United States Congress, House of Representatives, Committee on International Relations, *Israeli Settlements in the Occupied Territories,* 95th Congress, 1st session (Washington, D.C.: Government Printing Office, 1978), pp. 7–42; Ann Lesch, "Israeli Settlements in the Occupied Territories," *Journal of Palestine Studies,* Vol. 25, Autumn 1977, pp. 26–47, and Vol. 29, Autumn 1978, pp. 100–19.

16. Bernard Avishai, "The Victory of the New Israel," *New York Review of Books,* August 13, 1981, p. 45.

3 THE OCCUPATION

1. Ann Mosely Lesch, *Political Perceptions of the Palestinians on the West Bank and the Gaza Strip* (Washington, D.C., The Middle East Institute, 1980), p. 31.

2. William Claiborne and Edward Cody, *The West Bank: Hostage of History* (Washington, D.C.: Foundation for Middle East Peace, November 1980), p. 3.

3. Raja Shehadeh and Jonathan Kuttab, *The West Bank and the Rule of Law* (Geneva: International Commission of Jurists and Ramallah Law in the Service of Man, 1980), p. 3. For Israel's interpretation of its administrative and legal procedures, see: Israel National Section of the International Commission of Jurists, *The Rule of Law in the Areas Administered by Israel* (Tel Aviv: TZATZ, 1981).

4. Geneva Conventions of August 12, 1949, with commentary published under the direction of Jean Pictet (Geneva: International Committee of

the Red Cross, 1956), Fourth Convention: Relative to the Protection of Civilians in Times of War.

5. Shehadeh and Kuttab, op. cit., pp. 28–9.

6. Israel ICJ, op. cit., pp. 28–9, 37–42.

7. Figures on the number of arrests have been provided by AFSC field staff in the Middle East, and Israel ICJ, op. cit., pp. 71–3.

8. Amnesty International, *Report and Recommendations of an Amnesty International Mission to the State of Israel,* June 3–7, 1979 (London: Amnesty International Publications, 1980).

9. Shehadeh and Kuttab, op. cit., p. 123.

10. Claiborne and Cody, op. cit., pp. 26–7.

11. Salim Tamar, "The Palestinians in the West Bank and Gaza: Sociology of Dependence," *Sociology of the Palestinians,* Khalil Nakhleh and Elia Zurcik, eds. (New York: St. Martin's Press, 1980.)

12. *Jerusalem Post,* April 7, 1981.

13. From an Israeli report delivered at the United Nations Conference on Desertification, Nairobi, Kenya, August 1977, cited in the Economics Department of Jordan, "The Significance of Some West Bank Resources to Israel," February 1979, p. 6.

14. David K. Shipler, "Israel Plans to Take Over Arab-Run Power Company," *New York Times,* January 1, 1980, p. A2.

15. Yehuda Litani, "Vigilantes in the Wild West (Bank)," *Haaretz,* May 11, 1979.

16. Ann Lesch, "Israeli Deportation of Palestinians from the West Bank and the Gaza Strip, 1967–1978," *Journal of Palestine Studies,* Vol. 30, Winter 1979, pp. 101–31, and Vol. 31, Spring 1979, pp. 81–112, and the *Financial Times,* London, December 4, 1979.

17. Mohammed Milhem, "Autonomy: An Empty Plate," *New Outlook,* January 1981, p. 22, and Mohammed Milhem and Fahd Kawasmeh, *New York Times,* June 1, 1981.

18. Shehadeh and Kuttab, op. cit., pp. 90–1.

19. Naseer Aruri, "Repression in Academia: Palestinian Universities vs. the Israeli Military," unpublished paper, February 1981, pp. 13–14.

20. Milton Viorst, "Bir Zeit: The Search for National Identity," *Science,* Vol. 20, No. 5, December 1980, pp. 1101–2.

21. Aruri, op. cit., p. 12.

22. Excerpt from a paper by Sahar Khalifah delivered at the International Writers' Program, Iowa City, University of Iowa, November 29, 1978.

4   THE PALESTINIANS

1. American Friends Service Committee, op. cit., pp. 71–2.

2. Frank Epp, *The Palestinians, Portrait of a People in Conflict* (Scottsdale, Pa.: Herald Press, 1976); and: John Amos, *Palestinian Resistance: Orga-*

nization of a Nationalist Movement (New York: Pergamon Press, 1980), p. 9.

3. Edward Said, *The Question of Palestine* (New York: The New York Times Book Co., Inc., 1979), pp. 120–2.

4. For texts of U.N. Resolutions and 1947 Partition Plan see: *The Middle East and North Africa 1980–1981* (London: Europa Publications, Inc., 1980); UN 1947 Partition Plan, UN Security Council Resolution 242, November 22, 1967 (See Appendix I.); and UN Security Council Resolution 338, October 22, 1973. (See Appendix II.)

5. For the text of the Camp David agreements and the Israeli-Egyptian peace treaty, see: United States Congress, House of Representatives, Committee on Foreign Affairs, Subcommittee on Europe and the Middle East, *The Search for Peace in the Middle East: Documents and Statements, 1967–1979,* 96th Congress, 1st session (Washington, D.C.: Government Printing Office, 1979), pp. 20–90.

6. For the text of the 1974 Rabat Conference final resolution, see: *Middle East and North Africa,* op. cit., p. 73. For the text of the resolutions of the 1978 Baghdad Summit, see: "Final Statement issued by Summit Conference 5 Nov." *Middle East and North Africa Daily FBIS* (Washington, D.C.: Foreign Broadcasting and Information Service, November 6, 1978), p. A14.

7. For full discussion of Fatah, see: John Amos, op. cit.

8. Abu Iyad, *My Home, My Land: A Narrative of the Palestinian Struggle,* with Eric Rouleau, trans. Linda Butler Koseoglu (New York: Quadrangle/The New York Times Book Co., Inc., 1981), p. 106.

9. Fouad Ajami, *The Arab Predicament* (Cambridge: Cambridge University Press, 1981), pp. 150–1.

10. Walid Khalidi, "Thinking the Unthinkable: A Sovereign Palestinian State," *Foreign Affairs,* Vol. 56, No. 4, July 1978, p. 699.

11. Avi Plascov, *A Palestinian State? Examining the Alternatives,* Adelphi Papers, No. 163, 1981, p. 8.

12. Ibid.

13. Ibid., p. 9.

14. *Haolam Hazeh,* May 12, 1976.

15. "Statement by the West Bank National Conference which Met in Beit Hanina, Jerusalem, October 1, 1978," *Journal of Palestine Studies,* Vol. VII, No. 2, Winter 1979, pp. 194–5.

16. Trudy Rubin, "Exiled West Bank Mayors Hope to Go Home After Israeli Elections," *Christian Science Monitor,* April 30, 1981.

17. Anthony Lewis, "Arafat Says Ambush of Jews in Hebron Was like US Struggle Against British," *New York Times,* May 8, 1980.

18. Anthony Lewis, "Time Out of Joint," *New York Times,* May 12, 1980, p. A19.

19. See for example: Walid Khalidi, "Thinking the Unthinkable," op. cit.

20. Several different translations of the 1968 amended Palestine National Charter exist. We refer you to: "The Palestine National Charter Adopted by the Fourth Palestine National Assembly, Cairo, June 17, 1968," *International Documents on Palestine 1968* (Beirut: Institute for Palestine Studies, 1971), pp. 393–4, and Y. Harkabi, *The Palestinian Covenant and Its Meaning* (London: Vallentine, Mitchell, and Co. Ltd., 1979), pp. 119–29.

21. Walid Khalidi, "Regiopolitics: Towards a US Policy on the Palestine Problem," *Foreign Affairs*, Vol. 59, No. 5, Summer 1981, p. 1060.

22. "Political Programme for the PLO approved by the Palestine National Council 11th Session January 6–12, 1973," *International Documents on Palestine 1973* (Beirut: Institute for Palestine Studies, 1976), p. 401.

23. Eric Rouleau, "Les Dirigeants Palestiniens Accepteraient Un Compromis," *Le Monde*, November 6, 1973, p. 3. Abu Iyad in *My Home, My Land* (p. 138) notes that as early as 1967 Farouk Qaddoumi, director of foreign affairs for the PLO, advocated a ministate on the West Bank and Gaza.

24. "Political Programme for the Present Stage of the PLO drawn up by the PNC," *Journal of Palestine Studies*, Summer 1974, p. 224.

25. Said Hammami, *Trouw* (June 28, 1975) quoted in Mordech Nissan, "Palestinian Moderates," *Jerusalem Quarterly*, No. 1, Fall 1976, p. 73.

26. "Resolutions of the 13th Palestine National Council, Cairo, issued March 21–25, 1977," *Journal of Palestine Studies*, Spring 1977, p. 189.

27. "Joint statement issued by the governments of the US and the USSR specifying the necessary steps to be taken to ensure peace in the Middle East," *International Documents on Palestine 1977* (Beirut: Institute for Palestine Studies, 1980), p. 255. (See Appendix V.)

28. "6-Point Programme Agreed to by all Palestinian factions announced by Salah Khalaf, Tripoli, December 4, 1977," *Journal of Palestine Studies*, Spring 1978, p. 188.

29. Text drafted and supplied to the American Friends Service Committee by Khaled al-Hassan.

30. "Venice Statement on Middle East," June 13, 1980, *Middle East International*, No. 127, June 20, 1980, p. 13. (See Appendix VII.)

31. "What Arafat Really Said," *Israel et Palestine*, April–May, 1979, p. 9.

32. Nicholas B. Tatro, "Saudis in Gesture on Israel," *Boston Globe*, August 9, 1981, p. 1.

33. John Kifner, "Arafat Says Saudi Plan Could Indeed Lead to Lasting Middle East Peace," *New York Times*, August 17, 1981, and John Kifner, "Arafat Welcomes Saudi Proposal for Coexistence with Israelis," *New York Times*, October 31, 1981, p. 6. (See Appendix VI.)

34. Ibid.

35. Daniel Southerland, "Brzezinski: It's Time to Speak to the PLO," *Christian Science Monitor*, August 13, 1981, p. 4.

36. "Why Not Talk With the PLO?" *Christian Science Monitor,* August 7, 1981.
37. "Excerpts from News Conference by Ford and Carter on the Future of Egypt," *New York Times,* October 12, 1981.
38. Walid Khalidi, "Regiopolitics," op. cit., p. 1063.

5 SECURITY AND TERRORISM

1. Aharon Yariv, "Strategic Depth," *Jerusalem Quarterly,* No. 17, Fall 1980, p. 5.
2. Mattityahu Peled, "Dissociating Israeli Security from More Territory," *New York Times,* December 16, 1977.
3. Yariv, op. cit., p. 8.
4. Ezer Weizman, *The Battle for Peace* (Toronto: Bantam Books, 1981), p. 227.
5. Shai Feldman, "Israel's Security," *Foreign Affairs,* Vol. 59, No. 4, Spring 1981, p. 762.
6. Shai Feldman, "A Nuclear Middle East," *Survival,* Vol. 23, No. 3, May–June 1981, and Robert Shaplen, op. cit., p. 67.
7. Plascov, op. cit., p. 51.
8. Meir Pail, *The West Bank and Gaza: A Strategic Analysis for Peace,* New Outlook Discussion Paper No. 3 (Tel Aviv: New Outlook, 1981), pp. 10 –11.
9. Peled, op. cit.
10. Khalidi, "Thinking the Unthinkable," op. cit., p. 713.
11. Feldman, op. cit., p. 771.
12. Amos, op. cit., pp. 335–46.
13. In the following discussion of terrorism, we have relied in part on a paper entitled "A Judgement on Terror," prepared in 1974 by David McReynolds of the War Resisters League for the AFSC 1974 Middle East Peace Packet.
14. Simpha Flapan, "The Maalot Tragedy," *New Outlook,* June 1974, p. 13.

6 OPTIONS AND PROPOSALS

1. Statistics from a study conducted by Dov Friedlander and Calvin Goldscheider, "The Population of Israel," cited in *Washington Post,* September 8, 1980.
2. Nadav Safran, *Israel, the Embattled Ally* (Cambridge: Harvard University Press, 1978), p. 101.
3. Interview with Moshe Nissim, "Why Autonomy," *Middle East Review,* Winter 1979–1980, p. 9.
4. Heller, op. cit., p. 121.
5. Interview with Nissim, loc. cit.

6. "Begin Wins a Close Vote of Confidence," *Boston Globe*, August 6, 1981, p. 5.

7. "Extracts from the Preparatory Committee Recommendations for Political Resolutions Submitted to the 3rd elected Congress of the Israel Labor Party in December 1980," *Middle East International*, June 30, 1981, p. 15.

8. Shimon Peres, "A Strategy for Peace in the Middle East," *Foreign Affairs*, Vol. 58, No. 4, Spring 1980, pp. 887–901.

9. Brig. Gen. Aryeh Shalev, *The Autonomy—Problems and Possible Solutions* (Tel Aviv: Tel Aviv University Center for Strategic Studies, January 1980), p. 60.

10. Moshe Dayan, "Making a Move on Autonomy," *Jerusalem Post*, December 25, 1980, p. 8.

11. Yigal Allon, "Israel: the Case for Defensible Borders," *Foreign Affairs*, October 1976, pp. 38–53.

12. The Etzion block of settlements which dates from pre-1948 is located southwest of Bethlehem.

13. Abba Eban, "The Palestinian Problem—A New Approach," *New Outlook*, Vol. 23, No. 1.

14. Victor Shemtov, "The Sand Is Running Out," *New Outlook*, Vol. 23, No. 4, May 1980, p. 11.

15. David Richardson, "The Least Dangerous Alternative," *Jerusalem Post Magazine*, June 29–July 1, 1981.

16. "Begin Wins a Close Vote of Confidence," op. cit.

17. Rabbi Arthur Hertzberg, "The West Bank's Future," *New York Times*, June 30, 1981, p. A15.

18. For full discussion of rejectionists see Amos, op. cit.

19. This presentation of Palestinian views regarding a transition formula draws heavily on an important recent study: Ann Mosely Lesch, *Political Perceptions of the Palestinians of the West Bank and the Gaza Strip* (Washington, D.C.: Middle East Institute, 1980).

20. Trudy Rubin, "West Bank and Gaza May Produce Few Willing to Participate in Negotiations," *Christian Science Monitor*, March 29, 1979, p. 5.

21. Anthony Lewis, "Dissent on the West Bank from Israeli Insider," *New York Times*, May 25, 1980.

22. A number of thoughtful proposals have been advanced for the resolution of the complicated question of Jerusalem. One of these is found in a recent article by the current mayor of the city: Teddy Kollek, "Jerusalem: Past and Future," *Foreign Affairs*, Vol. 59, No. 5, Summer 1981, pp. 1041–9. Other studies of this issue from a variety of perspectives include: H. Eugene Bovis, *The Jerusalem Question 1917–1968* (Stanford: Hoover Institution Press, 1971); A. L. Tibawi, *Jerusalem: Its Place*

in Islam and Arab History, Monograph No. 19 (Beirut: Institute for Palestine Studies, 1969); and *Jerusalem: Problems and Prospects,* Joel Kraemer, ed. (New York: Praeger, 1980).

7   THE TRAGEDY OF LEBANON

1. "Chronology of the Lebanese War," *International IDOC New Series Bulletin,* No. 3–4, International Documentation and Center, Rome, March–April 1977, p. 17.
2. A good examination of the economic impact of the Lebanese civil war, particularly in the south, is: Elaine Hagopian and Samih Farsoun, *South Lebanon,* Special Report No. 2 (Detroit: Association of Arab American University Graduates, Inc., August 1978).
3. For greater detail on the Lebanese civil war, consult: John Bullock, *Death of a Country* (London: Weidenfeld and Nicolson, 1977); P. E. Haley and Lewis Snider, eds., *Lebanon in Crisis* (Syracuse: Syracuse University Press, 1979); Roger Owen, ed., *Essays on the Crisis in Lebanon* (London: Ithaca Press, 1976); and Walid Khalidi, *Conflict and Violence in Lebanon: Confrontation in the Middle East* (Cambridge: Harvard Studies in International Affairs, 1979).
4. Quoted in James Fine, "The Tragedy of Lebanon," Quaker International Affairs Report (Philadelphia: American Friends Service Committee, March 1981), p. 8.
5. Ibid., p. 4.
6. David Ottaway, "Lebanon Is Alarmed by Increasing Israeli Activity in its South," *Washington Post,* October 26, 1980; and Fine, op. cit., p. 10–11.
7. Fine, op. cit., pp. 15–16.
8. Ibid.
9. Ibid., p. 15.
10. Everett Mendelsohn, "Middle East Conflicts: Reflections on a Trip to the Middle East, Summer 1980" (Philadelphia: American Friends Service Committee, 1980), p. 23.
11. "Text of U.N. Council's Resolution," *New York Times,* March 20, 1978, p. A10. (See Appendix IV.)
12. For text of Cairo agreement, see Khalidi, *Conflict and Violence in Lebanon,* op. cit., pp. 185–7.
13. Ibid., p. 52.

8   OIL AND CONFLICT

1. For a useful background source on Middle Eastern oil, see: Joe Stork, *Middle East Oil and the Energy Crisis* (New York: Monthly Review Press, 1975).

2. These are EXXON, BP, Shell, Gulf, Texaco, Standard Oil of California, and Mobil.
3. Joseph Nye, "Energy Nightmares," *Foreign Policy,* No. 40, Fall 1980, pp. 132–54.
4. Ibid., p. 139.
5. "The Oil Crisis: Is there a Military Option?" *The Defense Monitor,* Vol. VIII, No. 11, December 1979, p. 1.
6. Nye, op. cit., p. 132.
7. For further information on immigrant labor in Gulf oil-producing countries, see: "Labor Migration in the Middle East," *MERIP Reports,* August, 1977.
8. For example, Saudi Arabia contributed 2.3 percent of GNP between 1975 and 1979; Kuwait 3.1 percent during the same period. U.S. contributions in 1979 were .2 percent of GNP, and France's .59 percent of GNP. The highest industrial country contribution was Sweden's at .94 percent of GNP. For further discussion of this issue, see: "Arab Aid," *Aramco World,* Vol. 3, No. 6, November–December 1979; and Paul Hallwood and Stuart Sinclair, *Oil, Debt and Development: OPEC in the Third World* (London: George Allen and Unwin, 1981).
9. For a thorough examination of the controversy surrounding projected Soviet oil production, see: Marshall Goldman, *The Enigma of Soviet Petroleum: Half Empty or Half Full?* (London: George Allen and Unwin, 1980); and Congressional Research Service, Library of Congress, *Energy in Soviet Policy,* A Study Prepared for the use of the Subcommittee on International Trade, Finance, and Security Economics of the Joint Economic Committee, Congress of the United States, June 11, 1981 (Washington, D.C.: Government Printing Office, 1981).
10. For example: H.E. Shaikh Ali Khalifah al Sabah (Kuwaiti oil minister) "Conceptual Perspective for a Long Range Oil Policy," *Middle East Economic Survey,* Vol. XXII, No. 48, September 17, 1979, p. 5.
11. It is interesting to note that the Kuwaiti oil minister in the speech cited in footnote 10 argues for a similar policy to the one here suggested.

9   THE ARMS RACE

1. These are: Iran, Libya, Iraq, Saudi Arabia, Israel, Syria, Egypt, and Ethiopia.
2. U.S. Department of State, *Congressional Presentation: Security Assistance,* FY 1980.
3. Arms Control and Disarmament Agency, *World Military Expenditures and Arms Transfers 1969–1978* (Washington, D.C.: ACDA, 1980).
4. Stockholm International Peace Research Institute, *World Armaments and Disarmament,* SIPRI Yearbook 1976 (London: Taylor and Francis Ltd., 1976), p. 65.

5. "The US Military in Saudi Arabia: Investing in Stability or Disaster?" *The Defense Monitor,* Vol. X, No. 4, (Washington, D.C.: Center for Defense Information, 1981), p. 1.
6. "Arms are Crucial Export for Israel," *New York Times,* August 24, 1981.
7. "US Military in Saudi Arabia," op. cit., p. 5.
8. For a study of Egypt's relationship with the U.S.S.R., see: Alvin Z. Rubinstein, *Red Star on the Nile* (Princeton: Princeton University Press, 1977); and Mohammed Heikal, *The Sphinx and the Commissar* (New York: Harper and Row, 1978).
9. For an examination of the Soviet-PLO relationship see: Rashid Khalidi, op. cit.
10. Central Intelligence Agency, *Communist Aid Activities in Non-Communist Less Developed Countries 1979 and 1954–1979* (National Foreign Assessment Center, April 1980).
11. "Tripartite Declaration Regarding Security in the Near East, May 25, 1950," *The Arab-Israeli Conflict: Readings and Documents,* John Norton Moore, ed. (Princeton: Princeton University Press, 1977), pp. 988–9.
12. U.S. Department of State, op. cit.
13. "Treaty on the Non-proliferation of Nuclear Weapons," July 1, 1968, *World Armaments and Disarmaments, SIPRI Yearbook 1981* (London: Taylor and Francis Ltd., 1981), pp. 415–16.
14. For a good recent study of nuclear weapons in the Middle East, see: Shai Feldman, "A Nuclear Middle East," op. cit., pp. 107–115.
15. "Dayan Says Israelis Have the Capacity to Produce A-Bombs," *New York Times,* June 25, 1981, p. 1.
16. Elliot Marshall, "Fallout from the Raid in Iraq," *Science,* Vol. 213, July 3, 1981, p. 116.

10 IRAN

1. Good background sources on the modern history and politics of Iran are: Richard Cottam, *Nationalism in Iran* (Pittsburgh: University of Pittsburgh, 1979), and Nikki R. Keddie, *Roots of Revolution: An Interpretive History of Modern Iran* (New Haven: Yale University Press, 1981).
2. For a firsthand account of these events and the CIA's involvement in them, see: Kermit Roosevelt, *Countercoup: The Struggle for the Control of Iran* (New York: McGraw-Hill, 1979).
3. Former SAVAK agents as well as former CIA analyst Jess Leaf (*New York Times,* 1/6/80) and Irish Nobel Peace Prize recipient Sean McBride (*The Nation,* 3/1/80) have made specific allegations in this regard.

4. Mohammed Reza Pahlavi, *Mission for My Country* (New York: McGraw-Hill, 1961).
5. The first prime minister appointed by Khomeini after his return to Iran in February 1979. Bazargan resigned after Iranian students seized the U.S. Embassy hostages.
6. A widely regarded educator who wrote and lectured on the sociology of Islam. Dr. Shariati was arrested and tortured by SAVAK. He died under suspicious circumstances in London in June 1977. For a sampling of his views, see: Ali Shariati, *On the Sociology of Islam,* trans. Hamid Algar (Berkeley: Mizan Press, 1979).
7. See "Iran in Revolution," *MERIP Reports,* No. 75–6, 1979, passim; Ervand Abrahamian, "Structural Causes of the Iranian Revolution," *MERIP Reports,* No. 87, May 1980, pp. 21–6. See also Nikki R. Keddie, op. cit.
8. William J. Butler and Georges Levasseur, *Human Rights and the Legal System in Iran* (Geneva: International Commission of Jurists, 1976).
9. The *Qur'an* (also spelled Koran) is Islam's holy scripture. Muslims believe the *Qur'an* contains God's words as revealed to the prophet Muhammad.
10. For a good introduction to Islam see: Kenneth Cross, *The House of Islam* (Belmont, Ca.: Wadsworth Press, 1975). For the more advanced reader, see: Fualur Rahman, *Islam,* 2nd ed. (Chicago: University of Chicago Press, 1979). For the most comprehensive history to date on Islam, see: Marshall Hodgson, *Venture of Islam,* 3 vols. (Chicago: University of Chicago Press, 1974).
11. For a collection of essays sympathetic to the Iranian revolution, consult: David Albert, ed., *Tell the American People: Perspectives on the Iranian Revolution* (Philadelphia: Movement for a New Society, 1980).
12. "The President's News Conference of October 1, 1981," *Weekly Compilation of Presidential Documents,* Vol. 17, No. 40, October 5, 1981, p. 1070.
13. Sunni Muslims represent the other major strand of Islam besides the Shi'ite Muslims. About 85 percent of the world's approximately 800,000 Muslims are Sunni.
14. "The State of the Union," Annual Message to the Congress, January 21, 1980, *Weekly Compilation of Presidential Documents,* Vol. 16, No. 4, January 28, 1980, pp. 170–1.
15. Richard Halloran, "Reagan Plan Looks to String of Bases in Mideast and Indian Ocean," *New York Times,* March 12, 1981, p. A8.

11 AFGHANISTAN

1. For an excellent background source on Afghanistan, we refer you to: Louis Dupree, *Afghanistan* (Princeton: Princeton University Press, 1980).

2. For a discussion of Amin's rule just prior to the Soviet invasion, see: Fred Halliday, "Afghanistan: A Revolution Consumes Itself," *The Nation,* November 17, 1979.

3. Joe Elder, Barbara Bowman, and Susan McCord, "Report of Quaker Visit to India, Pakistan and Afghanistan," AFSC Trip Report, May 20–June 8, 1980, pp. 10–11.

4. Rodney Tasker, "On the Frontiers of Fear," *Far Eastern Economic Review,* week of October 16–22, 1981, p. 42.

5. Ibid.

6. President Carter's 1980 state of the union address, op. cit., p. 164.

7. For an interesting discussion of the U.S. relationship with Pakistan, see: Alexandre Destarac and M. Levent, "Le Pakistan, Fragile Bastion dans la Stratégie Occidentale," *Le Monde Diplomatique,* March 1981; and Claudia Wright, "A Risky Bet on General Zia," *Atlantic Monthly,* June 1981, pp. 16–23.

8. Fred Halliday, *Soviet Policy in the Arc of Crisis.* (Washington, D.C.: Institute for Policy Studies, 1981).

12 THE SOVIET UNION

1. Fred Halliday, *Soviet Policy in the Arc of Crisis,* op. cit., Chap. 2, sec. 2.

2. Rashid Khalidi, *Soviet Middle East Policy in the Wake of Camp David,* Institute for Palestine Studies, Paper No. 3 (Beirut: IPS, 1979).

3. Halliday, *Soviet Policy,* op. cit.

4. For more in-depth consideration of the Soviet role in the Middle East, see: Robert O. Freedman, *Soviet Policy Toward the Middle East Since 1970* (New York: Praeger, 1978); Ilana Kass, *Soviet Involvement in the Middle East—Policy Formulation 1966–1973* (Boulder: Westview Press, 1978).

13 UNITED STATES POLICY

1. For the text of the Rogers Plan, see: U.S. Congress, "Search for Peace in the Middle East Documents," op. cit., p. 296.

2. For a detailed discussion of Kissinger's shuttle diplomacy in the Middle East, see: Safran, op. cit., pp. 506–60, and 588–94.

3. For views of the early Reagan administration, see: "U.S. Would Resist a Mideast Shift," *Washington Post,* March 19, 1981, p. 1.

4. "Text of Draft Resolution at UN on Israel's Raid on Iraqi Reactor," *New York Times,* June 19, 1981.

Bibliography

DOCUMENTS

Moore, John Norton, ed. *The Arab Israeli Conflict: Readings and Documents.* Princeton: Princeton University Press, 1977.
A valuable source book for documents and interpretive essays on the Arab-Israeli conflict until 1975.

U.S. House of Representatives, Committee on Foreign Affairs, Subcommittee on Europe and the Middle East. *The Search for Peace in the Middle East: Documents and Statements 1967–1979.* 96th Congress, 1st session. Washington, D.C.: Government Printing Office, 1979.
A useful collection of documents pertaining to the conflict, with particular emphasis on official U.S. administration positions and comments.

ISRAEL

Avineri, Shlomo. *The Making of Modern Zionism, The Intellectual Origins of the Jewish State.* New York: Basic Books, Inc., 1981.
A thoughtful new analysis of Zionism written by a former member of the Israeli Labor government.

Eliav, Arie Lova. *Land of the Hart: Israelis, Arabs, the Territories and a Vision of the Future.* trans., Judith Yalon. Philadelphia: Jewish Publication Society, 1974.
A sensitive assessment of the situation of Israel and its neighbors by a key figure in Israel's Sheli party. Lova Eliav has participated in a number of secret talks with moderate PLO leaders.

Elon, Amos. *The Israelis: Founders and Sons.* New York: Holt, Rinehart and Winston, 1971.
The work of one of Israel's leading authors on two generations of Israelis, those who came from abroad and founded the country, and their sons who were raised there. An interesting analysis full of detail.

Flapan, Simha, ed. *When Enemies Dare to Talk: An Israeli-Palestinian Debate.* London: Croom Helm Ltd., 1979.
The edited transcript of a dialogue held between Israelis and West Bank Palestinians in Jerusalem in September 1978 under the auspices of New Outlook magazine.

Harkabi, Yehoshafat. *Arab Strategies and Israel's Response.* New York: Free Press, Macmillan Publishing Co., Inc., 1977.
An examination of the spectrum of Israeli views toward the Arabs and toward an eventual settlement of the conflict by a former chief of military intelligence for Israel.

Hertzberg, Rabbi Arthur, ed. *The Zionist Idea.* New York: Atheneum, 1975.
A collection of essays on Zionism.

Lustick, Ian. *Arabs in the Jewish State: Israel's Control of a National Minority.* Austin: University of Texas Press, 1980.
An important new study of the situation of Israel's Arab minority by a professor at Dartmouth College.

Peretz, Don. *The Government and Politics and Israel.* Boulder: Westview Press, 1979.
A useful basic text on Israel's political parties and the structure of the Israeli government.

Sachar, Howard M. *A History of Israel: From the Rise of Zionism to Our Time.* New York: Alfred A. Knopf, 1979.
A comprehensive text on the history of Israel.

Safran, Nadav. *Israel: The Embattled Ally.* Cambridge: Belknap Press, Harvard University Press, 1981.
A penetrating analysis of the recent history of Israel, with a thorough examination of how domestic and international factors influence policy and action.

PALESTINIANS

Amos, John W., II. *Palestinian Resistance: Organization of a Nationalist Movement.* New York: Pergamon Press, Inc., 1980.
A thorough examination of the various groups that make up the Palestine Liberation Organization, their orientations and organization.

Iyad, Abu with Eric Rouleau. *My Home, My Land: A Narrative of the Palestinian Struggle.* trans., Linda Butler Koseoglu. New York: Times Books, 1981.
A first-person account as told to a leading French journalist of the life of Abu Iyad, a key Fatah leader. Illuminating in its coverage of Palestinian history from the mid-1950's from an insider's point of view.

Lesch, Ann Mosely. *Political Perceptions of the Palestinians on the West Bank and the Gaza Strip.* Washington, D.C., Middle East Institute, 1980.
A recent study of the range of views of Palestinians in the occupied territories regarding a range of questions, particularly formulas for a settlement of the

Arab-Israeli conflict. Ann Lesch was an AFSC representative in Jerusalem for a number of years.

Migdal, Joel S., ed. *Palestinian Society and Politics.* Princeton: Princeton University Press, 1980.
An interesting study of the sociology of the Palestinian people.

Quandt, William B., Jabber, Fuad, and Lesch, Ann Mosely. *The Politics of Palestinian Nationalism.* Berkeley: University of California Press, 1973.
Perhaps the seminal work on the subject, this text serves as a useful introduction to the development of the Palestinian national movement from 1947 to 1970.

Said, Edward. *The Question of Palestine.* New York: Times Books, 1979.
A sequel volume to Said's Orientalism, this book examines how the West has consistently misunderstood the Arab-Israeli conflict. Illuminating analysis by a leading Palestinian intellectual, a professor at Columbia University.

Tawil, Raymonda Hawa. *My Home, My Prison.* New York: Holt, Rinehart and Winston, 1979.
The moving personal account of a Palestinian journalist who has been a central figure in the politics of the West Bank. A nationalist and an advocate of womens' issues, Ms. Tawil gives the reader in this compelling narrative a window on affairs in the occupied territories.

Van Arkadie, Brian. *Benefits and Burdens: A Report on the West Bank and Gaza Strip Economies Since 1967.* New York: Carnegie Endowment for International Peace, 1977.
An analysis of the economic impact of occupation on the West Bank and Gaza, describing the character of the economies of these areas at present.

ARAB WORLD

Ajami, Fouad. *The Arab Predicament: Arab Political Thought and Practice Since 1967.* Cambridge: Cambridge University Press, 1981.
An excellent recent work examining Arab attitudes to the issues confronting the region.

Polk, William R. *The Arab World.* Cambridge: Harvard University Press, 1980.
A useful basic text.

LEBANON

Bulloch, John. *Death of a Country.* London: Weidenfeld and Nicolson, 1977.
The account of a journalist of the Lebanese Civil War. Clear and readable.

Haley, P. Edward, and Snider, Lewis W., eds. *Lebanon in Crisis: Participants and Issues.* Syracuse: Syracuse University Press, 1979.
A collection of essays on various aspects of the conflict in Lebanon.

Khalidi, Walid. *Conflict and Violence in Lebanon: Confrontation in the Middle East.* Cambridge: Harvard Center for International Affairs, 1979.

A thoughtfully written analysis of the Lebanese Civil War by a leading Palestinian scholar.

IRAN

Akhavi, Shahrough. *Religion and Politics in Contemporary Iran: Clergy-State Relations in the Pahlavi Period.* Albany: State University of New York, 1980.
A scholarly analysis of the role of religion in Iranian politics as it developed from the midnineteenth century until the revolution and the fall of the Shah.

Banisadr, Abolhassan. *The Fundamental Principles and Precepts of Islamic Government.* trans., Mohammed R. Ghanoonparvar. Lexington: Mazda Publishers, 1981.
A discussion of the application of Islamic principles to running a state in the contemporary world written by the former president of revolutionary Iran, currently in exile in France.

Cottam, Richard W. *Nationalism in Iran.* Pittsburgh: University of Pittsburgh Press, 1979.
An early study of the workings of Iranian politics prior to the revolution by one of the leading American scholars on Iran.

Fischer, Michael M. J. *Iran: From Religious Dispute to Revolution.* Cambridge: Harvard University Press, 1980.
A sociologist's perspective on factors contributing to the Iranian revolution.

Halliday, Fred. *Iran: Dictatorship and Development.* Middlesex: Penguin Books, Ltd., 1979.

Keddie, Nikki R. *Roots of Revolution: An Interpretive History of Modern Iran.* New Haven: Yale University Press, 1981.
A penetrating study of the Iranian revolution and what contributed to it.

Roosevelt, Kermit. *Countercoup: The Struggle for the Control of Iran.* New York: McGraw-Hill Book Company, 1979.
An account of the 1953 overthrow of Mossadegh by the CIA agent who engineered it.

AFGHANISTAN

Dupree, Louis. *Afghanistan.* Princeton: Princeton University Press, 1980.
A comprehensive resource on Afghanistan, its people, history, and culture. The final section examines the Soviet invasion in December 1979.

SOVIET POLICY IN THE MIDDLE EAST

Halliday, Fred. *Soviet Policy in the Arc of Crisis.* Washington, D.C.: Institute for Policy Studies, 1981.
A comprehensive new study of Soviet policy in the Middle East.

Heikal, Mohamed. *The Sphinx and the Commissar: The Rise and Fall of Soviet Influence in the Middle East.* New York: Harper and Row, 1978.
An interesting analysis of the role of the Soviet Union in the Middle East, particularly in Egypt, by a leading Egyptian opposition figure.

Leitenberg, Milton and Sheffer, Gabriel, eds. *Great Power Intervention in the Middle East.* New York: Pergamon Press, 1979.
A good selection of essays on superpower involvement in the Middle East.

OIL

Deese, David A. and Nye, Joseph A., eds. *Energy and Security.* New York: Harper and Row, 1981.
An insightful analysis of the interplay of Middle Eastern oil and international security.

ARMS

Jabber, Paul. *Not by War Alone: Security and Arms Control in the Middle East.* Berkeley: University of California Press, 1981.
A discussion of a series of questions related to the Middle East arms balances, considering both conventional and nuclear weaponry, with a view to the future.

U.S. MIDDLE EAST POLICY

Quandt, William B. *Decade of Decisions: American Policy Toward the Arab-Israeli Conflict 1967–1976.* Berkeley: University of California Press, 1977.
A study of U.S. Middle East policy as it developed in the decade after the Six Day War by a former National Security Council expert on the Middle East.

Appendixes

I Security Council Resolution 242 Concerning Principles for a Just and Lasting Peace in the Middle East, November 22, 1967

The Security Council.
Expressing its continuing concern with the grave situation in the Middle East,
Emphasizing the inadmissibility of the acquisition of territory by war and the need to work for a just and lasting peace in which every State in the area can live in security,
Emphasizing further that all Member States in their acceptance of the Charter of the United Nations have undertaken a commitment to act in accordance with Article 2 of the Charter,
1. *Affirms* that the fulfilment of Charter principles requires the establishment of a just and lasting peace in the Middle East which should include the application of both the following principles:
  (i) Withdrawal of Israel armed forces from territories occupied in the recent conflict;
  (ii) Termination of all claims or states of belligerency and respect for and acknowledgement of the sovereignty, territorial integrity and political independence of every State in the area and their right to live in peace within secure and recognized boundaries free from threats or acts of force;
2. *Affirms further* the necessity
  (a) For guaranteeing freedom of navigation through international waterways in the area;
  (b) For achieving a just settlement of the refugee problem;
  (c) For guaranteeing the territorial inviolability and political

independence of every State in the area, through measures including the establishment of demilitarized zones;

3. *Requests* the Secretary-General to designate a Special Representative to proceed to the Middle East to establish and maintain contacts with the States concerned in order to promote agreement and assist efforts to achieve a peaceful and accepted settlement in accordance with the provisions and principles in this resolution;

4. *Requests* the Secretary-General to report to the Security Council on the progress of the efforts of the Special Representative as soon as possible.

*Adopted unanimously at the
1382nd meeting.*

II Security Council Resolutions 338, 339 Concerning the October War, October 22–27, 1973

Resolution 338 (October 22, 1973)

The Security Council
1. *Calls upon* all parties to the present fighting to cease all firing and terminate all military activity immediately, no later than 12 hours after the moment of the adoption of this decision, in the positions they now occupy;

2. *Calls upon* the parties concerned to start immediately after the cease-fire the implementation of Security Council resolution 242 (1967) in all of its parts:

3. *Decides* that, immediately and concurrently with the cease-fire, negotiations start between the parties concerned under appropriate auspices aimed at establishing a just and durable peace in the Middle East.

Resolution 339 (October 23, 1973)

The Security Council
Referring to its resolution 338 (1973) of 22 October 1973,
1. *Confirms* its decision on an immediate cessation of all kinds of firing and of all military action, and urges that the forces of the two sides be returned to the positions they occupied at the moment the cease-fire became effective;

2. *Requests* the Secretary-General to take measures for immediate

dispatch of United Nations observers to supervise the observance of the cease-fire between the forces of Israel and the Arab Republic of Egypt, using for this purpose the personnel of the United Nations now in the Middle East and first of all the personnel now in Cairo.

III General Assembly Resolution 3236 Concerning the Question of Palestine, November 22, 1974

The General Assembly,

Having considered the question of Palestine,

Having heard the statement of the Palestine Liberation Organization, the representative of the Palestinian people,

Having also heard other statements made during the debate,

Deeply concerned that no just solution to the problem of Palestine has yet been achieved and recognizing that the problem of Palestine continues to endanger international peace and security,

Recognizing that the Palestinian people is entitled to self-determination in accordance with the Charter of the United Nations,

Expressing its grave concern that the Palestinian people has been prevented from enjoying its inalienable rights, in particular its right to self-determination,

Guided by the purposes and principles of the Charter,

Recalling its relevant resolutions which affirm the right of the Palestinian people to self-determination,

1. *Reaffirms* the inalienable rights of the Palestinian people in Palestine, including:

   (a) The right to self-determination without external interference;

   (b) The right to national independence and sovereignty;

2. *Reaffirms* also the inalienable right of the Palestinians to return to their homes and property from which they have been displaced and uprooted, and calls for their return;

3. *Emphasizes* that full respect for and the realization of these inalienable rights of the Palestinian people are indispensable for the solution of the question of Palestine;

4. *Recognizes* that the Palestinian people is a principal party in the establishment of a just and durable peace in the Middle East;

5. *Further recognizes* the right of the Palestinian people to regain its rights by all means in accordance with the purposes and principles of the Charter of the United Nations;

6. *Appeals* to all States and international organizations to extend their

support to the Palestinian people in its struggle to restore its rights, in accordance with the Charter;

7. *Requests* the Secretary-General to establish contacts with the Palestine Liberation Organization on all matters concerning the question of Palestine;

8. *Requests* the Secretary-General to report to the General Assembly at its thirtieth session on the implementation of the present resolution;

9. *Decides* to include the item entitled "Question of Palestine" in the provisional agenda of its thirtieth session.

2296th plenary meeting
22 November 1974

IV UN Security Council Resolution 425, 19 March 1978

THE SECURITY COUNCIL,

TAKING NOTE of the letters of the permanent representative of Lebanon and the permanent representative of Israel, having heard the statements of the permanent representatives of Lebanon and Israel,

GRAVELY CONCERNED at the deterioration of the situation in the Middle East, and its consequences to the maintenance of international peace,

CONVINCED that the present situation impedes the achievement of a just peace in the Middle East,

1. CALLS for strict respect for the territorial integrity, sovereignty and political independence of Lebanon within its territorially recognized boundaries;

2. CALLS upon Israel immediately to cease its military action against Lebanese territorial integrity and withdraw forthwith its forces from all Lebanese territory;

3. DECIDES, in the light of the request of the government of Lebanon, to establish immediately under its authority a United Nations interim force for southern Lebanon for the purpose of confirming the withdrawal of Israeli forces, restoring international peace and security and assisting the government of Lebanon in ensuring the return of its effective authority in the area, the force to be composed of personnel drawn from state members of the United Nations;

4. REQUESTS the secretary general to report to the Council within 24 hours on the implementation of this resolution.

UN Security Council Resolution 426 (Excerpts) 19 March 1978

. . . 1. The present report is submitted in pursuance of Security Council resolution 425 (1978) of 19 March 1978 in which the Council, among other things, decided to set up a United Nations Force in Lebanon under its authority and requested the Secretary General to submit a report to it on the implementation of the resolution.

Terms of reference

2. The terms of reference of the United Nations Interim Force in Lebanon (UNIFIL) are:

a) The Force will determine compliance with paragraph 2 of Security Council resolution 425 (1978).

b) The Force will confirm the withdrawal of Israeli forces, restore international peace and security, and assist the Government of Lebanon in ensuring the return of its effective authority in the area.

c) The Force will establish and maintain itself in an area of operation to be defined in the light of paragraph 2 (b) above.

d) The Force will use its best efforts to prevent the recurrence of fighting and to ensure that its area of operation is not utilized for hostile activities of any kind.

e) In the fulfillment of this task, the Force will have the cooperation of the Military Observers of UNTSO, who will continue to function on the Armistice Demarcation Line after the termination of the mandate of UNIFIL.

V Joint Statement Issued by the Governments of the U.S. and the U.S.S.R. New York, October 1, 1977

Having exchanged views regarding the unsafe situation which remains in the Middle East, U.S. Secretary of State Cyrus Vance and Member of the Politbureau of the Central Committee of the CPSU, Minister for Foreign Affairs of the USSR A.A. Gromyko have the following statement to make on behalf of their countries, which are cochairmen of the Geneva Peace Conference on the Middle East:

1. Both governments are convinced that vital interests of the peoples of this

area, as well as the interests of strengthening peace and international security in general, urgently dictate the necessity of achieving, as soon as possible, a just and lasting settlement of the Arab-Israeli conflict. This settlement should be comprehensive, incorporating all parties concerned and all questions.

The United States and the Soviet Union believe that, within the framework of a comprehensive settlement of the Middle East problem, all specific questions of the settlement should be resolved, including such key issues as withdrawal of Israeli Armed Forces from territories occupied in the 1967 conflict; the resolution of the Palestinian question, including insuring the legitimate rights of the Palestinian people; termination of the state of war and establishment of normal peaceful relations on the basis of mutual recognition of the principles of sovereignty, territorial integrity, and political independence.

The two governments believe that, in addition to such measures for insuring the security of the borders between Israel and the neighboring Arab states as the establishment of demilitarized zones and the agreed stationing in them of U.N. troops or observers, international guarantees of such borders as well as of the observance of the terms of the settlement can also be established should the contracting parties so desire. The United States and the Soviet Union are ready to participate in these guarantees, subject to their constitutional processes.

2. The United States and the Soviet Union believe that the only right and effective way for achieving a fundamental solution to all aspects of the Middle East problem in its entirety is negotiations within the framework of the Geneva peace conference, specially convened for these purposes, with participation in its work of the representatives of all the parties involved in the conflict including those of the Palestinian people, and legal and contractual formalization of the decisions reached at the conference.

In their capacity as cochairmen of the Geneva conference, the United States and the USSR affirm their intention, through joint efforts and in their contacts with the parties concerned, to facilitate in every way the resumption of the work of the conference not later than December 1977. The cochairmen note that there still exist several questions of a procedural and organizational nature which remain to be agreed upon by the participants to the conference.

3. Guided by the goal of achieving a just political settlement in the Middle East and of eliminating the explosive situation in this area of the world, the United States and the USSR appeal to all the parties in the conflict to understand the necessity for careful consideration of each other's legitimate rights and interests and to demonstrate mutual readiness to act accordingly.

VI A Framework for Peace in the Middle East Agreed at Camp David* September 17, 1978

Muhammad Anwar al-Sadat, President of the Arab Republic of Egypt, and Menachem Begin, Prime Minister of Israel, met with Jimmy Carter, President of the United States of America, at Camp David from September 5 to September 17, 1978, and have agreed on the following framework for peace in the Middle East. They invite other parties to the Arab-Israeli conflict to adhere to it.

Preamble

The search for peace in the Middle East must be guided by the following:

—The agreed basis for a peaceful settlement of the conflict between Israel and its neighbors is United Nations Security Council Resolution 242, in all its parts.†

—After four wars during thirty years, despite intensive human efforts, the Middle East, which is the cradle of civilization and the birthplace of three great religions, does not yet enjoy the blessings of peace. The people of the Middle East yearn for peace so that the vast human and natural resources of the region can be turned to the pursuits of peace and so that this area can become a model for coexistence and cooperation among nations.

—The historic initiative of President Sadat in visiting Jerusalem and the reception accorded to him by the Parliament, government and people of Israel, and the reciprocal visit of Prime Minister Begin to Ismailia, the peace proposals made by both leaders, as well as the warm reception of these missions by the peoples of both countries, have created an unprecedented opportunity for peace which must not be lost if this generation and future generations are to be spared the tragedies of war.

—The provisions of the Charter of the United Nations and the other accepted norms of international law and legitimacy now provide accepted standards for the conduct of relations among all states.

—To achieve a relationship of peace, in the spirit of Article 2 of the United Nations Charter, future negotiations between Israel and any neighbor prepared to negotiate peace and security with it, are necessary for the purpose of carrying out all the provisions and principles of Resolutions 242 and 338.

—Peace requires respect for the sovereignty, territorial integrity and political independence of every state in the area and their right to live in peace within secure and recognized boundaries free from threats or acts of force.

---

*Accompanying letters may be found in: *The Camp David Summit, September 1978,* Department of State Publication 8954, Near East and South Asian Series 88 (Washington, D.C.: USGPO, 1978).

†The texts of Resolutions 242 and 338 are annexed to this document.

Progress toward that goal can accelerate movement toward a new era of reconciliation in the Middle East marked by cooperation in promoting economic development, in maintaining stability, and in assuring security.

—Security is enhanced by a relationship of peace and by cooperation between nations which enjoy normal relations. In addition, under the terms of peace treaties, the parties can, on the basis of reciprocity, agree to special security arrangements such as demilitarized zones, limited armaments areas, early warning stations, the presence of international forces, liaison, agreed measures for monitoring, and other arrangements that they agree are useful.

Framework

Taking these factors into account, the parties are determined to reach a just, comprehensive, and durable settlement of the Middle East conflict through the conclusion of peace treaties based on Security Council Resolutions 242 and 338 in all their parts. Their purpose is to achieve peace and good neighborly relations. They recognize that, for peace to endure, it must involve all those who have been most deeply affected by the conflict. They therefore agree that this framework as appropriate is intended by them to constitute a basis for peace not only between Egypt and Israel, but also between Israel and each of its other neighbors which is prepared to negotiate peace with Israel on this basis. With that objective in mind, they have agreed to proceed as follows:

A. West Bank and Gaza

1. Egypt, Israel, Jordan and the representatives of the Palestinian people should participate in negotiations on the resolution of the Palestinian problem in all its aspects. To achieve that objective, negotiations relating to the West Bank and Gaza should proceed in three stages:

(a) Egypt and Israel agree that, in order to ensure a peaceful and orderly transfer of authority, and taking into account the security concerns of all the parties, there should be transitional arrangements for the West Bank and Gaza for a period not exceeding five years. In order to provide full autonomy to the inhabitants, under these arrangements the Israeli military government and its civilian administration will be withdrawn as soon as a self-governing authority has been freely elected by the inhabitants of these areas to replace the existing military government. To negotiate the details of a transitional arrangement, the Government of Jordan will be invited to join the negotiations on the basis of this framework. These new arrangements should give due consideration both to the principle of self-government by the inhabitants of these terrorities and to the legitimate security concerns of the parties involved.

(b) Egypt, Israel, and Jordan will agree on the modalities for establishing the elected self-governing authority in the West Bank and Gaza. The delegations of Egypt and Jordan may include Palestinians from the West Bank and Gaza or other Palestinians as mutually agreed. The parties will negotiate an agreement which will define the powers and responsibilities of the self-governing authority to be exercised in the West Bank and Gaza. A withdrawal of Israeli armed forces will take place and there will be a redeployment of the remaining Israeli forces into specified security locations. The agreement will also include arrangements for assuring internal and external security and public order. A strong local police force will be established, which may include Jordanian citizens. In addition, Israeli and Jordanian forces will participate in joint patrols and in the manning of control posts to assure the security of the borders.

(c) When the self-governing authority (administrative council) in the West Bank and Gaza is established and inaugurated, the transitional period of five years will begin. As soon as possible, but not later than the third year after the beginning of the transitional period, negotiations will take place to determine the final status of the West Bank and Gaza and its relationship with its neighbors, and to conclude a peace treaty between Israel and Jordan by the end of the transitional period. These negotiations will be conducted among Egypt, Israel, Jordan, and the elected representatives of the inhabitants of the West Bank and Gaza. Two separate but related committees will be convened, one committee, consisting of representatives of the four parties which will negotiate and agree on the final status of the West Bank and Gaza, and its relationship with its neighbors, and the second committee, consisting of representatives of Israel and representatives of Jordan to be joined by the elected representatives of the inhabitants of the West Bank and Gaza, to negotiate the peace treaty between Israel and Jordan, taking into account the agreement reached on the final status of the West Bank and Gaza. The negotiations shall be based on all the provisions and principles of UN Security Council Resolution 242. The negotiations will resolve, among other matters, the location of the boundaries and the nature of the security arrangements. The solution from the negotiations must also recognize the legitimate rights of the Palestinian people and their just requirements. In this way, the Palestinians will participate in the determination of their own future through:

1) The negotiations among Egypt, Israel, Jordan and the representatives of the inhabitants of the West Bank and Gaza to agree on the final status of the West Bank and Gaza and other outstanding issues by the end of the transitional period.

2) Submitting their agreement to a vote by the elected representatives of the inhabitants of the West Bank and Gaza.

3) Providing for the elected representatives of the inhabitants of the West Bank and Gaza to decide how they shall govern themselves consistent with the provisions of their agreement.

4) Participating as stated above in the work of the committee negotiating the peace treaty between Israel and Jordan.

2. All necessary measures will be taken and provisions made to assure the security of Israel and its neighbors during the transitional period and beyond. To assist in providing such security, a strong local police force will be constituted by the self-governing authority. It will be composed of inhabitants of the West Bank and Gaza. The police will maintain continuing liaison on internal security matters with the designated Israeli, Jordanian, and Egyptian officers.

3. During the transitional period, representatives of Egypt, Israel, Jordan, and the self-governing authority will constitute a continuing committee to decide by agreement on the modalities of admission of persons displaced from the West Bank and Gaza in 1967, together with necessary measures to prevent disruption and disorder. Other matters of common concern may also be dealt with by this committee.

4. Egypt and Israel will work with each other and with other interested parties to establish agreed procedures for a prompt, just and permanent implementation of the resolution of the refugee problem.

B. Egypt-Israel

1. Egypt and Israel undertake not to resort to the threat or the use of force to settle disputes. Any disputes shall be settled by peaceful means in accordance with the provisions of Article 33 of the Charter of the United Nations.

2. In order to achieve peace between them, the parties agree to negotiate in good faith with a goal of concluding within three months from the signing of this Framework a peace treaty between them, while inviting the other parties to the conflict to proceed simultaneously to negotiate and conclude similar peace treaties with a view to achieving a comprehensive peace in the area. The Framework for the Conclusion of a Peace Treaty between Egypt and Israel will govern the peace negotiations between them. The parties will agree on the modalities and the timetable for the implementation of their obligations under the treaty.

C. Associated Principles

1. Egypt and Israel state that the principles and provisions described below should apply to peace treaties between Israel and each of its neighbors—Egypt, Jordan, Syria and Lebanon.

2. Signatories shall establish among themselves relationships normal to states at peace with one another. To this end, they should undertake to abide by all the provisions of the Charter of the United Nations. Steps to be taken in this respect include:

(a) full recognition;

(b) abolishing economic boycotts;

(c) guaranteeing that under their jurisdiction the citizens of the other parties shall enjoy the protection of the due process of law.

3. Signatories should explore possibilities for economic development in the context of final peace treaties, with the objective of contributing to the atmosphere of peace, cooperation and friendship which is their common goal.

4. Claims Commissions may be established for the mutual settlement of all financial claims.

5. The United States shall be invited to participate in the talks on matters related to the modalities of the implementation of the agreements and working out the timetable for the carrying out of the obligations of the parties.

6. The United Nations Security Council shall be requested to endorse the peace treaties and ensure that their provisions shall not be violated. The permanent members of the Security Council shall be requested to underwrite the peace treaties and ensure respect for their provisions. They shall also be requested to conform their policies and actions with the undertakings contained in this Framework.

FRAMEWORK FOR THE CONCLUSION OF A PEACE TREATY BETWEEN EGYPT AND ISRAEL

In order to achieve peace between them, Israel and Egypt agree to negotiate in good faith with a goal of concluding within three months of the signing of this framework a peace treaty between them.

It is agreed that:

The site of the negotiations will be under a United Nations flag at a location or locations to be mutually agreed.

All of the principles of U.N. Resolution 242 will apply in this resolution of the dispute between Israel and Egypt.

Unless otherwise mutually agreed, terms of the peace treaty will be implemented between two and three years after the peace treaty is signed.

The following matters are agreed between the parties:

(a) the full exercise of Egyptian sovereignty up to the internationally recognized border between Egypt and mandated Palestine;

(b) the withdrawal of Israeli armed forces from the Sinai;

(c) the use of airfields left by the Israelis near El Arish, Rafah, Ras en Naqb, and Sharm el Sheikh for civilian purposes only, including possible commercial use by all nations;

(d) the right of free passage by ships of Israel through the Gulf of Suez and the Suez Canal on the basis of the Constantinople Convention of 1888 applying to all nations; the Strait of Tiran and the Gulf of Aqaba are international waterways to be open to all nations for unimpeded and nonsuspendable freedom of navigation and overflight;

(e) the construction of a highway between the Sinai and Jordan near Elat with guaranteed free and peaceful passage by Egypt and Jordan; and

(f) the stationing of military forces listed below.

Stationing of Forces

A. No more than one division (mechanized or infantry) of Egyptian armed forces will be stationed within an area lying approximately 50 kilometers (km) east of the Gulf of Suez and the Suez Canal.

B. Only United Nations forces and civil police equipped with light weapons to perform normal police functions will be stationed within an area lying west of the international border and the Gulf of Aqaba, varying in width from 20 km to 40 km.

C. In the area within 3 km east of the international border there will be Israeli limited military forces not to exceed four infantry battalions and United Nations observers.

D. Border patrol units, not to exceed three battalions, will supplement the civil police in maintaining order in the area not included above.

The exact demarcation of the above areas will be as decided during the peace negotiations.

Early warning stations may exist to insure compliance with the terms of the agreement.

United Nations forces will be stationed: (a) in part of the area in the Sinai lying within about 20 km of the Mediterranean Sea and adjacent to the international border, and (b) in the Sharm el Sheikh area to ensure freedom of passage through the Strait of Tiran; and these forces will not be removed unless such removal is approved by the Security Council of the United Nations with a unanimous vote of the five permanent members.

After a peace treaty is signed, and after the interim withdrawal is complete, normal relations will be established between Egypt and Israel, including: full recognition, including diplomatic, economic and cultural relations; termination of economic boycotts and barriers to the free movement of goods and people; and mutual protection of citizens by the due process of law.

Interim Withdrawal

Between the three months and nine months after the signing of the peace treaty, all Israeli forces will withdraw east of a line extending from a point east of El Arish to Ras Muhammad, the exact location of this time to be determined by mutual agreement.

VII   The Egyptian-Israeli Peace Treaty

TREATY OF PEACE BETWEEN
THE ARAB REPUBLIC OF EGYPT AND THE STATE OF ISRAEL*
March 26, 1979

The Government of the Arab Republic of Egypt and the Government of the State of Israel:

Preamble

Convinced of the urgent necessity of the establishment of a just, comprehensive and lasting peace in the Middle East in accordance with Security Council Resolutions 242 and 338;

Reaffirming their adherence to the "Framework for Peace in the Middle East Agreed at Camp David," dated September 17, 1978;

Noting that the aforementioned Framework as appropriate is intended to constitute a basis for peace not only between Egypt and Israel but also between Israel and each of its other Arab neighbors which is prepared to negotiate peace with it on this basis;

Desiring to bring to an end the state of war between them and to establish a peace in which every state in the area can live in security;

Convinced that the conclusion of a Treaty of Peace between Egypt and Israel is an important step in the search for comprehensive peace in the area and for the attainment of the settlement of the Arab-Israeli conflict in all its aspects;

Inviting the other Arab parties to this dispute to join the peace process with Israel guided by and based on the principles of the aforementioned Framework;

Desiring as well to develop friendly relations and cooperation between themselves in accordance with the United Nations Charter and the principles of international law governing international relations in times of peace;

Agree to the following provisions in the free exercise of their sovereignty, in order to implement the "Framework for the Conclusion of a Peace Treaty Between Egypt and Israel":

---

*The additional Treaty Protocols may be found in: *The Egyptian-Israeli Peace Treaty, March 26, 1979,* Department of State Publication 8976, Near Eastern and South Asian Series 91, Selected Documents no. 11 (Washington, D.C.: USGPO, 1979).

Article I

1. The state of war between the Parties will be terminated and peace will be established between them upon the exchange of instruments of ratification of this Treaty.

2. Israel will withdraw all its armed forces and civilians from the Sinai behind the international boundary between Egypt and mandated Palestine, as provided in the annexed protocol (Annex I), and Egypt will resume the exercise of its full sovereignty over the Sinai.

3. Upon completion of the interim withdrawal provided for in Annex I, the Parties will establish normal and friendly relations, in accordance with Article III (3).

Article II

The permanent boundary between Egypt and Israel is the recognized international boundary between Egypt and the former mandated territory of Palestine, as shown on the map at Annex II, without prejudice to the issue of the status of the Gaza Strip. The Parties recognize this boundary as inviolable. Each will respect the territorial integrity of the other, including their territorial waters and airspace.

Article III

1. The Parties will apply between them the provisions of the Charter of the United Nations and the principles of international law governing relations among states in times of peace. In particular:

a. They recognize and will respect each other's sovereignty, territorial integrity and political independence;

b. They recognize and will respect each other's right to live in peace within their secure and recognized boundaries;

c. They will refrain from the threat or use of force, directly or indirectly, against each other and will settle all disputes between them by peaceful means.

2. Each Party undertakes to ensure that acts or threats of belligerency, hostility, or violence do not originate from and are not committed from within its territory, or by any forces subject to its control or by any other forces stationed on its territory, against the population, citizens or property of the other Party. Each Party also undertakes to refrain from organizing, instigating, inciting, assisting or participating in acts or threats of belligerency, hostility, subversion or violence against the other Party, anywhere, and undertakes to ensure that perpetrators of such acts are brought to justice.

3. The Parties agree that the normal relationship established between them will include full recognition, diplomatic, economic and cultural relations, termination of economic boycotts and discriminatory barriers to the free movement of people and goods, and will guarantee the mutual enjoyment by

citizens of the due process of law. The process by which they undertake to achieve such a relationship parallel to the implementation of other provisions of this Treaty is set out in the annexed protocol (Annex III).

Article IV

1. In order to provide maximum security for both Parties on the basis of reciprocity, agreed security arrangements will be established including limited force zones in Egyptian and Israeli territory, and United Nations forces and observers, described in detail as to nature and timing in Annex I, and other security arrangements the Parties may agree upon.

2. The Parties agree to the stationing of United Nations personnel in areas described in Annex I. The Parties agree not to request withdrawal of the United Nations personnel and that these personnel will not be removed unless such removal is approved by the Security Council of the United Nations, with the affirmative vote of the five Permanent Members, unless the Parties otherwise agree.

3. A Joint Commission will be established to facilitate the implementation of the Treaty, as provided for in Annex I.

4. The security arrangements provided for in paragraphs 1 and 2 of this Article may at the request of either party be reviewed and amended by mutual agreement of the Parties.

Article V

1. Ships of Israel, and cargoes destined for or coming from Israel, shall enjoy the right of free passage through the Suez Canal and its approaches through the Gulf of Suez and the Mediterranean Sea on the basis of the Constantinople Convention of 1888, applying to all nations. Israeli nationals, vessels and cargoes, as well as persons, vessels and cargoes destined for or coming from Israel, shall be accorded non-discriminatory treatment in all matters connected with usage of the canal.

2. The Parties consider the Strait of Tiran and the Gulf of Aqaba to be international waterways open to all nations for unimpeded and non-suspendable freedom of navigation and overflight. The Parties will respect each other's right to navigation and overflight for access to either country through the Strait of Tiran and the Gulf of Aqaba.

Article VI

1. This Treaty does not affect and shall not be interpreted as affecting in any way the rights and obligations of the Parties under the Charter of the United Nations.

2. The Parties undertake to fulfill in good faith their obligations under this Treaty, without regard to action or inaction of any other party and independently of any instrument external to this Treaty.

3. They further undertake to take all the necessary measures for the application in their relations of the provisions of the multilateral conventions to which they are parties, including the submission of appropriate notification to the Secretary General of the United Nations and other depositaries of such conventions.

4. The Parties undertake not to enter into any obligation in conflict with this Treaty.

5. Subject to Article 103 of the United Nations Charter, in the event of a conflict between the obligations of the Parties under the present Treaty and any of their other obligations, the obligations under this Treaty will be binding and implemented.

Article VII

1. Disputes arising out of the application or interpretation of this Treaty shall be resolved by negotiations.

2. Any such disputes which cannot be settled by negotiations shall be resolved by conciliation or submitted to arbitration.

Article VIII

The Parties agree to establish a claims commission for the mutual settlement of all financial claims.

Article IX

1. This Treaty shall enter into force upon exchange of instruments of ratification.

2. This Treaty supersedes the Agreement between Egypt and Israel of September, 1975.

3. All protocols, annexes, and maps attached to this Treaty shall be regarded as an integral part hereof.

4. The Treaty shall be communicated to the Secretary General of the United Nations for registration in accordance with the provisions of Article 102 of the Charter of the United Nations.

VIII   The European Declaration

Following is the text of the declaration on the Middle East by the European Economic Community issued at the conclusion of a two-day summit in Venice, June 13, 1981.

1. The heads of state and government and the ministers of foreign affairs held a comprehensive exchange of views on all aspects of the present situation in the Middle East, including the state of negotiations resulting from the agreements signed between Egypt and Israel in March 1979. They agreed that growing tensions affecting this region constitute a serious danger and render a comprehensive solution to the Israeli-Arab conflict more necessary and pressing than ever.

2. The nine member states of the European Community consider that the traditional ties and common interests which link Europe to the Middle East oblige them to play a special role and now require them to work in a more concrete way toward peace.

3. In this regard the nine countries of the Community base on Security Council Resolutions 242 and 338 and the positions which they have expressed on several occasions, notably in their declarations of 29 June 1977, 19 September 1978, 26 March and 18 June 1979, as well as the speech made on their behalf on 25 September 1979 by the Irish Minister of Foreign Affairs at the 34th United Nations General Assembly.

4. On the bases thus set out, the time has come to promote the recognition and implementation of the two principles universally accepted by the international community: the right to existence and to security of all the states in the region, including Israel, and justice for all the peoples, which implies the recognition of the legitimate rights of the Palestinian people.

5. All of the countries in the area are entitled to live in peace within secure, recognized and guaranteed borders. The necessary guarantees for a peace settlement should be provided by the United Nations by a decision of the Security Council and, if necessary, on the basis of other mutually agreed procedures. The Nine declare that they are prepared to participate within the framework of a comprehensive settlement in a system of concrete and binding international guarantees, including guarantees on the ground.

6. A just solution must finally be found to the Palestinian problem, which is not simply one of refugees. The Palestinian people, which is conscious of existing as such, must be placed in a position, by an appropriate process defined within the framework of the comprehensive peace settlement, to exercise fully its right to self-determination.

7. The achievement of these objectives requires the involvement and support of all the parties concerned in the peace settlement which the Nine are endeavoring to promote in keeping with the principles formulated in the declaration referred to above. These principles apply to all the parties concerned, and thus the Palestinian people, and to the Palestine Liberation Organization, which will have to be associated with the negotiations.

8. The Nine recognize the special importance of the role played by the question of Jerusalem for all the parties concerned. The Nine stress that they will not accept any unilateral initiative designed to change the status of Jerusalem and that any agreement on the city's status should guarantee freedom of access of everyone to the holy places.

9. The Nine stress the need for Israel to put an end to the territorial occupation which it has maintained since the conflict of 1967, as it has done for part of Sinai. They are deeply convinced that the Israeli settlements constitute a serious obstacle to the peace process in the Middle East. The Nine consider that these settlements, as well as modifications in population and property in the occupied Arab territories, are illegal under international law.

10. Concerned as they are to put an end to violence, the Nine consider that only the renunciation of force or the threatened use of force by all the parties can create a climate of confidence in the area, and constitute a basic element for a comprehensive settlement of the conflict in the Middle East.

11. The Nine have decided to make the necessary contacts with all the parties concerned. The objective of these contacts would be to ascertain the position of the various parties with respect to the principles set out in this declaration and in the light of the results of this consultation process to determine the form which such an initiative on their part could take.

IX Saudi Arabia's Peace Plan

Following is an unofficial translation from the Arabic of the Middle East peace plan proposed by Crown Prince Fahd of Saudi Arabia and published by the Saudi press agency.

1. Israeli evacuation of all Arab territories seized during the 1967 Middle East war, including the Arab sector of Jerusalem.

2. Dismantling the settlements set up by Israel on the occupied lands after the 1967 war.

3. Guaranteeing freedom of religious practices for all religions in the Jerusalem holy shrines.

4. Asserting the rights of the Palestinian people and compensating those Palestinians who do not wish to return to their homeland.

5. Commencing a transitional period in the West Bank of Jordan and the Gaza Strip under United Nations supervision for a duration not exceeding a few months.

6. Setting up a Palestinian state with East Jerusalem as its capital.

7. Affirming the right of all countries of the region to live in peace.

8. Guaranteeing the implementation of these principles by the United Nations or some of its member states.

DATE DUE